ATP 3-20.98

Reconnaissance Platoon

APRIL 2013

DISTRIBUTION RESTRICTION: Approved for public release; distribution is unlimited.

Headquarters, Department of the Army

This publication is available at Army Knowledge Online
(https://armypubs.us.army.mil/doctrine/index.html).
To receive publishing updates, please subscribe at
http://www.apd.army.mil/AdminPubs/new_subscribe.asp.

*ATP 3-20.98

Army Techniques and Procedures
No. 3-20.98

Headquarters
Department of the Army
Washington, DC, 5 April 2013

Reconnaissance Platoon

Contents

		Page
	PREFACE	viii
Chapter 1	INTRODUCTION	1-1
	Section I – Overview	1-1
	Operational Environment	1-1
	Decisive Action	1-2
	Combat Power	1-2
	Leadership	1-3
	Information	1-3
	Warfighting Functions	1-3
	Section II – Mission Command	**1-3**
	Command	1-4
	Control	1-5
	Communication	1-7
	Section III – Command and Support Relationships	**1-9**
	Command Relationships	1-9
	Support Relationships	1-9
	Section IV – Planning Considerations	**1-10**
	Operational Variables	1-10
	Mission Variables	1-10
	Troop-Leading Procedures	1-11
	Risk Management	1-12
	Fratricide Avoidance	1-12

DISTRIBUTION RESTRICTION: Approved for public release; distribution is unlimited.

*This manual supersedes FM 7-92, 23 December 1992 and FM 3-21.94, 18 April 2003.

Contents

Chapter 2	**RECONNAISSANCE PLATOON** **2-1**	
	Section I – Role of the Reconnaissance Platoon 2-1	
	Fundamental Role 2-1	
	Section II – Organization and Capabilities 2-1	
	Reconnaissance Squadron and Combined Arms Battalion Reconnaissance Platoon in the ABCT 2-1	
	IBCT Mounted Reconnaissance Platoon 2-4	
	IBCT Dismounted Reconnaissance Troop and Infantry Battalion Reconnaissance Platoons 2-7	
	SBCT Reconnaissance Platoon and Infantry Battalion Scout Platoon 2-10	
	Battlefield Surveillance Brigade Reconnaissance Platoon 2-14	
	Section III – Key Personnel 2-16	
	Duties and Responsibilities 2-16	
Chapter 3	**RECONNAISSANCE** **3-1**	
	Section I – Overview 3-1	
	Platoon Missions 3-2	
	Fundamentals of Reconnaissance 3-2	
	Section II – Reconnaissance Planning Considerations 3-2	
	Reconnaissance Planning Guidance 3-2	
	Operational Considerations 3-5	
	Reconnaissance Techniques 3-5	
	Section III – Forms of Reconnaissance 3-8	
	Zone Reconnaissance 3-9	
	Obstacle Reconnaissance 3-13	
	Area Reconnaissance 3-14	
	Route Reconnaissance 3-17	
	Section IV - Reconnaissance Handover 3-33	
	Operational Considerations for Reconnaissance Handover 3-33	
	Section V – Dismounted Reconnaissance Patrols 3-37	
Chapter 4	**SECURITY** **4-1**	
	Section I – Overview 4-1	
	Section II – Fundamentals of Security Tasks 4-1	
	Section III – Forms of Security 4-2	
	Five Forms of Security 4-2	

Contents

	Positioning the Observation Post	4-8
	Manning the Observation Post	4-11
	Perform Counter Reconnaissance	4-15
	Route Security tasks	4-25
	Convoy Escort	4-30
	Local Security	4-41
Chapter 5	**STABILITY**	**5-1**
	Section I – Fundamentals of Stability	5-1
	Purpose of Stability	5-1
	Section II – Planning	5-3
	Considerations	5-3
	Rules of Engagement	5-7
	Section III – Preparation	5-8
	Precombat Checks and Inspections	5-8
	Training for Stability	5-8
	Section IV – Execute and Assess	5-9
	Detained Persons	5-14
Chapter 6	**OTHER TACTICAL OPERATIONS**	**6-1**
	Section I – Platoon Tactical Movement	6-1
	Planning and Operational Considerations	6-1
	Fundamentals of Movement	6-2
	Platoon Formations	6-8
	Movement Techniques	6-12
	Section II – Infiltration/Exfiltration	6-17
	Infiltration	6-17
	Exfiltration	6-20
	Section III – Patrol Bases and Combat Outposts	6-23
	Patrol Bases	6-23
	Combat Outposts	6-26
	Section IV – Direct Fire Planning	6-26
	Direct Fire Standard Operating Procedure	6-27
	Engagement Area Development	6-28
	Section V – Assembly Areas	6-31
	Characteristics	6-31
	Quartering Party Responsibilities	6-31
	Occupation of an Assembly Area	6-33
	Section VI – Linkup	6-34
	Forms of Linkup	6-34

Contents

	Section VII – Passage of Lines 6-37
	Overview 6-37
	Planning 6-37
	Preparation 6-40
	Section VIII – Relief in Place 6-46
Chapter 7	AUGMENTING COMBAT POWER 7-1
	Section I – Fires 7-1
	Overview 7-1
	Fire Support Personnel 7-2
	Mortar Employment 7-5
	Field Artillery Support 7-6
	Close Combat Attack 7-11
	Air Ground Intergration 7-14
	Sniper Employment 7-17
	Section II – Engineers 7-18
	Support in Reconnaissance Tasks 7-18
	Section III – Intelligence 7-19
	Sensor Teams 7-19
	Ground Surveillance Systems 7-20
	Human Intelligence Collection 7-20
	Unmanned Aircraft System tasks 7-21
	Military Intelligence Company 7-25
	Section IV – Chemical, Biological, Radiological, Nuclear, and High-Yield Explosives 7-26
	Reconnaissance Support 7-26
	Section V – Other Combat Augmentation 7-26
	Military Working Dogs 7-27
	Interpreters 7-27
	Tactical Military Information Support Teams 7-27
	Explosive Ordnance Disposal 7-27
	Civil Affairs Team 7-28
Chapter 8	SUSTAINMENT 8-1
	Section I – Planning and Responsibilities 8-1
	Planning Considerations 8-1
	Individual Responsibilities 8-3
	Section II – Supply tasks 8-5
	Classes of Supply 8-5
	Section III – Functions of Sustainment 8-10

	Maintenance	8-10
	Force Health Protection	8-11
Appendix A	**ANALOG REPORTS**	**A-1**
	Contact and Blue Reports	A-1
	Intelligence Reports	A-6
	Logistics Reports	A-8
	Personnel Reports	A-13
	Chemical, Biological, Radiological, Nuclear, and High Yield Explosives Reports	A-15
Glossary		Glossary-1
References		References-1
Index		Index-1

Figures

Figure 2-1. Reconnaissance squadron and CAB reconnaissance platoons in the ABCT 2-2
Figure 2-2. IBCT mounted reconnaissance platoon 2-5
Figure 2-3. DRT reconnaissance platoon and Infantry battalion reconnaissance platoons 2-8
Figure 2-4. Infantry battalion reconnaissance platoon 2-9
Figure 2-5. SBCT reconnaissance platoon 2-10
Figure 2-6. SBCT Infantry battalion scout platoon 2-12
Figure 2-7. BFSB reconnaissance platoon 2-14
Figure 3-1. Area reconnaissance 3-15
Figure 3-2. Example of overlay graphics 3-21
Figure 3-3. Reconnaissance overlay symbols 3-22
Figure 3-4. Route width 3-27
Figure 3-5. Formula method for determining curve radius 3-30
Figure 3-6. Formula for slope percentage 3-31
Figure 3-7. Pace method for percentage slope 3-31
Figure 3-8. Map method for percentage slope 3-32
Figure 3-9. Example of reconnaissance platoon handover (phase one) 3-36
Figure 3-10. Example of reconnaissance platoon handover (phase two) 3-36

Contents

Figure 3-11. Example of reconnaissance platoon handover (phase three) 3-37
Figure 3-12. Primary and alternate routes 3-41
Figure 4-1. Use of redundancy in surveillance tasks 4-5
Figure 4-2. Use of cueing in surveillance tasks 4-6
Figure 4-3. Linear positioning of observation posts 4-9
Figure 4-4. In-depth positioning of observation posts 4-9
Figure 4-5. Vehicles overwatching a potential observation post site . 4-11
Figure 4-6. Counterreconnaissance (part one) 4-16
Figure 4-7. Counterreconnaissance (part two) 4-17
Figure 4-8. Use of patrol, observation post, and ambush site to enhance area security 4-25
Figure 4-9. Convoy security (possible locations/tasks that can be executed by a reconnaissance platoon within the overall convoy security mission) 4-29
Figure 4-10. Convoy security with combat outposts 4-29
Figure 4-11. Establishing outposts 4-30
Figure 4-12. ABCT or CAB reconnaissance platoon escorts a convoy 4-32
Figure 4-13. Convoy escort takes action toward ambush 4-33
Figure 4-14. Convoy continues to move out of kill zone 4-35
Figure 4-15. Convoy escort suppresses ambush for reaction force .. 4-36
Figure 4-16. Convoy escort vehicles assault ambush position without reaction force 4-37
Figure 4-17. Escort vehicles break contact without reaction force 4-37
Figure 4-18. Convoy moves to herringbone formation 4-38
Figure 4-19. Convoy moves back into column formation 4-39
Figure 4-20. Escort vehicles rejoin column 4-39
Figure 4-21. Escort teams conduct obstacle reconnaissance and reconnoiter for a bypass 4-41
Figure 5-1. Sample tag for captured documents and equipment 5-17
Figure 6-1. Use of natural terrain for concealment 6-2
Figure 6-2. Column formation (SBCT reconnaissance platoon) 6-9
Figure 6-3. Column formation (ABCT reconnaissance platoon) 6-10
Figure 6-4. Staggered column formation (SBCT reconnaissance platoon) 6-10
Figure 6-5. Coil formation (SBCT reconnaissance platoon) 6-11
Figure 6-6. Coil formation (ABCT reconnaissance platoon) 6-11
Figure 6-7. Herringbone formation (SBCT reconnaissance platoon) . 6-12

Figure 6-8. SBCT reconnaissance platoon traveling formation 6-14
Figure 6-9. ABCT reconnaissance platoon conducts traveling overwatch formation - start 6-15
Figure 6-10. ABCT reconnaissance platoon conducts traveling overwatch formation - stop 6-15
Figure 6-11. Patrol base occupation... 6-25
Figure 6-12. Reconnaissance handover... 6-38
Figure 6-13. Forward passage line... 6-42
Figure 6-14. Rearward passage line 6-43
Figure 7-1. Example of a call for fire.. 7-8
Figure 7-2. UAS complementing a ground screen 7-23
Figure 7-3. UAS providing additional security for a reconnaissance platoon 7-24
Figure 7-4. UAS reconnoitering for a bypass 7-25
Figure 8-1. Tailgate resupply... 8-7
Figure 8-2. Service station resupply 8-8

Tables

Table 3-1. Traffic flow capability based on route width...................... 3-27
Table 3-2. Example of patrol time schedule (backward planning) 3-39
Table 4-1. Reconnaissance platoon observation post organization and manning capabilities 4-8
Table 7-1. Example of a GRID mission 7-10
Table 7-2. Example of a shift from known point 7-11
Table 7-3. Close combat attack briefing 7-13
Table 7-4. Close air support nine-line request format....................... 7-16
Table 7-4. Close air support nine-line request format (continued) 7-17
Table 7-5. UAS sensor characteristics 7-22

Preface

Purpose
Army Techniques and Procedures (ATP) 3-20.98 provides the techniques for employment of reconnaissance platoons of the reconnaissance squadrons in the Armored brigade combat team (ABCT), Infantry brigade combat team (IBCT), Stryker brigade combat team (SBCT), and battlefield surveillance brigade (BFSB). This manual also applies to the reconnaissance platoons of the combined arms battalion (CAB), Stryker Infantry battalion, and the Infantry battalion of the IBCT, and provides techniques for the employment of the reconnaissance platoons throughout the range of military operations.

Scope
This ATP provides doctrinal guidance for commanders, staff, and leaders who are responsible for planning, preparing, executing, and assessing operations of the reconnaissance platoons. It also serves as an authoritative reference for personnel developing materiel and force structure, institutional and unit training, and standard operating procedures (SOPs) for reconnaissance platoon organizations. These doctrinal techniques are to be used as a guide and are not to be considered prescriptive. This manual outlines the framework in which the five types of reconnaissance platoons operate: by themselves, or as part of the troop or combined arms organization. It also includes discussions of doctrine that apply to each specific type of platoon.

Intended Audience
This ATP is directed toward the reconnaissance platoon leader, platoon sergeant, section sergeant, team leaders, subordinate leaders, and all supporting units.

Applicability
This ATP applies to the Active Army, the United States Army National Guard/Army National Guard of the United States (ARNGUS), and the United States Army Reserve (USAR) unless otherwise stated.

Feedback
The proponent for this publication is the U.S. Army Training and Doctrine Command (TRADOC). The preparing agency is the U.S. Army Maneuver Center of Excellence (MCoE). Comments and recommendations can be sent by any means-U.S. mail, e-mail, fax, or telephone-using or following the format of DA Form 2028 (*Recommended Changes to Publications and Blank Forms)*. Point of contact information follows:

    E-mail: usarmy.benning.mcoe.mbx.doctrine@mail.mil
    Phone: COM 706-545-7114 or DSN 835-7114
    Fax: COM 706-545-7500 or DSN 835-7500
    US Mail: Commanding General, MCoE
              Directorate of Training and Doctrine
              Doctrine and Collective Training Division
              ATTN: ATZB-TDD
              Fort Benning, GA 31905-5410

Unless otherwise stated in this publication, masculine nouns and pronouns refer to both men and women.

Chapter 1

Introduction

Serving as the eyes and ears of the commander, a reconnaissance platoon is a versatile force conducting tasks across the range of military operations. Information gathered by the platoon enables commanders to make rapid, well-informed tactical decisions within highly variable threat profiles and operational areas. The reconnaissance platoon—
- Provides a significant dismounted, mounted, and reconnaissance capability.
- Maximizes security with timely, accurate, and relevant combat information.
- Enables higher headquarters to quickly and decisively employ combat power.

Planning considerations for the reconnaissance platoon and the doctrine that forms basic platoon missions, mission command, and command and support relationships is thoroughly explored in this publication.

SECTION I – OVERVIEW

OPERATIONAL ENVIRONMENT

1-1. The conditions, circumstances, and influences that affect the employment of capabilities and bear on the decisions of the commander are known as the operational environment (OE). These influences include all adversarial, friendly, and neutral systems across the range of military operations. For more information refer to ADP 3-0.

THREATS

1-2. Threats are nation-states, organizations, people, groups, conditions, or natural phenomena able to damage or destroy life, vital resources, or institutions. There are four major categories of threats (or threat challenges):
- Traditional.
- Irregular.
- Catastrophic.
- Disruptive.

HYBRID THREATS

1-3. Hybrid threats are characterized by the combination of regular forces governed by international law, military tradition, and custom merging with irregular

Chapter 1

forces that are unregulated and act with no restrictions on the amount of violence or the targets of violence. These unregulated forces include militias, terrorists, guerillas, and criminals.

1-4. Such forces combine their abilities to use and transition between regular and irregular tactics and weapons, enabling hybrid threats to effectively capitalize on perceived vulnerabilities. For more information refer to TC 7-100.

DECISIVE ACTION

1-5. Army forces combine offensive, defensive, and stability or civil support tasks simultaneously as part of an interdependent joint force to seize, retain, and exploit the initiative, accepting prudent risk to create opportunities to achieve decisive results. For more information refer to ADP 3-0.

1-6. Decisive action requires continuous, simultaneous combinations of offensive, defensive, and stability or civil support tasks. The reconnaissance platoon is prepared to conduct any combination of these primary tasks independently or as part of a larger force:

- **Offensive tasks** are conducted to defeat and destroy enemy forces and seize terrain, resources, and population centers.
- **Defensive tasks** are conducted to defeat an enemy attack, gain time, economize forces, and develop conditions favorable for offensive or stability tasks.
- **Stability tasks** encompass various missions, tasks, and activities conducted outside the United States. In coordination with other instruments of national power, these tasks maintain or reestablish a safe and secure environment, restore essential government services, reconstruct emergency infrastructure, and provide humanitarian aid.
- **Department of Defense Support to Civilian Authorities** assists with domestic emergencies. Civil support includes operations that address the consequences of natural or man-made disasters, accidents, terrorist attacks, and other incidents in the United States and its territories. Army forces conduct these operations when the size and scope of events exceed the capabilities or capacities of domestic civilian agencies. There are three primary tasks:
  - Provide support in response to disaster.
  - Support civil law enforcement.
  - Provide other support as required.

COMBAT POWER

1-7. Combat power is the total means of a unit's destructive, constructive, and information capabilities that Soldiers can apply at a given time. Army forces generate combat power by converting potential into effective action. Commanders conceptualize their capabilities in terms of the eight elements of combat power. For more information refer to ADP 3-0.

Introduction

LEADERSHIP

1-8. Good leaders are the catalyst for success. Confident, competent, and informed leadership increases the effectiveness of all other warfighting functions by formulating sound concepts and ensuring discipline and motivation in the force. As the most dynamic element of combat power, effective leadership can compensate for deficiencies in all warfighting functions.

1-9. The Army requires self-aware, adaptive leaders who can defeat the enemy in combat and master complex operations dominated by stability or civil support missions. Leaders in the platoon strive for cooperation with multinational military and civilian partners.

INFORMATION

1-10. In modern conflict, information is as important as lethal action in determining success or failure, and is effective at all levels of an operation. Leaders rely on information to understand, visualize, describe, direct, and increase the effectiveness of warfighting functions. Engagements, battles, and major operations require informative and influential activities that improve morale within the area of operations (AO) and complement the mission. For more information refer to ADP 3-0.

WARFIGHTING FUNCTIONS

1-11. Commanders use the group of tasks and systems (people, organizations, information, and processes) to accomplish missions and training objectives. There are six warfighting functions:
- Mission command.
- Movement and maneuver.
- Intelligence.
- Fires.
- Sustainment.
- Protection.

SECTION II – MISSION COMMAND

1-12. Mission command applies to all operations across the range of military operations and allows subordinates the greatest possible freedom of action. Commanders focus their orders on the purpose of the operation rather than on the details of how to perform assigned tasks. Mission command emphasizes timely decision making, understanding the higher commander's intent, and clearly identifying the tasks to be performed by subordinates to achieve the desired end-state. This improves Soldier's abilities to act effectively in fluid, chaotic situations. For more information refer to ADP 3-0.

Chapter 1

1-13. When exercising mission command, the reconnaissance platoon leader, assisted by the platoon sergeant (PSG), uses a variety of techniques to prepare for missions, issue orders, employ the platoon, and communicate. The success of this process rests on decisive leadership, realistic training, a thorough understanding of the SOP, and the effective use of communications equipment. For maximum efficiency, the platoon leader keeps plans as simple as possible while ensuring the platoon has the necessary information and instructions. There are three tasks that the platoon leader completes to ensure mission accomplishment:

- Understand, visualize, describe, direct, lead, and assess.
- Develop teams.
- Lead, inform, and influence activities.

COMMAND

1-14. Command is an individual and personal function that combines imaginative problem solving, communication skills, and a thorough understanding of operations. Command during operations requires understanding the complex relationships among friendly and enemy forces and the environment, including the local population. This understanding helps commanders visualize and describe their intent and develop focused planning guidance.

1-15. Authority refers to the right and power to judge, act, or command. It includes responsibility, accountability, and delegation. Leaders rely on their education, experience, knowledge, and judgment as they plan the end state and lead their forces during preparation and execution.

1-16. Decision-making is a conscious process for selecting a course of action (COA). At the platoon level, many decisions are based upon SOP and standard unit drills that cover a wide range of routine and emergency actions. Evacuation of wounded Soldiers, rearming and resupply procedures, and actions on contact are a few examples. This enables the platoon to operate quickly and efficiently without constant guidance from the platoon leader. Standard operating procedures are especially critical in maintaining combat preparedness when leaders are tired or under stress as a result of continuous operations. This is the main reason why everyone in the platoon has a thorough understanding of the drills and SOP.

1-17. Leadership is the process of influencing people with purpose, direction, and motivation while accomplishing the mission and improving the organization. The reconnaissance platoon leader is an expert in Armor and Infantry tasks, proficient in mounted and dismounted missions, and knowledgeable of company operations. (Refer to FM 6-22 for more information.)

1-18. The platoon leader, assisted by the PSG, uses a variety of techniques to plan missions, issue orders, employ the platoon, and communicate. At platoon level, effective use of command is a function of several critical factors:

- The commander's intent.

Introduction

- Leadership.
- Training.
- Sound and thorough understanding of standard operating procedures.
- Tactically sound employment of graphic control measures, communications equipment, and techniques.

MISSION ORDERS

1-19. The use of mission orders is a technique for completing combat orders while allowing subordinates maximum freedom for planning and actions that accomplish objectives. Mission orders state the task organization, mission of the force, and the commander's intent. A brief concept of the operations, platoon missions, and essential coordinating instructions are also contained in the mission order. A mission assigned to subordinates includes the normal elements (who, what, when, where, and why), but the commander leaves out "how" the mission is conducted. (Refer to FM 3-20.971 for more information.)

CONTROL

1-20. Control is the regulation of forces and warfighting functions to accomplish the mission according to the commander's intent. This is the science of defining limits, computing requirements, allocating resources, monitoring performance, and directing subordinate actions. Time-distance factors, the time required initiating certain actions, and the inclusion of operational terms and graphics are also taken into consideration. Control also includes the physical capabilities and limitations of friendly and enemy organizations and systems. The science of control drives the commander's tasks and integrates the warfighting functions.

SITUATIONAL AWARENESS

1-21. Situational awareness (SA) is immediate knowledge about the conditions of the operation, constrained geographically and in time. Leaders begin their visualization of the battlefield with SA. Knowledge of the location, and the orientation and locations of friendly, threat, neutral, or noncombatant elements in the AO are the keys to making sound, quick, tactical decisions. It allows leaders to form logical conclusions for making decisions that anticipate future events and information. For the reconnaissance platoon, SA can be increased with the use of technological equipment inherent in each team, squad, and section.

Friendly Situational Awareness

1-22. The position of each vehicle in the unit is displayed on the Force XXI Battle Command Brigade and Below (FBCB2) screen. This provides the vehicle commander (VC) a clear picture of his location in relationship to the rest of the unit. While the system functions automatically for vehicles equipped to operate on the tactical internet, it does not provide locations for every friendly element on the battlefield. Dismounted Infantry squads from company Infantry platoons, scout observation posts (OPs), or multinational troops may be operating in, or adjacent to, the platoon's battle space. Icons representing these formations can be added into FBCB2 based on frequency modulation transmitted reports but are not updated

Chapter 1

in real time. As a result, the FBCB2 System cannot be the sole instrument used for clearing fires, and does not substitute for the commander's judgment in preventing fratricide.

Enemy Situational Awareness

1-23. Situational awareness of the threat is created from top down and bottom up feeds. The battalion S-2 populates the FBCB2 with threat icons based on spot reports (SPOTREPs) generated by assets outside the squadron, such as an unmanned aircraft system (UAS). Based on intelligence preparation of the battlefield (IPB), the S-2 augments actual locations with a situation template pinpointing the locations.

1-24. As the platoon conducts missions, it increases SA by sending an initial frequency modulation SPOTREP, followed by a digital SPOTREP via FBCB2, which uses the far target locator. When a VC sends a SPOTREP, he automatically populates the FBCB2 Systems in the task force with an icon that represents the threat (digital report recipients are based on the domain of the system). The unit commander, executive officer (XO), and first sergeant (1SG) evaluate the validity of the SPOTREP, remove additional icons if necessary (icon management), and forward the SPOTREP to the rest of the unit and higher headquarters (HQ) such as the battalion or squadron via FBCB2.

1-25. Reports concerning enemy formations represented by icons on the FBCB2 are updated as the enemy location changes or if the enemy is destroyed. Icons fade and eventually disappear from the FBCB2 screen as their information ages. The unit SOP governs the rate at which icons fade.

1-26. Situational awareness derived from FBCB2 is only as good as the reports it receives, and does not give a complete picture of the threats. The VCs and platoon leader makes sure vehicle scan techniques and platoon fire control plans enable friendly troops to detect threat forces not yet reported by digital means. The dismounted units receive constant updated information regarding SA from the platoon leader through frequency modulation communications.

GRAPHIC CONTROL MEASURES

1-27. Reconnaissance platoon leaders often generate platoon-level graphic control measures because of the decentralized nature of reconnaissance and security missions. It is essential that platoon graphic control measures be routinely incorporated into the graphics of the troop fire support team (FIST) and troop HQ element. Graphic control measures are considered rigid and unchangeable. Placement of platoon battle positions should be dictated by the terrain and commander's intent, as opposed to battle positions drawn on the map. For example, if the map location of a screen mission position does not allow the platoon leader to conduct proper surveillance on the enemy, the platoon leader can usually inform the commander and adjust the position as needed to accomplish the platoon mission. Control measures assist the platoon leader in identifying the necessary coordination that is accomplished with adjacent units. (Refer to FM 1-02 for more information.)

COMMUNICATION

1-28. The primary mission of reconnaissance platoons is to provide information to the commander about the enemy and other conditions of the area of operation. Because of the extended frontages and distances over which the platoon operates, it relies heavily on effective communication techniques. These techniques include wire, visual signals, or radio and digital system communication. This also includes the proper way of using the equipment and the effective application of operational terms, radiotelephone procedures, and digital tactics, techniques, and procedures (TTP).

1-29. The platoon leader ensures that Soldiers understand the communications procedures. For radio systems, including tactical satellite (TACSAT), this includes the different nets on which the platoon operates, positioning considerations, field-expedient communications techniques, and visual signals. In employing the platoon's digital systems (including FBCB2), scouts understand how to use hot keys: and prepare and send reports, orders, and overlays.

MEANS OF TACTICAL COMMUNICATION

1-30. The reconnaissance platoon has several available means of communication. Whether it is using messenger, wire, visual, sound, radio signals, or digital systems, the platoon remains flexible in order to react quickly to new situations. Use of communication methods are carefully planned and rehearsed to avoid dependence on a single technique. The SOP can give the platoon a tremendous advantage in mission accomplishment. Hand and arm/flag signals aid in controlling platoon movement. Clear and concise radio transmissions can reduce transmission times.

Net Control

1-31. The platoon net is the key for controlling the reconnaissance platoon. The smooth functioning of the net allows accurate information to be passed quickly to and from the platoon leader. This information flow is critical in maintaining the platoon leader's SA and enhancing mission command. When contact is made, the volume of traffic on the platoon net increases drastically. The platoon is organized to control, understand, and process this vast amount of information while engaging the enemy and possibly being engaged in turn. The following guidelines help ensure that the information flowing over the net is organized and controlled.

Net Discipline

1-32. The PSG is responsible for net discipline. In this capacity, he identifies and corrects any violation of procedure as it occurs. An improper or inefficient radio procedure, even in routine administrative reports, inhibits effective control. All scouts are experts in communications procedures. This ensures efficient communication within the platoon and allows effective communication with outside elements such as the squadron, battalion, troop command posts, other platoons, and subordinate or supporting elements.

1-33. During most maneuver and combat tasks, dispersion forces the reconnaissance platoon to rely heavily on effective communications by means of

FBCB2, wire, visual signals, and radio. The tactical situation dictates which type of communications system the reconnaissance platoon employs.

1-34. Standard operating procedures play a critical role in ensuring that platoon communications enhance situational understanding. The platoon leader and platoon sergeant should develop the SOP that contains the tactics, techniques, and procedures needed for combat. The SOP can describe prearranged signals that aid platoon movement by reducing frequency modulation radio and digital transmission times.

Reconnaissance Platoon Nets

1-35. All leaders in the platoon employ and monitor designated radio nets based on unit organization, mission requirements, and mission orders. The reconnaissance platoon may monitor or use several different nets during a mission. At a minimum the platoon uses the following radio nets:
- **Platoon.** This is the primary net for all platoon missions. All scouts within the platoon monitor and transmit on this net unless directed to use an alternate net.
- **Company/troop command.** The commander uses this net to maneuver the company or troop, and to process routine administrative/logistic (A/L) reports. The platoon leader and PSG monitor this net to acquire current tactical information based on reports from the commander, XO, and other platoon leaders. They transmit on the company net to keep the commander informed and to cross talk with other platoon leaders. The platoon leader and PSG have the authority to monitor and transmit on this net, and all leaders are able to switch to this net to send reports and receive guidance if they are unable to contact their platoon leader or PSG.

1-36. Every reconnaissance Soldier is an expert in the technical aspects of their voice and digital communications systems. In particular, he understands how to maintain each system, how to place it into mission, and how to troubleshoot it whenever it is not functioning properly. A properly functioning platoon net allows accurate information to be passed quickly to and from the platoon leader. This information flow is critical in maintaining the platoon leader's SA.

Routing Traffic

1-37. The PSG normally receives and consolidates A/L reports from section/squads, and other routine communications from the unit commanders. These reports are passed to the platoon leader or higher HQ using the procedures prescribed in the unit SOP. (Refer to FM 6-02.53 for more information.)

Introduction

SECTION III – COMMAND AND SUPPORT RELATIONSHIPS

COMMAND RELATIONSHIPS

1-38. Command relationships define superior and subordinate relationships between unit(s) and leaders. By specifying a chain of command, command relationships unify effort and give leaders the ability to employ subordinate forces with maximum flexibility. Command relationships identify the degree of control of the supported commander. The type of command relationship often relates to the expected longevity of the relationship between the units involved and quickly identifies the degree of support that the gaining and losing commanders provide.

- **Organic.** The platoon is assigned to and forms an essential part of the military organization. Organic units are listed in the higher unit's table of organization and equipment (TOE) or modified table of organization and equipment.
- **Assigned.** The platoon remains subordinate to a higher HQ for an extended period of time, typically years.
- **Attached.** The platoon is temporarily subordinated to the gaining HQ and the period may be lengthy, often months or years.
- **Operational control (OPCON).** This authority allows the gaining commander to task-organize and direct forces. The parent unit retains responsibility for training, maintenance, resupply, and unit-level reporting.
- **Tactical control.** This authority allows the gaining commander to direct but not to task-organize forces. The parent unit retains responsibility for training, maintenance, resupply, and unit-level reporting.

1-39. During most tactical missions, the reconnaissance platoon can be organized to operate with units such as Armor, Infantry or Stryker. The platoon can also have units or teams attached to them such as engineers, civil affairs teams, tactical military information support teams, human intelligence (HUMINT) collection teams, explosive ordinance disposal (EOD) teams, electronic warfare assets, and Army aviation.

SUPPORT RELATIONSHIPS

1-40. Supporting and supported units share specific relationships and responsibilities. For example, the assigning HQ retains logistic support responsibility and the authority to reorganize or reassign all or part of a supporting force. Although support relationships usually do not occur at the platoon level, it is important to understand how they affect the type of support it provides or receives. For further information refer to ADP 3-0. The three types of support relationships are—

- **Direct.** The reconnaissance platoon provides support to the unit. The platoon is under the command of the supported unit, and is required to report directly to that unit and provide any requested support.

Chapter 1

- **Reinforcing.** In this type of support, the platoon provides reinforcing support for another unit. As a secondary mission, it remains responsive for direct support requests.
- **General.** The reconnaissance platoon can provide general support to the unit as a whole or to any particular subunit.

SECTION IV – PLANNING CONSIDERATIONS

1-41. Planning is the process by which the platoon leader translates his visualization into a specific course of action, focusing on the expected results. This begins with the analysis and assessment of the conditions in the operational environment, with particular emphasis on the enemy to determine the relationship among the mission variables. Planning also involves understanding and framing the problem and envisioning the set of conditions that represent the desired end-state. Based on the commander's guidance, the platoon leader's plan includes formulating one or more suitable courses of action to accomplish the mission. (Refer to ADP 5-0 and ADRP 5-0 for more information.)

OPERATIONAL VARIABLES

1-42. Army forces use operational variables to understand and visualize the broad environment in which they are conducting operations. Operational variables are those broad aspects of the military and nonmilitary environment that may differ from one operational area to another, affecting major operations. They describe the military aspects of an operational environment and the population's influence on it. For more information refer to ADP 3-0.

MISSION VARIABLES

1-43. Mission variables are mission, enemy, terrain and weather, troops and support available, time available and civil considerations (METT-TC). These are the categories of relevant information used for mission analysis. The platoon leader uses the mission variables to synthesize operational variables and tactical-level information with local knowledge about conditions relevant to their mission.

1-44. Upon receipt of a warning order (WARNORD) or mission, the platoon leader narrows his focus to the six mission variables. Commanders analyze the civil considerations of areas, structures, capabilities, organizations, people, and events (ASCOPE).

1-45. Incorporating the analysis of the operational variables into METT-TC emphasizes the operational environment's human aspects. This emphasis is most obvious in civil considerations, but it affects the other METT-TC variables as well.

1-46. Incorporating human factors into mission analysis requires critical thinking, collaboration, continuous learning, and adaptation. It also requires analyzing local and regional perceptions.

1-47. Many factors influence perceptions of the enemy, adversaries, supporters, and neutrals. These include—
- Language.
- Culture.
- Geography.
- History.
- Education.
- Beliefs.
- Perceived objectives and motivation.
- Communications media.
- Personal experience.

1-48. The reconnaissance platoon interacts with people at many levels. In general, the people in an area of operations can be categorized as:—
- **Enemy.** This is a party identified as hostile. The use of force is authorized. An enemy is also called a combatant and is treated as such under the law of war.
- **Adversary.** This is a party acknowledged as potentially hostile to a friendly party and against which the use of force may be needed. Adversaries include members of the local population who sympathize with the enemy.
- **Supporter.** This is a party who sympathizes with friendly forces and who may or may not provide materiel assistance to them.
- **Neutrals.** This is a party who does not support or oppose friendly or enemy forces.

1-49. One reason land operations are complex is that all four categories are intermixed, often with no easy means to distinguish one from another. For more information refer to ADP 3-0.

TROOP-LEADING PROCEDURES

1-50. Troop-leading procedures (TLPs) are a dynamic process used by small-unit leaders to analyze a mission, develop a plan, and prepare for a mission. TLPs consist of eight steps and are supported by composite risk management. The step sequence of TLP is not rigid. Leaders can modify the sequence to meet the mission, situation, and available time. Some steps are done concurrently while others may go on continuously throughout the mission. (Refer to ADP 5-0 and ADRP 5-0 for more information.) The steps are:
- Step 1 – Receive the mission.
- Step 2 – Issue a warning order.
- Step 3 – Make a tentative plan.
- Step 4 – Initiate movement.
- Step 5 – Conduct reconnaissance.
- Step 6 – Complete the plan.

Chapter 1

- Step 7 – Issue the order.
- Step 8 – Supervise and refine.

RISK MANAGEMENT

1-51. The primary objective of risk management (RM) is to help units protect their combat power through accident prevention. The platoon leader and platoon sergeant gather the knowledge during the TLP to implement a protection measure for risk. RM entails making informed decisions that balance risk with mission benefits and provides all leaders with a systematic mechanism to identify risk associated with a COA during planning. (Refer to FM 5-19 for more information.)

FRATRICIDE AVOIDANCE

1-52. Leaders at all levels are responsible for preventing fratricide. They lower the probability of fratricide without discouraging boldness and audacity. Good leadership that results in positive weapons control, control of Soldier movements, and disciplined operational procedures helps achieve this goal. Situational understanding, friendly personnel, and combat identification methods are also key factors to fratricide avoidance. Most host nation contractors, day laborers, and nongovernmental organization (NGO) personnel who support Army operations face the same risks as U.S. forces. Since these personnel work and often live among U.S. forces, commanders include them in protection and combat identification plans. This may significantly increase the protection responsibility of commanders.

1-53. Fratricide avoidance is normally accomplished through a protection strategy emphasizing prevention centered on two fundamental areas—situational awareness and target identification. Fratricide may also be more prevalent during joint and coalition operations when communications and interoperability challenges are not fully resolved.

- **Situational awareness** is the immediate knowledge of the operation conditions constrained geographically and in time. It includes the real-time, accurate knowledge of one's own location and orientation; and the locations, activities, and intentions of other friendly, enemy, neutral, or noncombatant elements in the AO, sector, zone, or immediate vicinity.
- **Target identification** is the accurate and timely characterization of a detected object on the battlefield as friend, neutral, enemy, or unknown. (Refer to FM 3-20.15 for more information.) Unknown objects should not be engaged. The target identification process continues until positive identification has been made. An exception to this is a weapons-free zone where units can fire at anything that is not positively identified as friendly.

1-54. The potential for fratricide may increase with the fluid nature of the nonlinear operational environment and the changing disposition of attacking and defending forces. The presence of noncombatants in the AO further complicates operations. Simplicity and clarity are often more important than a complex, detailed plan when developing fratricide avoidance methods.

Chapter 2

Reconnaissance Platoon

Reconnaissance platoons are fundamental components of the armored brigade combat team, Infantry brigade combat team, and Stryker brigade combat team. They also serve as essential support in the reconnaissance and surveillance squadron of the battlefield surveillance brigade. This chapter discusses the role of the reconnaissance platoon, task organization, capabilities, duties, and responsibilities of key personnel.

SECTION I – ROLE OF THE RECONNAISSANCE PLATOON

FUNDAMENTAL ROLE

2-1. The fundamental role of the reconnaissance platoon is to conduct aggressive and stealthy missions that satisfy the commander's critical information requirements (CCIRs). The commander gives missions to the platoon and the platoon progressively builds SA of the OE for the commander. The critical information provided by the platoon enables the commander to develop situational understanding (SU), make comprehensive plans and decisions, and direct follow-on or future operations.

2-2. The CCIR is an information requirement identified by the commander as being critical for facilitating timely decision-making and successful execution of military operations. Two key elements are friendly force information requirements and priority intelligence requirements (PIR). The commander chooses whether to designate an information requirement as a CCIR based on likely decisions and visualization of the mission's course, which may support one or more decisions.

SECTION II – ORGANIZATION AND CAPABILITIES

RECONNAISSANCE SQUADRON AND COMBINED ARMS BATTALION RECONNAISSANCE PLATOON IN THE ABCT

2-3. Armored brigade combat team platoons are equipped with three cavalry fighting vehicles (CFVs) and five armored high-mobility multipurpose wheeled vehicles (HMMWVs) outfitted with long-range advanced scout surveillance systems (LRAS3s). (See Figure 2-1.)

Chapter 2

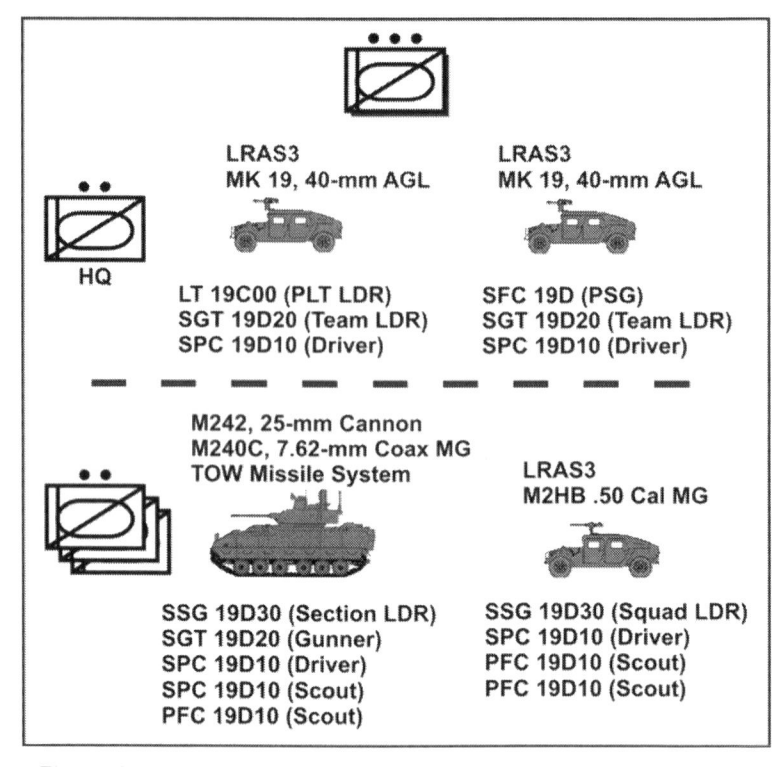

```
         •••
        ┌─────┐
        │  ⌀  │
        └─────┘
              LRAS3                      LRAS3
              MK 19, 40-mm AGL           MK 19, 40-mm AGL
  ••
┌─────┐       [HMMWV]                    [HMMWV]
│  ⌀  │
└─────┘
  HQ          LT 19C00 (PLT LDR)         SFC 19D (PSG)
              SGT 19D20 (Team LDR)       SGT 19D20 (Team LDR)
              SPC 19D10 (Driver)         SPC 19D10 (Driver)
─ ─ ─ ─ ─ ─ ─ ─ ─ ─ ─ ─ ─ ─ ─ ─ ─ ─ ─ ─ ─ ─ ─ ─ ─ ─ ─
              M242, 25-mm Cannon
              M240C, 7.62-mm Coax MG
  ••          TOW Missile System         LRAS3
┌─────┐                                  M2HB .50 Cal MG
│  ⌀  │       [CFV]                      [HMMWV]
└─────┘

              SSG 19D30 (Section LDR)    SSG 19D30 (Squad LDR)
              SGT 19D20 (Gunner)         SPC 19D10 (Driver)
              SPC 19D10 (Driver)         PFC 19D10 (Scout)
              SPC 19D10 (Scout)          PFC 19D10 (Scout)
              PFC 19D10 (Scout)
```

Figure 2-1. Reconnaissance squadron and CAB reconnaissance platoons in the ABCT

CAPABILITIES

2-4. The reconnaissance squadron and combined arms battalion reconnaissance platoons in the ABCT have the following capabilities:
- The M3A3 CFV provides firepower and survivability in decisive action.
- The CFV has a stabilized turret employing 25-mm cannon, 7.62-mm coaxial machine gun, and a tube-launched, optically tracked, wire-guided (TOW) missile system.
- Each CFV carries two scouts to execute dismounted tasks.
- The LRAS3 provides real-time ability to detect, recognize, identify, and geo-locate distant targets while transmitting data directly to digital information systems such as FBCB2.

LIMITATIONS

2-5. These squadrons and platoons have the following limitations:
- They are vulnerable to enemy counterreconnaissance and security measures, and fighting for information in decisive action is limited.

Reconnaissance Platoon

- The M1114/M1152 HMMWV provides inadequate survivability against direct and indirect fires in missions teamed with the more survivable M3A3.
- Limited dismounts reduce the capability of the platoon to conduct long-term OPs, continuous screening ability, or to concurrently conduct multiple dismounted tasks associated with route, zone, or area reconnaissance.

ORGANIZATION

2-6. There are several organizational options the reconnaissance squadron and CAB reconnaissance platoons in the ABCT have, including the basic options covered in this discussion. The troop commander and platoon leader may develop other combinations to meet unique METT-TC requirements and to accommodate attachments.

2-7. In most missions, reconnaissance squadron and CAB reconnaissance platoons are employed in sections, with each section made up of section/squad leaders and team leaders, and their vehicle crews (or teams). These elements may be further organized into designated dismounted teams and squads as outlined in previous paragraphs.

Four-Section (Two-Vehicle) Organization

2-8. When observing multiple avenues of approach or when multiple reconnaissance missions are required, the four-section (two-vehicle) organization is effective. This grouping provides security at the section level and gives sufficient maneuver and mission command capability to conduct limited separate missions. However, the ability to conduct dismounted patrols is very limited and these organizational considerations apply:

- The headquarters section consists of the platoon leaders and PSGs HMMWVs.
- Three reconnaissance sections (A, B, and C) that consist of one section leader's CFV and one squad leader's HMMWV.
- This configuration provides six personnel per reconnaissance section for dismounted tasks.

Three-Section Organization

2-9. The three-section organization is ideal for reconnaissance along a single route. It allows employment of two short-duration OPs, although the ability to concurrently conduct dismounted patrols is very limited. These organizational considerations apply:

- The headquarters section includes the platoon leader mounted in a CFV and the PSG mounted in a HMMWV.
- Two reconnaissance sections (A and B) that consist of one section leader's CFV and two team leader's HMMWVs.
- This configuration provides eight personnel per reconnaissance section for dismounted tasks.

5 April 2013 ATP 3-20.98 2-3

Chapter 2

Two-Section Organization

2-10. Considered ideal for reconnaissance when vehicle weight/size restrictions or armor protection is a key factor for the mission, the two-section organization maximizes security at the section level. This gives the sections sufficient maneuver and mission command capability to conduct limited separate missions, and allows for maximum dismounted capabilities. In certain scenarios the CFV section may be left out of the mission if METT-TC and RM factors allow this organization. These organizational considerations apply:

- Alpha section consists of the platoon leader and a team leader mounted in CFVs, and two team leaders mounted in two HMMWVs.
- Bravo section is the PSG and two team leaders mounted in HMMWVs, and one team leader mounted in a CFV.
- If weight or size restrictions apply as a mission constraint, the platoon leader and the PSG are mounted in a HMMWV.

Teams

2-11. The platoon may also be task-organized for maneuver purposes into smaller reconnaissance teams. These normally consist of a single vehicle and its crew, but may require combining personnel from multiple vehicles/crews in accordance with METT-TC requirements.

IBCT MOUNTED RECONNAISSANCE PLATOON

2-12. The three reconnaissance platoons are each organized with six armored, mounted HMMWVs. (See Figure 2-2.)

Reconnaissance Platoon

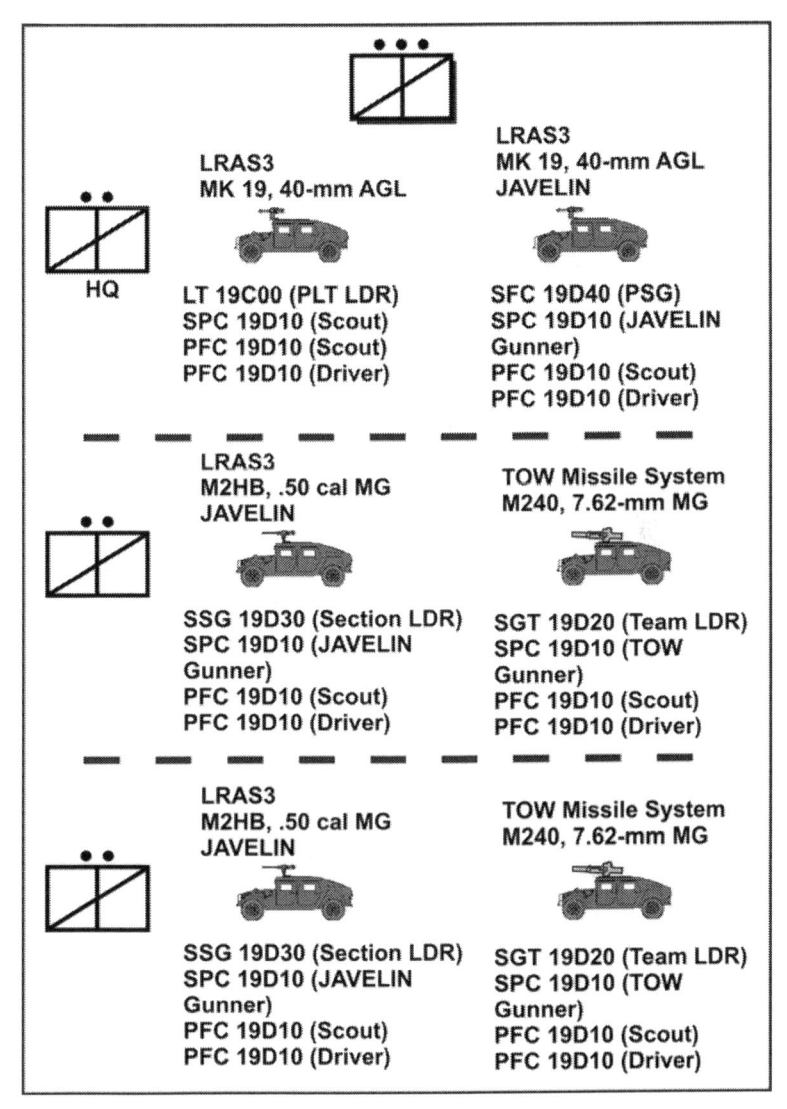

```
                          •••
                         ┌────┐
                         │ ╱  │
                         └────┘
                                    LRAS3
              LRAS3                 MK 19, 40-mm AGL
  ••          MK 19, 40-mm AGL      JAVELIN
┌────┐
│ ╱  │
└────┘
 HQ           LT 19C00 (PLT LDR)    SFC 19D40 (PSG)
              SPC 19D10 (Scout)     SPC 19D10 (JAVELIN
              PFC 19D10 (Scout)     Gunner)
              PFC 19D10 (Driver)    PFC 19D10 (Scout)
                                    PFC 19D10 (Driver)

              LRAS3
              M2HB, .50 cal MG      TOW Missile System
  ••          JAVELIN               M240, 7.62-mm MG
┌────┐
│ ╱  │
└────┘
              SSG 19D30 (Section LDR)   SGT 19D20 (Team LDR)
              SPC 19D10 (JAVELIN        SPC 19D10 (TOW
              Gunner)                   Gunner)
              PFC 19D10 (Scout)         PFC 19D10 (Scout)
              PFC 19D10 (Driver)        PFC 19D10 (Driver)

              LRAS3
              M2HB, .50 cal MG      TOW Missile System
  ••          JAVELIN               M240, 7.62-mm MG
┌────┐
│ ╱  │
└────┘
              SSG 19D30 (Section LDR)   SGT 19D20 (Team LDR)
              SPC 19D10 (JAVELIN        SPC 19D10 (TOW
              Gunner)                   Gunner)
              PFC 19D10 (Scout)         PFC 19D10 (Scout)
              PFC 19D10 (Driver)        PFC 19D10 (Driver)
```

Figure 2-2. IBCT mounted reconnaissance platoon

CAPABILITIES

2-13. The IBCT mounted reconnaissance platoon has the following capabilities:
- Possesses two mounted TOW systems.

Chapter 2

- Is highly mobile and responsive.
- Provides all-weather, continuous, accurate, and timely information gathering through the combined use of LRAS3.

LIMITATIONS
2-14. The following limitations apply to the IBCT mounted reconnaissance platoon:
- Due to vulnerability by enemy counterreconnaissance and security measures, fighting for information in decisive action is limited.
- The HMMWV provides inadequate survivability and mobility.
- The platoon possesses limited dismounted capability.
- Limited dismounts reduce the capability of the platoon to conduct long-term OPs, continuous screening, or to conduct the dismounted tasks associated with route, zone, or area reconnaissance.

ORGANIZATION
2-15. The IBCT reconnaissance platoon has a wide variety of organizational choices, including the basic options covered in the following discussion. The troop commander and platoon leader may develop other combinations to meet unique METT-TC requirements and to accommodate attachments.

2-16. In most missions, the IBCT reconnaissance platoon is employed by reconnaissance sections. Each section is made up of a section leader, team leaders, and their vehicle crews.

Two-Section Organization
2-17. A two-section organization is effective when only two maneuver corridors have to be observed, or when two distinct reconnaissance missions are required. This organization maximizes security at the section level, giving the sections sufficient maneuver and mission command capability to conduct limited separate missions. This allows the following dismounted capabilities:
- Twelve personnel for dismounted tasks, such as a reconnaissance patrol.
- Six personnel (two per vehicle) for performing reconnaissance tasks while conducting mounted tasks.
- Six personnel to man OPs or conduct patrols.

Three-Section Organization
2-18. This organization is ideal for reconnaissance along a single route. It allows employment of three short-duration OPs. However, the ability to concurrently conduct dismounted patrols is very limited.

Six-Vehicle Organization
2-19. The six-vehicle organization is the most difficult to control. The platoon leader employs this method when he has six separate information sources at the

same time. This allows only one dismount to provide local security. The platoon may also be task organized for maneuver purposes into smaller reconnaissance teams, each normally consisting of a single vehicle and its crew.

IBCT DISMOUNTED RECONNAISSANCE TROOP AND INFANTRY BATTALION RECONNAISSANCE PLATOONS

CAPABILITIES

2-20. The dismounted reconnaissance troop (DRT) and Infantry battalion reconnaissance platoons have the following capabilities:

- Provides all-weather, continuous, accurate, and timely reconnaissance and security in complex, close, and urban terrain.
- Employs the UAS to enhance reconnaissance efforts.
- Conducts stealthy reconnaissance and security tasks.
- Rapidly assesses situations and directs combat power, reconnaissance, and security capabilities to meet PIR.
- Employs integrated and synchronized reconnaissance to detect threat deception, decoys, and cover and concealment that otherwise would not be detected by single-capability surveillance methods.
- Supports targeting and target acquisition through available ground and aerial assets.
- Assists in shaping the AO by providing information or directing fires to disrupt the threat.
- Conduct ground, water, and air insertion.

LIMITATIONS

2-21. The DRT and Infantry battalion reconnaissance platoons have the following limitations, which can be mitigated with careful employment or augmentation:

- Limited mounted capability, requiring augmentation of mobility platforms for rapid movement.
- Limited direct-fire standoff, lethality, and survivability.
- More time required to plan and employ.
- Dismounted tasks associated with zone, area, and route reconnaissance.
- Only has the Force XXI BCB2 System in the vehicles.
- May require augmentation to perform offense or defense missions.
- Requires augmentation from engineer assets to perform technical engineer tasks.
- Limited organic sustainment assets.
- Requires vehicle augmentations to perform convoy security.

Chapter 2

ORGANIZATIONS

2-22. Each reconnaissance platoon has three sections. Each section consists of two four-man teams and a leader's vehicle carrying four personnel. (See Figure 2-3.)

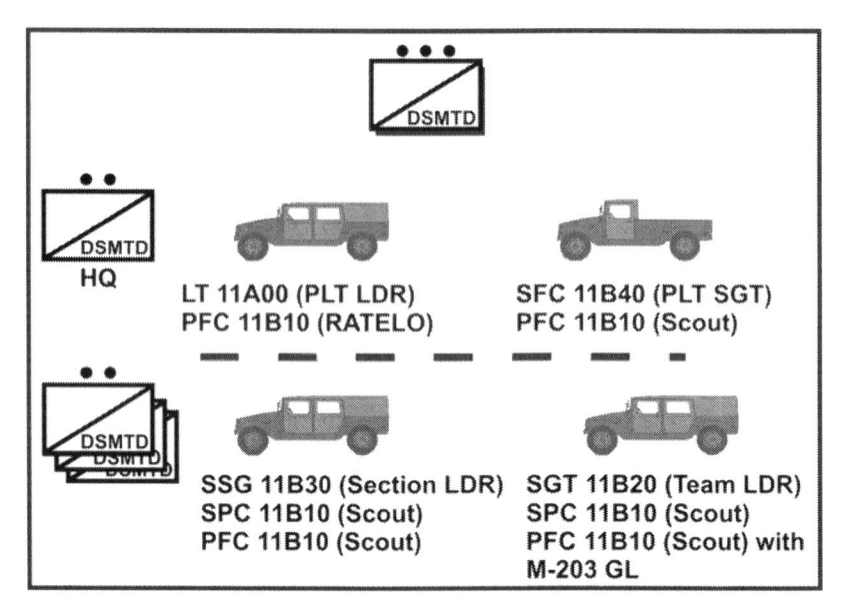

Figure 2-3. DRT reconnaissance platoon and Infantry battalion reconnaissance platoons

EQUIPMENT

2-23. The DRT and Infantry battalion reconnaissance platoons are designed as a foot-mobile unit with few organic vehicles. The unit is equipped with weapon systems and equipment suited to dismounted reconnaissance and security tasks. The Infantry battalion platoon has no organic crew-served weapons, and most Soldiers within the unit are equipped with the M4 rifle. (See Figure 2-4.) Currently, other major equipment issued includes:

- 1 – HMMWV with trailer.
- 1 – FBCB2 computer.
- 6 – M249 SAW machine guns.
- 6 – 40-mm grenade launchers.
- 3 – Javelin command launch units.

Reconnaissance Platoon

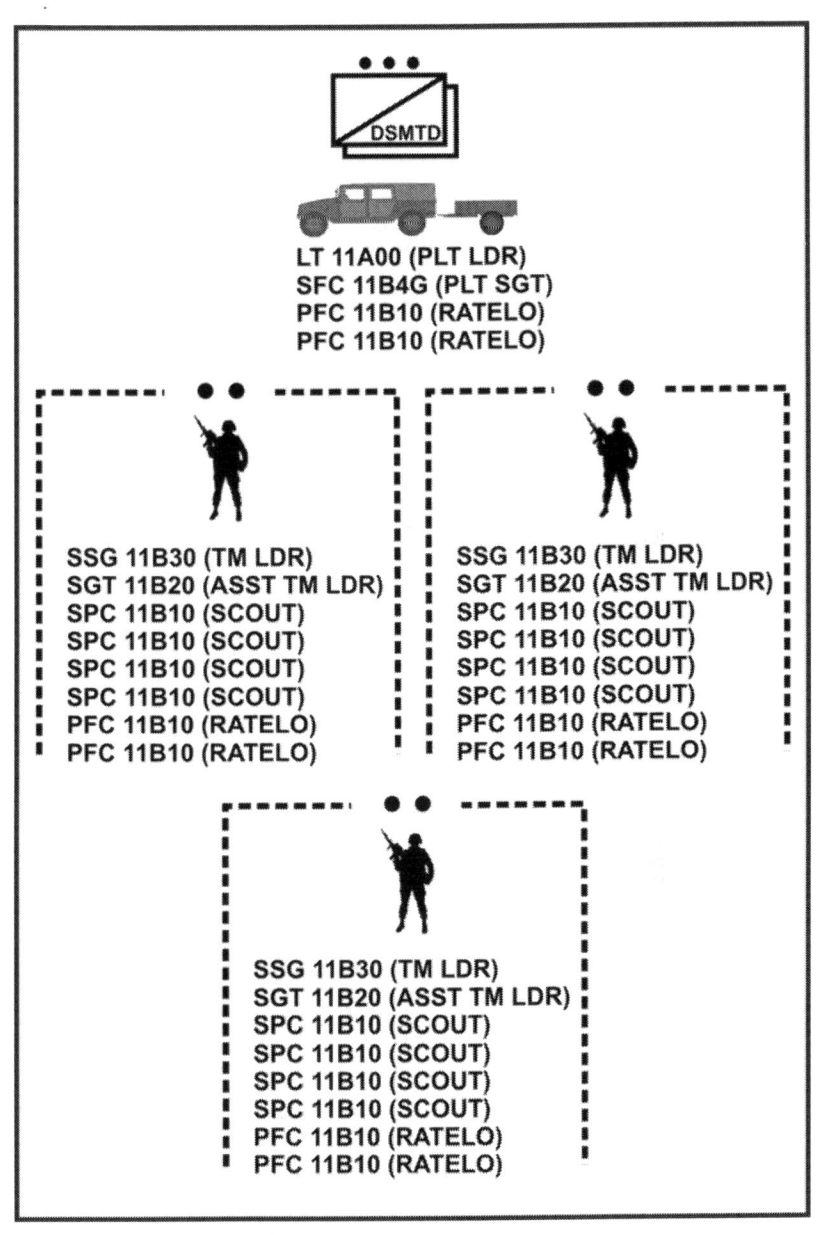

```
                    DSMTD

         LT 11A00 (PLT LDR)
         SFC 11B4G (PLT SGT)
         PFC 11B10 (RATELO)
         PFC 11B10 (RATELO)
```

SSG 11B30 (TM LDR)
SGT 11B20 (ASST TM LDR)
SPC 11B10 (SCOUT)
SPC 11B10 (SCOUT)
SPC 11B10 (SCOUT)
SPC 11B10 (SCOUT)
PFC 11B10 (RATELO)
PFC 11B10 (RATELO)

SSG 11B30 (TM LDR)
SGT 11B20 (ASST TM LDR)
SPC 11B10 (SCOUT)
SPC 11B10 (SCOUT)
SPC 11B10 (SCOUT)
SPC 11B10 (SCOUT)
PFC 11B10 (RATELO)
PFC 11B10 (RATELO)

SSG 11B30 (TM LDR)
SGT 11B20 (ASST TM LDR)
SPC 11B10 (SCOUT)
SPC 11B10 (SCOUT)
SPC 11B10 (SCOUT)
SPC 11B10 (SCOUT)
PFC 11B10 (RATELO)
PFC 11B10 (RATELO)

Figure 2-4. Infantry battalion reconnaissance platoon

Chapter 2

SBCT RECONNAISSANCE PLATOON AND INFANTRY BATTALION SCOUT PLATOON

2-24. This platoon is organized with four Stryker reconnaissance vehicles (RVs). (See Figures 2-5 and 2-6.)

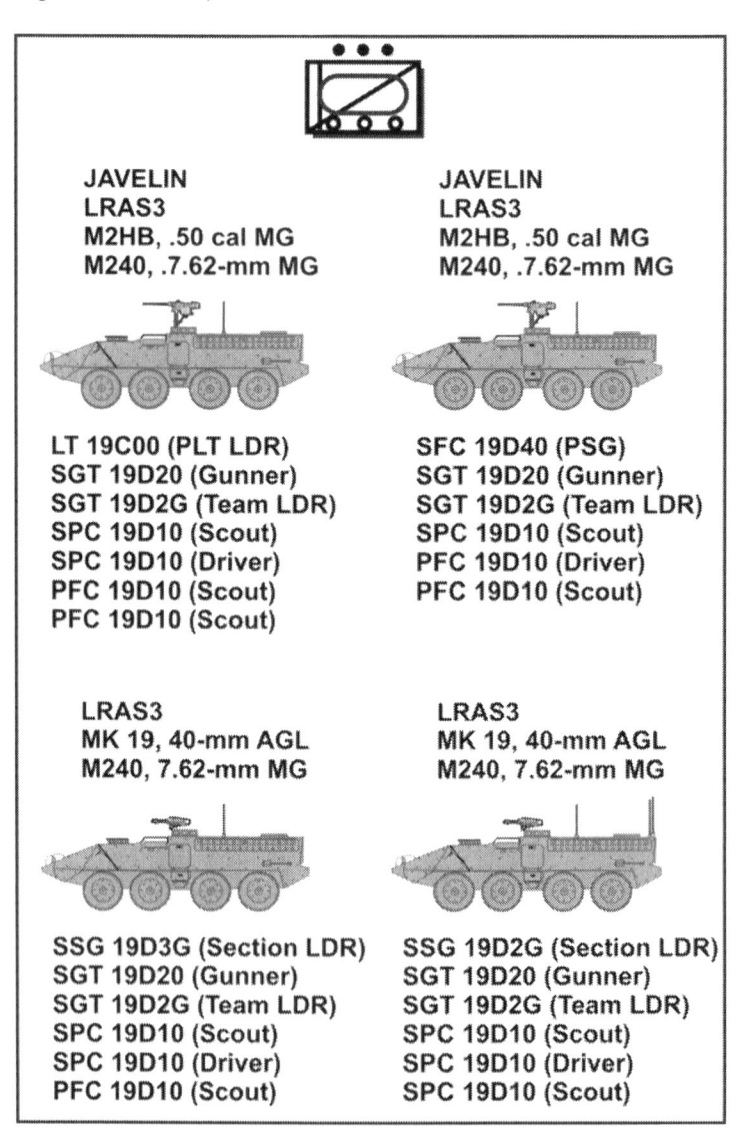

JAVELIN
LRAS3
M2HB, .50 cal MG
M240, .7.62-mm MG

JAVELIN
LRAS3
M2HB, .50 cal MG
M240, .7.62-mm MG

LT 19C00 (PLT LDR)
SGT 19D20 (Gunner)
SGT 19D2G (Team LDR)
SPC 19D10 (Scout)
SPC 19D10 (Driver)
PFC 19D10 (Scout)
PFC 19D10 (Scout)

SFC 19D40 (PSG)
SGT 19D20 (Gunner)
SGT 19D2G (Team LDR)
SPC 19D10 (Scout)
PFC 19D10 (Driver)
PFC 19D10 (Scout)

LRAS3
MK 19, 40-mm AGL
M240, 7.62-mm MG

LRAS3
MK 19, 40-mm AGL
M240, 7.62-mm MG

SSG 19D3G (Section LDR)
SGT 19D20 (Gunner)
SGT 19D2G (Team LDR)
SPC 19D10 (Scout)
SPC 19D10 (Driver)
PFC 19D10 (Scout)

SSG 19D2G (Section LDR)
SGT 19D20 (Gunner)
SGT 19D2G (Team LDR)
SPC 19D10 (Scout)
SPC 19D10 (Driver)
SPC 19D10 (Scout)

Figure 2-5. SBCT reconnaissance platoon

CAPABILITIES

2-25. The SBCT reconnaissance platoon has the following capabilities:

- Provides all-weather, continuous, accurate, and timely reconnaissance and security in complex, close, and urban terrain.
- Possesses four Javelin systems.
- Has access to information and intelligence provided by assets in the squadron surveillance troop, such as the UAS, and chemical, biological, radiological, nuclear, and high-yield explosives (CBRNE) reconnaissance platoon.
- Provides all-weather, continuous, accurate, and timely information gathering through the combined use of LRAS3s.

LIMITATIONS

2-26. The SBCT reconnaissance platoon has the following limitations:

- Fighting for information is limited due to enemy counterreconnaissance and security measures vulnerability.
- Four-vehicle/two-section platoons accept risk when individual Stryker's reconnoiter lateral routes and the terrain adjacent to the route when performing route reconnaissance.
- With limited dismounts within sections, the two sections are combined to generate the required dismounts needed to execute a long-term OP, continuous screening, or conduct the dismounted tasks associated with route, zone, or area reconnaissance.

Chapter 2

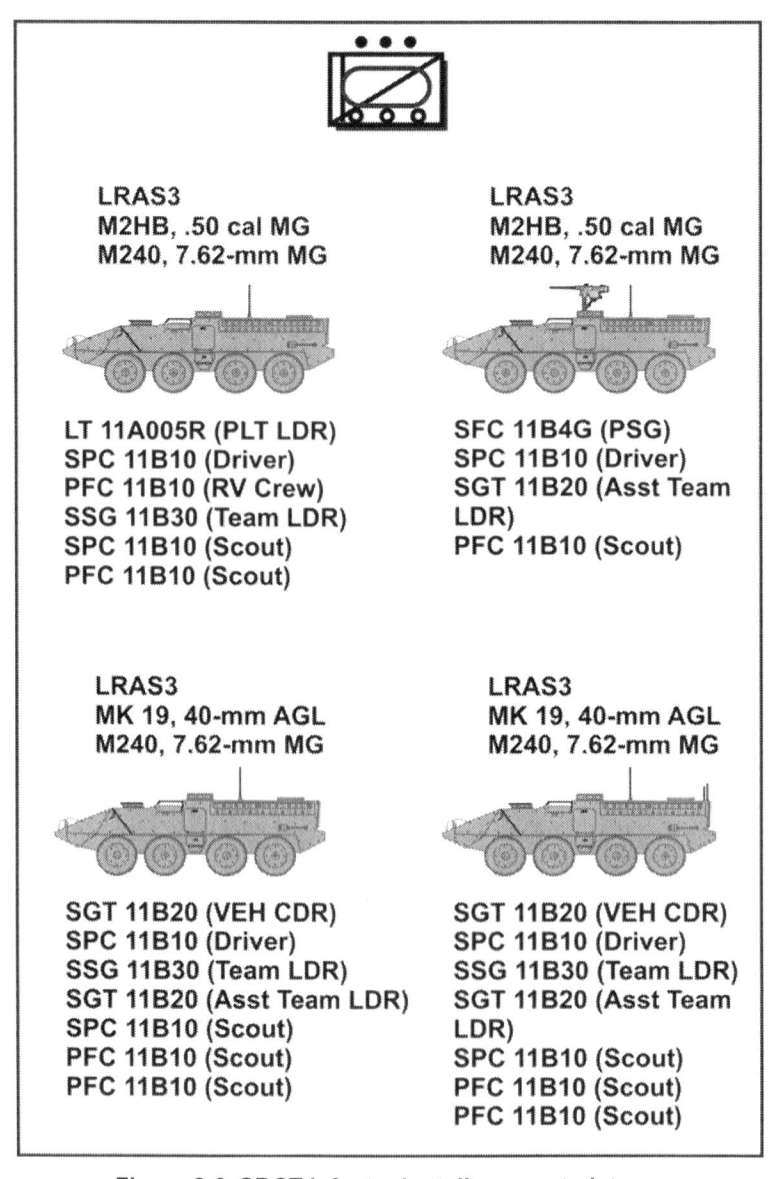

```
          LRAS3                        LRAS3
          M2HB, .50 cal MG             M2HB, .50 cal MG
          M240, 7.62-mm MG             M240, 7.62-mm MG

          LT 11A005R (PLT LDR)         SFC 11B4G (PSG)
          SPC 11B10 (Driver)           SPC 11B10 (Driver)
          PFC 11B10 (RV Crew)          SGT 11B20 (Asst Team
          SSG 11B30 (Team LDR)         LDR)
          SPC 11B10 (Scout)            PFC 11B10 (Scout)
          PFC 11B10 (Scout)


          LRAS3                        LRAS3
          MK 19, 40-mm AGL             MK 19, 40-mm AGL
          M240, 7.62-mm MG             M240, 7.62-mm MG

          SGT 11B20 (VEH CDR)          SGT 11B20 (VEH CDR)
          SPC 11B10 (Driver)           SPC 11B10 (Driver)
          SSG 11B30 (Team LDR)         SSG 11B30 (Team LDR)
          SGT 11B20 (Asst Team LDR)    SGT 11B20 (Asst Team
          SPC 11B10 (Scout)            LDR)
          PFC 11B10 (Scout)            SPC 11B10 (Scout)
          PFC 11B10 (Scout)            PFC 11B10 (Scout)
                                       PFC 11B10 (Scout)
```

Figure 2-6. SBCT Infantry battalion scout platoon

Reconnaissance Platoon

CAPABILITIES

2-27. The SBCT Infantry battalion scout platoon has the following capabilities:
- Provides all-weather, continuous, accurate, and timely reconnaissance and security in complex, close, and urban terrain.
- Provides all-weather, continuous, accurate, and timely information gathering through the combined use of LRAS3s.

LIMITATIONS

2-28. The SBCT Infantry battalion scout platoon has the following limitations:
- Fighting for information is limited due to enemy counterreconnaissance and security measures vulnerability.
- Four-vehicle/two-section platoons accept risk when individual Stryker's reconnoiter lateral routes and the terrain adjacent to the route when performing route reconnaissance.

MOUNTED ORGANIZATION

2-29. The SBCT reconnaissance platoon is limited in organizational configurations because it has only four organic vehicles. Regardless of the mission it is executing, or the formation or movement technique it is using, the platoon normally operates in one of three organizations during mounted tasks:
- Three sections with one vehicle in each section and the platoon leader's vehicle providing mission command.
- Two sections with two vehicles in each section.
- Four-vehicle platoon.

Two-Section Organization

2-30. The two-section organization is used when increased security is required, the AO can be covered efficiently with only two elements, or the threat situation is unknown. This type of organization limits the amount of terrain the platoon covers and decreases the speed with which the platoon performs its tasks. On the other hand, it increases internal section security by providing mutually supporting fires, and gives the platoon leader and PSG greater flexibility in performing mission command and sustainment requirements.

Three-Section Organization

2-31. The four-vehicle organization is the most difficult to control. The platoon leader employs this organization when he has four separate information sources at the same time, or when the platoon is executing certain surveillance missions. This organization should be used when the threat is low or nonexistent. This formation may also be implemented during short-duration security missions.

Dismounted Organization

2-32. Dismounted tasks are the SBCT reconnaissance platoon's primary means for gathering information. The basic dismounted elements are the team, section, and platoon. Each vehicle has a designated dismounted team.

Chapter 2

BATTLEFIELD SURVEILLANCE BRIGADE RECONNAISSANCE PLATOON

2-33. The BFSB reconnaissance platoon is a lightly armed organization that relies on stealth versus aggressive methods to conduct reconnaissance and surveillance, and to avoid combat. The light composition of vehicles and weapons dictates that if an asset is compromised, it withdraws or exfiltrates to preserve its information collecting capability. If an asset becomes decisively engaged it relies on its limited firepower, and Army or joint fires for protection and to break contact. This platoon is organized with six armored HMMWVs. (See Figure 2-7.)

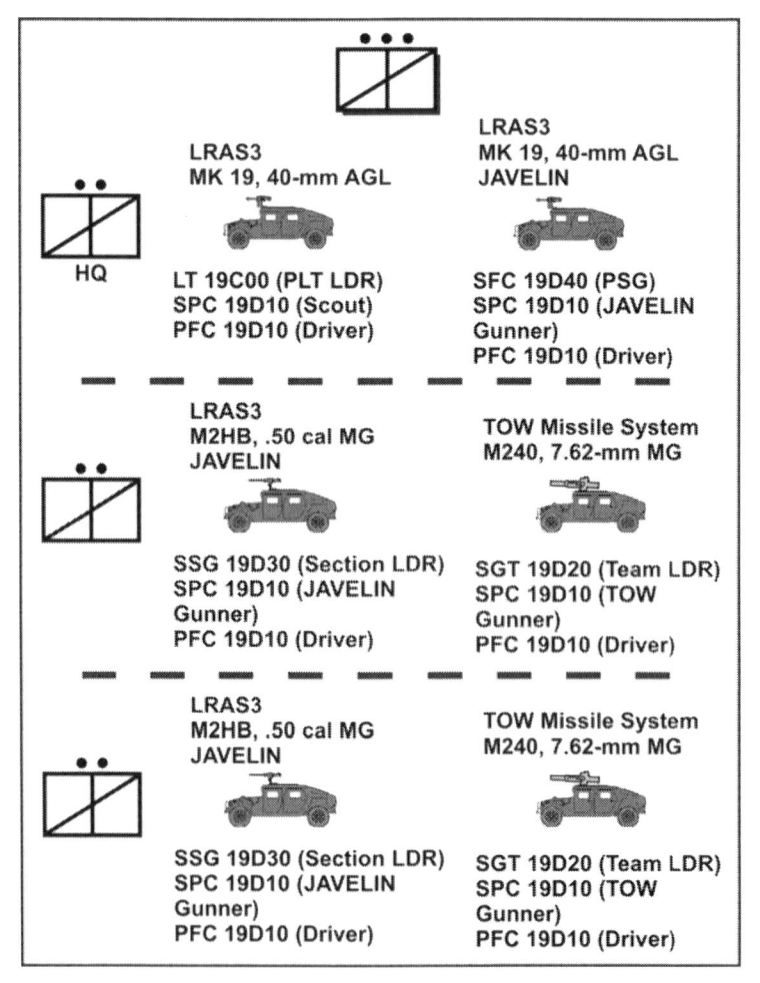

Figure 2-7. BFSB reconnaissance platoon

CAPABILITIES

2-34. The BFSB reconnaissance platoon has the following capabilities:
- It is integrated into the BFSB architecture and has access to information and intelligence collected by brigade assets.
- Possesses multiple Javelin missile systems.
- It is highly mobile and responsive.
- Provides all-weather, continuous, accurate, and timely information gathering through the combined use of LRAS3s.

LIMITATIONS

2-35. The BFSB reconnaissance platoon has the following limitations:
- Fighting for information in decisive action is limited.
- Security missions in decisive action are limited.
- Does not have organic mortars.
- The platoon possesses limited dismounted capability. The HMMWV provides inadequate survivability and mobility and carries a crew of three, one of whom is tasked to perform dismounted reconnaissance tasks.
- With limited dismounts within sections, the two reconnaissance sections are combined to generate the required dismounts to execute a long-term OP, continuous screening, or to conduct the dismounted tasks associated with route, zone, or area reconnaissance.

ORGANIZATION

2-36. Much like the IBCT reconnaissance platoon, the BFSB reconnaissance platoon has a wide variety of organizational options, including the basic options covered in the following discussion. The troop commander and platoon leader may develop other combinations to meet unique METT-TC requirements and to accommodate attachments.

Two-Section Organization

2-37. This is an effective organization when only two maneuver corridors have to be observed, or when two distinct reconnaissance or surveillance missions are required. This organization maximizes security at the section level and gives the sections sufficient maneuver and mission command capability to conduct limited separate missions. This organization allows the following dismounted capabilities:
- Three personnel (one per vehicle) for performing reconnaissance tasks while conducting mounted tasks.
- Five personnel to man OPs or conduct patrols.

Three-Section Organization

2-38. This organization is ideal for reconnaissance along a single route. It allows employment of three short-duration OPs, but the ability to concurrently conduct dismounted patrols is very limited.

Chapter 2

Six-Vehicle Organization
2-39. The six-vehicle organization is the least secure and most difficult to control. It should be used only when there are simultaneous multiple surveillance requirements. This organization allows only one dismount to provide local security.

SECTION III – KEY PERSONNEL

DUTIES AND RESPONSIBILITIES
2-40. The reconnaissance platoon leader and the platoon's noncommissioned officers (NCOs) are experts in the use of organic weapons, indirect fires, land navigation, supporting fires, demolitions, obstacles, communications, reconnaissance, HUMINT collection, liaison, and security techniques. They are familiar with Infantry, Armor, mortar, and combined arms tactics; and be able to react to rapidly changing situations. They also know how to employ sustainment assets that are attached or supporting the platoon. Because of the many missions the platoon is capable of performing, the reconnaissance platoon leader and PSG are proficient in tasks at all skill levels of their military occupational specialty (MOS). Additionally, they are familiar with the capabilities, limitations, and deployment of surveillance techniques, and reconnaissance security surveillance assets, such as ground sensors and the UAS.

PLATOON LEADER
2-41. The platoon leader is responsible to the higher commander for the discipline, combat readiness, and training of the platoon; and the maintenance of its equipment. He has a thorough knowledge of reconnaissance and security tasks, and works closely with the higher commander during the mission analysis portion of the planning process. A solid understanding of troop-leading procedures, and the ability to apply them quickly and efficiently in the field are essential. The platoon leader is proficient in the tactical employment of the platoon, knows the capabilities and limitations of personnel and equipment, and is an expert in threat organizations, doctrine, and equipment.

2-42. Most of all, the platoon leader is versatile, able to exercise sound judgment, and makes correct decisions quickly based on the commander's intent and the tactical situation. It is the platoon leader's responsibility to ensure that every member of the platoon understands and can successfully accomplish the following leadership competencies:
- Troop-leading procedures.
- Deployment.
- Tactical movement.
- Observation post establishment and operation.
- Patrolling and local security.
- Proper use and maintenance of all organic equipment and communications, including digital assets.

Reconnaissance Platoon

- Employment of fires.
- Actions on contact.
- The multidimensional aspects of reconnaissance, security, and surveillance.
- Reporting procedures.
- Employment of reconnaissance security surveillance assets such as PROPHET and UAS.

PLATOON SERGEANT
2-43. The PSG leads elements of the platoon as directed by the platoon leader, and assumes command in the absence of the platoon leader. During tactical missions, the PSG may assist in the control of the platoon, requiring personal proficiency in all of the platoon's leadership competencies. The PSG assists the platoon leader in maintaining discipline, coordinating training, and controlling the platoon. Supervising equipment maintenance, logistics tasks, and other sustainment activities is also the PSGs responsibility.

SECTION AND TEAM LEADERS
2-44. All leaders have a thorough knowledge of reconnaissance and security tasks. Section/squad and team leaders are experts in:

- Dismounted patrolling.
- Mounted tasks.
- Employment of reconnaissance security surveillance assets.
- Conducting surveillance and establishing OPs.
- Employment of fires.
- Training and discipline of their sections.
- Tactical employment and control of the section, requiring proficiency in the platoon's leadership.
- Maintenance and operation of all vehicles and equipment organic to their sections.

Note. Team leaders have the same responsibilities for their teams as section leaders have for sections.

GUNNER
2-45. Gunners in a reconnaissance platoon are subject matter experts of their vehicle and its weapons system. While serving as a gunner, a Soldier mentors the other Soldiers assigned to his vehicle. The gunner is responsible for the operation of the assigned vehicle, and for maintaining his and other reconnaissance platoons' proficiency in gunnery, dismounted and mounted maneuver, and other MOS skills.

DRIVER
2-46. Drivers in a reconnaissance platoon are tasked to be technically competent on their assigned vehicle, and tactically proficient at driving in all mission

Chapter 2

environments. The driver is initially responsible for operation and maintenance of the assigned vehicle, and maintaining other perishable reconnaissance skills. While assigned to a vehicle, the driver is responsible for the following:

- Observation of his sector of responsibility.
- Maintenance for the vehicle—preventative maintenance checks and services (PMCS).
- Maintaining and improving all scout skills.
- Preparing for positions of increased responsibility within the platoon.

Chapter 3

Reconnaissance

SECTION I – OVERVIEW

3-1. The primary mission for the reconnaissance platoon is to gain information and survey enemy territory. This is conducted as part of security, stability, and other missions; and can be performed mounted or dismounted. Mounted reconnaissance is conducted when time is critical and there is a need to cover a large area quickly. This allows a fast tempo in combat that makes maximum use of the optics, firepower, communications, and protection provided by reconnaissance vehicles. Dismounted reconnaissance allows platoons to gather detailed information, enhance security, and move with stealth in rugged terrain.

3-2. Scouts reconnoiter terrain to determine movement and maneuver conditions relevant to friendly and enemy forces. Reconnaissance platoons thoroughly understand how the enemy deploys its forces, and the sequence and timing of their entry into the AO. When they find the enemy, these platoons determine the enemy's composition, disposition, strengths, and weaknesses in detail. The accurate and timely reporting of enemy locations and strength can make the difference between success and failure for the mission. At the same time, it is critical that reconnaissance platoons never lose sight of their objectives or become committed in engagements that eliminate their freedom to maneuver.

3-3. Reconnaissance platoons conduct reconnaissance based on their commander's intent and guidance. Their mission is to provide current, accurate information about the enemy, terrain, weather, and civil considerations such as culture, infrastructure, and physical resources within a specified AO. In simplest terms, the reconnaissance platoon and its higher HQ take steps to link the purpose of the reconnaissance to one or more of the following requirements:
- Obtaining information to answer the commander's CCIR.
- Obtaining information to fill voids in the unit planning analysis by answering PIR and specific information requirements (SIR).
- Supporting targeting requirements by conducting target acquisition and surveillance.

3-4. These actions provide follow-on forces with an opportunity for freedom of maneuver and rapid closure to their objective. Reconnaissance platoons use the fundamentals of reconnaissance to prevent maneuver elements from being surprised or interrupted, which protects these forces from losing Soldiers and equipment.

Chapter 3

PLATOON MISSIONS

3-5. The primary missions of the reconnaissance platoon, in support of troop/company, squadron/battalion, and brigade missions include the following three forms of reconnaissance:

- Zone.
- Area.
- Route.

3-6. The reconnaissance platoon may conduct these primary missions during offensive or defensive tasks, stability tasks, or civil support tasks. To execute their primary missions in decisive action, the platoon is flexible, well trained, and fully manned.

FUNDAMENTALS OF RECONNAISSANCE

3-7. There are seven fundamentals that are common to all successful reconnaissance tasks. (Refer to FM 3-20.971 and FM 3-90-1 for more information.) Platoon leaders and all members of the reconnaissance platoon make certain their planning, preparation, and execution of reconnaissance missions adhere to these fundamentals:

- Ensure continuous reconnaissance.
- Do not keep reconnaissance assets in reserve.
- Orient on the reconnaissance objective.
- Report all information rapidly and accurately.
- Retain freedom of maneuver.
- Gain and maintain threat contact.
- Develop the situation rapidly.

SECTION II – RECONNAISSANCE PLANNING CONSIDERATIONS

RECONNAISSANCE PLANNING GUIDANCE

3-8. The purpose of this section is to outline the planning, methods, and tactical employment involved in executing reconnaissance missions. Critical to the platoon leader's ability to execute the mission is a clear understanding of the focus, tempo, and engagement criteria of the mission. This information is essential commander's guidance and is an extension of the commander's intent. It is meant to fully clarify the reconnaissance effort. It should be received from higher HQ and issued to subordinates.

3-9. Focus allows the platoon leader to determine which critical tasks the platoon needs to accomplish first. This helps narrow the scope of operations to the information that is most important to squadron and brigade missions. In small-scale contingency operations, the platoon focus might be terrain-oriented or enemy

Reconnaissance

security force-oriented. In an environment involving stability tasks, the platoon might be focused on determining the local populace sentiment or on identifying local paramilitary leaders. While all critical tasks have some degree of applicability in any given mission, certain tasks are more important for specific missions and are clearly articulated at each level. (Refer to FM 3-20.971 or ATTP 3-20.97 for more information.) Considerations related to the focus include:

- Threat/enemy (conventional and nonconventional forces, terrorist organizations, and criminal elements).
- Society/human demographics (HUMINT, civilian considerations).
- Terrain (bridges, routes, and defensible terrain).
- Infrastructure (facilities and food distribution).
- Any other aspects of METT-TC that is directly relevant to the mission.
- The critical reconnaissance tasks that are to be conducted or deleted.

3-10. Tempo is the relative speed and rhythm of military operations over time with respect to the enemy. This allows the platoon leader to establish associated time requirements and correlate them with planning time, movement formations, engagement criteria, and methods such as dismounted or mounted reconnaissance. The platoon leader establishes the tempo by determining whether the reconnaissance is stealthy or aggressive.

STEALTHY, FORCEFUL, DELIBERATE, AND RAPID RECONNAISSANCE

3-11. Reconnaissance can be characterized as stealthy, forceful, deliberate, or rapid. Through his intent, the commander defines when key reconnaissance tasks are accomplished in relationship to the end-state of the missions. This allows the platoon leader to exercise initiative in determining how to meet the commander's intent.

3-12. Stealthy reconnaissance occurs when the platoon conducts a methodical, time-consuming mission that minimizes chance enemy contact. It is usually conducted dismounted, and stealth is strongly emphasized. The lighter an organization, the more stealth becomes essential. Stealthy reconnaissance takes maximum advantage of covered and concealed terrain, and reduced battlefield signatures. However, stealth cannot be guaranteed and units attempting to conduct stealthy reconnaissance must have immediate access to supporting fires, and be drilled to react correctly once the enemy makes contact. The platoon can expect to operate over extended distances long before combat is executed.

3-13. Forceful reconnaissance is the opposite of stealthy, and involves mounted tasks conducted at a faster pace. Because the units are less concerned with being detected by the enemy, CFV and motorized reconnaissance platoons are better suited for this type of reconnaissance. Dismounted reconnaissance platoons may need vehicle augmentation. A platoon conducting aggressive reconnaissance uses movement to rapidly develop the situation. Direct and indirect fire systems are also employed. Firepower, aggressive exploitation of actions on contact,

Chapter 3

operations security, and training are required for the unit to survive and accomplish the mission.

3-14. Deliberate reconnaissance entails slow, detailed, broad-based operations where the platoon may accomplish several tasks. Mounted reconnaissance platoon leaders ensure that subordinates understand the slower tempo and the use of dismounted scouts to collect the required information.

3-15. Rapid reconnaissance focuses on collecting a few key pieces of information required by the troop commander. CFV and motorized reconnaissance platoons are better suited for this type of reconnaissance. Dismounted reconnaissance platoons may need vehicle augmentation.

3-16. The platoon leader's instruction for tempo should be based on the higher commander's guidance. Specific information for the execution should include:
- Planning timelines.
- Tasks to subordinate units.
- Specific information requirements.
- Latest time information.
- Movement techniques.
- Reconnaissance methods (mounted, dismounted, aerial, sensor).
- Tactical risk.

3-17. A key factor in reconnaissance execution is the time available to conduct the mission. Platoon leaders recognize and accept the increased risk to the reconnaissance element and the main body when the pace is accelerated. This risk can be offset by employing air reconnaissance and technical means to cover open terrain or areas of lower threat.

Engagement Criteria

3-18. Engagement criteria establish which targets and circumstances the platoon is expected to defeat, and which targets they are expected to hand off to higher elements. Understanding what the commander wants the platoon to destroy, and the awareness of the enemy's most likely COA, helps the platoon leader identify section/team capabilities. This enables the platoon leader to—
- Conduct the platoon's direct fire planning.
- Develop engagement areas.
- Plan for the destruction of specific enemy vehicles.

3-19. Engagement criteria are generally defined using the terms aggressive and discreet. An aggressive reconnaissance is primarily a mounted, fast-paced mission with permissive engagement criteria that allows the force to fight for information. A discreet reconnaissance is characterized by restraint in initiating combat to gain information. Merely defining engagement criteria using the terms "aggressive" or "discreet" is not sufficient in today's OE. Engagement criteria should be defined using precise doctrinal terms. The commander issues specific planning guidance to define the engagement criteria and execution information, such as:

- Engagement criteria.
- Bypass criteria.
- Reconnaissance handover.
- Priority of fires.
- Rules of engagement or rules for use of force.
- Weapons control status.
- Inform and influence activities guidance.

3-20. The platoon leader plans for and rehearses escalation of force (EOF) procedures for missions within the AO. Escalation of force is a tool to determine if a person is demonstrating hostile intent. Reconnaissance platoons may consider a wide range of steps before using any lethal force which results in weapons discharge, or damage to individuals or property. Platoons following EOF procedures can make quick and reasonable decisions to protect themselves. This prevents unnecessary death and collateral damage during the application of force without limiting the reconnaissance platoon's ability to protect themselves.

3-21. By using the correct equipment and current intelligence information, leaders reduce the unnecessary use of lethal force and promote a positive image of the Army. Rehearsal during troop-leading procedures ensures everyone understands how an EOF supports the rules of engagement (ROE), and the difference between the two. A thorough understanding also includes the impact of EOF incidents on local nationals and the negative perceptions which may complicate the AO.

OPERATIONAL CONSIDERATIONS

3-22. Reconnaissance platoons adjust their traditional roles in order to fulfill the broader mission of collecting information. They are prepared to operate beyond the traditional roles of reconnaissance, surveillance, and target acquisition of enemy forces in decisive action. This involves the surrounding political, economic, social, information, infrastructure, physical environment, and time variables of the area.

3-23. This multidimensional requirement means that the reconnaissance platoon develops an understanding of what is happening and why. In the operational environment, collecting information that may identify enemy centers of gravity, decisive points, and the means to influence their will and behavior are some of the most important contributions the reconnaissance platoon can make to ensure successful mission accomplishment.

RECONNAISSANCE TECHNIQUES

3-24. Techniques are directed by the commander. There are several avenues of consideration for reconnaissance platoons. Push and pull are two techniques used by the reconnaissance platoon.

Chapter 3

RECONNAISSANCE PUSH AND PULL

3-25. Reconnaissance push emphasizes development of a detailed plan to focus the effort on an evolving maneuver sequel, or several sequels, prior to the deployment of the reconnaissance assets. The plan often encompasses several branches or COAs that are understood by leaders at all levels and are well rehearsed.

3-26. Reconnaissance pull defers committing to a specific plan or COA prior to deployment of reconnaissance elements. It focuses on collecting enemy strength and weakness information that is critical in formulating the future plan or COA. Reconnaissance pull emphasizes opportunity at the expense of a detailed, well-rehearsed plan. Upon discovering enemy strengths and weaknesses, the platoon, as part of the reconnaissance squadron and brigade, "pulls" the brigade combat team (BCT) along the path of least resistance into positions of tactical advantage. When weaknesses are discovered during execution, a change in the scheme of maneuver can help the units to exploit opportunities. (Refer to FM 3-20.96 for more information.)

RECONNAISSANCE METHODS

3-27. There are four reconnaissance methods:
- Aerial.
- Sensor.
- Mounted.
- Dismounted.

3-28. Whenever possible, the platoon uses a combination of all methods when employing reconnaissance fundamentals. This provides depth and redundancy throughout the AO, and helps the platoon accomplish the reconnaissance mission based on the factors of METT-TC, reconnaissance guidance, and the commander's intent. Mounted and dismounted surveillance can be employed simultaneously, providing flexibility and capitalizing on the strengths of both methods. The most valuable reconnaissance asset is still the platoon directly observing the target.

Aerial Reconnaissance

3-29. Aerial reconnaissance conducted by UAS or Army aviation assets provides a flexible, low-risk means for gaining basic information in the least amount of time. It serves as a link between sensors and mounted or dismounted reconnaissance.

3-30. The UAS is organic to the troop and squadron for surveillance and reconnaissance of the SBCT, IBCT, and ABCT. Complex terrain, adverse weather, and enemy deception/countermeasures can degrade the UAS effectiveness. The reconnaissance platoon can employ the UAS forward in its AO to facilitate reconnaissance in complex terrain, or to maximize the UAS operational range.

3-31. Normally, aerial assets are controlled by the reconnaissance platoon higher HQ. The higher HQ may direct aerial reconnaissance, or the platoon leader may determine the requirement for it when:
- Time is extremely limited or information is required quickly.

Reconnaissance

- Ground reconnaissance elements are not available.
- The objective is at an extended range.
- Verification of a target is needed.
- Enemy locations are known and extremely dangerous (high risk) to ground assets.
- Enemy locations are vague, but are identified as high risk to ground assets.
- Terrain is complex and weather conditions are favorable.

Mounted Reconnaissance

3-32. Mounted reconnaissance enables a more rapid tempo at the expense of stealth and security. This increases the probability of enemy detection, and can compromise reconnaissance efforts. Information in mounted surveillance is primarily gathered using the LRAS3 to observe from a greater distance. Though a reconnaissance mission can be primarily mounted, dismounted activities such as confirming or denying enemy activity in dead space may be required during the maneuver for security reasons. Using dismounted assets also increases the stealth and security of a mounted reconnaissance, and should be used whenever possible while staying within mission timelines.

3-33. The platoon leader directs platoons to conduct mounted reconnaissance when—

- Time is limited.
- Distances require mounted movement.
- Stealth and security are not primary concerns.
- Detailed information is not required or the mounted method affords the same opportunity to collect information as the dismounted method.
- The nature of the surveillance target allows vehicles to approach (such as a terrain feature or road intersection in stability tasks).
- Enemy locations are known.

Dismounted Reconnaissance

3-34. Dismounted reconnaissance is the most time-consuming means of inspection for ground units, but it permits collection of the most detailed information about the enemy, terrain, society, and infrastructure within a given area or zone, or along a route. The platoon can use dismounted reconnaissance to collect detailed information about a fixed site or enemy from close proximity, although the platoon may be limited in the number of dismounted scouts it can employ at any time. For example, when a section is required to operate a long-duration OP, the mounted reconnaissance platoon may have to leave a vehicle in the assembly area or forward operating base (FOB) to increase the number of dismounts available. Engineer augmentation is desirable during dismounted reconnaissance to support terrain and infrastructure assessment.

Chapter 3

3-35. The platoon leader directs the platoon to conduct dismounted reconnaissance when:
- Stealth is required or security is the primary concern.
- Time is available.
- Detailed information is required.
- The reconnaissance target is a stationary enemy, fixed site, or terrain feature.
- Enemy contact is expected or has been achieved through visual/electronic means.
- Reconnaissance vehicles cannot move through an area because of terrain or enemy presence.

3-36. Sensor operations cue a combination of aerial and dismounted/mounted methods. They allow flexibility in economizing reconnaissance assets and can observe areas where contact is likely but cannot be observed. They can maintain surveillance of areas that need to be observed over extended periods and may be employed as the "cue" for aerial, dismounted, and mounted reconnaissance. Sensors provide redundancy when assets are pushed forward to facilitate ground reconnaissance, and can extend surveillance distance between ground reconnaissance and the enemy. Some sensor elements, such as PROPHET, may operate under higher HQ control within the reconnaissance AO, while other elements, such as ground sensors, may be attached to the platoon to facilitate ground inspection.

3-37. The platoon leader needs to know the capabilities and limitations of the various sensor systems. These systems are susceptible to countermeasures, lack the ability to convey the human dimension of the AO in terms of assessing the enemy's morale, and cannot make crucial decisions or judgment calls.

3-38. The higher HQ may direct the use of sensors to—
- Expand the scope of missions in a larger AO.
- Conduct missions of an extended duration.
- Conduct CBRNE reconnaissance.
- Trigger (cue) a more thorough ground or aerial reconnaissance of a given area.

SECTION III – FORMS OF RECONNAISSANCE

3-39. The primary missions of the reconnaissance platoon is to conduct the following four forms of reconnaissance:
- Zone.
- Area.

- Route.
- Reconnaissance in force.

ZONE RECONNAISSANCE

3-40. The commander normally assigns a zone reconnaissance when detailed information before maneuvering forces through a region defined by boundaries is needed. This information provides the commander with a detailed picture of how the enemy plans to defend the zone, enabling the commander to choose the appropriate COA. The platoon normally scouts an area as part of a larger force, but may conduct a zone reconnaissance with proper augmentation. The scope of an area reconnaissance may include the execution of route and area reconnaissance tasks.

3-41. Zone reconnaissance focuses on one or more of the following types of missions:
- Terrain.
- Force-oriented (threat or enemy).
- Society-oriented.
- Infrastructure-oriented.

3-42. The techniques and objectives of terrain-oriented and force-oriented zone reconnaissance are not mutually exclusive. The commander's guidance on the focus of the reconnaissance and METT-TC factors dictates the priorities and critical tasks for the mission.

3-43. Terrain-oriented zone reconnaissance is used to gain detailed information about routes, topography, and resources within the assigned zone. This is the most comprehensive type of reconnaissance mission. It is common for a platoon executing a zone reconnaissance in highly restrictive terrain to advance at approximately 1 kilometer (km) per hour, whereas a reconnaissance mission in open and rolling terrain can cover more than 40 kms per hour.

3-44. Force-oriented zone reconnaissance is employed to gain detailed information about enemy forces within the region. As the platoon conducts this type of mission, its focus is on determining the enemy's locations, strengths, and weaknesses. ABCT reconnaissance platoons are more suited to missions against enemies that are heavily equipped.

3-45. When augmented with the appropriate assets, a reconnaissance platoon can conduct the multidimensional aspect of zone reconnaissance to gain information about the civilian population and infrastructure in a particular area.

CRITICAL TASKS FOR ZONE RECONNAISSANCE

3-46. Zone reconnaissance is usually conducted over a larger physical space and may include a route or area reconnaissance (with the associated critical tasks). Unless the commander directs otherwise, the critical tasks include:
- Find and report all enemy forces.
- Reconnoiter and determine trafficability of all terrain.

- Inspect and classify all bridges.
- Locate fords or crossing sites near all bridges.
- Inspect and classify all overpasses, underpasses, and culverts.
- Within capability, locate all minefields and other obstacles, reduce or breach them, and clear and mark lanes.
- Locate and identify bypasses around built-up areas, obstacles, and contaminated areas.
- Report information.

3-47. In addition to these tasks, the reconnaissance platoon is prepared to conduct other tasks deemed critical by the higher commander. Additional tasks may include:

- Identifying threat activities (including insurgent and opposition leaders), countermeasures, and probable COAs.
- Determining the size, location, and composition of society/human demographics. Examples include race, sex, age, religion, language, tribe, clan, class, education, history, government, and factions.
- Establishing and maintaining contact with local civilian and military leadership.
- Investigating the society with HUMINT teams to determine the needs of the population, which includes the—
  - Regional, local, and neighborhood situations.
  - Organizations and operational methods of terrorists, transnational groups, and ethnic centers of gravity.
  - Financial and economic systems.
  - Media activities (local, U.S., and international).
- Identifying key municipal infrastructure that can affect military operations, including sewage, water, electricity, academic, trash, medical, safety, and other considerations (SWEAT-MSO).
- Identifying the allegiances of the local population to factions, religious groups, or other organizations.

Planning

3-48. Zone reconnaissance is very time-consuming. Unless the orders specify which tasks to omit, all critical tasks listed in the previous discussion are implied in the mission statement. When speed is the primary concern, commanders modify the focus, tempo, and engagement criteria to prioritize the critical tasks for the platoon leader. The width of the zone is determined by the road network, terrain features, anticipated enemy activity, and time available to accomplish the mission. UAS assets can be used in an economy of force role to observe areas beyond the operational reach of ground reconnaissance elements.

3-49. The parent unit's order includes phase lines and other graphic control measures within the area that control the maneuver of the units during the zone reconnaissance mission. The platoon leader verifies mission requisites by identifying

Reconnaissance

information requirements, CCIR, SIR, and develops a visualization of the higher commander's plan.

Preparation

3-50. To allow subordinates time to prepare for the zone reconnaissance, the platoon leader issues a detailed WARNORD as quickly as possible. This enables the subordinates to begin their own planning and preparations. The platoon leader also passes any other instructions or information that may help subordinates prepare for the mission. The minimum information that should be included in the WARNORD is:

- Mission or nature of the reconnaissance.
- Time and place for issuing the operation order (OPORD).
- Elements participating in the reconnaissance.
- Specific tasks not addressed by the SOP.
- Timeline for the reconnaissance.

3-51. After issuing a WARNORD for the mission, the platoon leader analyzes the mission to determine what needs to be accomplished. The following considerations are taken into account:

- Commander's guidance on focus. (The reconnaissance objective of threat/enemy, terrain, social/human demographics, infrastructure, or a combination of factors.)
- Tempo. (Time allowed for mission accomplishment, and the use of stealthy or forceful tempo.)
- Engagement criteria. (What situations constitute a platoon fight? In what situation does the platoon defer the fight to a higher element? What are the bypass criteria?)
- Information received about the threat during the IPB to determine what enemy activity is expected in the encounter.
- Terrain. (Conduct a map reconnaissance and examine any imagery intelligence [IMINT], signal intelligence [SIGINT], HUMINT, or information from other units to determine what types of terrain the reconnaissance platoon is to operate over.)
- Need for requesting and integrating outside assets such as HUMINT, counterintelligence (CI), civil affairs (CA), and military police (MP).

3-52. This analysis is important to identify areas the enemy could occupy based on observation capability, fields of fire, and natural obstacles. From these factors the platoon leader determines the manner in which the reconnaissance platoon accomplishes the mission.

3-53. The platoon leader develops a COA and contingencies, and completes troop-leading procedures to accomplish the assigned mission. Phase lines on easily identifiable terrain through the zone may be added to help control movement. Checkpoints are placed in specific areas that are reconnoitered or aid in controlling

Chapter 3

the mission. If the terrain is mixed with extensive dead space and easily identifiable features, boundaries may be used to designate areas of responsibility for each section. The platoon leader places contact points at critical areas to ensure the sections maintain contact; and determine when conditions support the employment of the UAS ahead or on the flanks of the reconnaissance platoon. This provides early warning or acts as an additional set of eyes behind the reconnaissance. If the UAS is used, coordinating air space usage to prevent coverage redundancy or collision with other aircraft is required. The platoon leader adds additional control measures to aid in the control of the sections, including the—

- Start point (SP).
- Release point (RP).
- Line of departure (LD).
- Grid Index Reference System (GIRS)/Terrain Index Reference System (TIRS).
- Named areas of interest (NAIs).
- Limit of advance (LOA).
- Reconnaissance objective.

3-54. The platoon leader works with the fire support officer (FSO) to plan and refine indirect fire targets that support the reconnaissance platoon's scheme of maneuver. At a minimum, they should plan targets on known or suspected enemy positions to increase the responsiveness of indirect fires. Enemy detection by UAS that results in the employment of indirect fires may require the UAS to be moved out of the area. Considerations are similar for helicopters when indirect fires are inbound.

3-55. Depending on applicable METT-TC considerations, the reconnaissance platoon can conduct the zone reconnaissance using a two-section, three-section, or single-vehicle/team organization. They deploy to cover the entire zone. Usually operating in an area it knows very little about, the COA allows for flexibility, responsiveness, and security as the platoon moves. If attachments are present, planning their location and enforcing formation discipline in the scheme of maneuver are critical factors in preventing navigational errors, searching for lost vehicles or Soldiers, reducing fratricide risk, and preventing elements from bunching up and affecting the rate of movement.

3-56. Another consideration is movement techniques. Depending on the time available and the likelihood of enemy contact, the platoon leader may choose one or a combination of three movement techniques to conduct the zone reconnaissance:

- Traveling.
- Traveling overwatch.
- Bounding overwatch.

Execution

3-57. In order to maximize reconnaissance assets and be prepared for chance contact, the platoon leader deploys the sections before reaching the LD. This also

Reconnaissance

aligns the sections with their designated AOs. The platoon is in position early enough to conduct observation of the LD. To do this, the platoon leader designates a section or team to conduct a reconnaissance of the route from the SP to the RP, and capture the time it takes to complete the movement. This time is used in deciding when to execute the SP, allowing the platoon enough time to complete movement to the LD and establish initial OPs.

3-58. Once the reconnaissance platoon has occupied their initial positions before the LD, vehicle commanders direct team members to scan the zone beyond the LD for enemy movement. Vehicles are turned off to allow for sound observation. During this time, the platoon leader requests SU from the commander or S-2 on enemy activity prior to moving across the LD. The platoon remains in observation positions until the time prescribed in the OPORD and then crosses the LD, or on order from the commander.

3-59. The reconnaissance platoon executes zone reconnaissance by using the technique of movement described in the OPORD. The sections move into section AOs within the zone for which the platoon is responsible. The platoon leader uses phase lines, checkpoints, contact points, or GIRS/TIRS to direct movement so the platoon can reconnoiter the entire zone. The platoon leader ensures the sections remain generally on line while maintaining adequate security through overwatch. This prevents development of significant gaps that a moving enemy could exploit and is accomplished by section/team leaders submitting location reports on a timely and regular basis.

3-60. In mounted reconnaissance platoons, scouts dismount to gather detailed information, reconnoiter danger areas, or move through areas that are not accessible to the vehicles. The sections maneuver through their sectors in a zigzag pattern to ensure that the zone is properly explored, and to accomplish all critical tasks. The platoon continues to inspect the zone until it reaches the LOA or the final reconnaissance objective. After completing actions on the objective, the reconnaissance platoon may transition to a follow-on assignment which may include moving into a screen mission. This allows the reconnaissance platoon to provide early warning of enemy activities; send Class I, III, and V reports; and conduct consolidation and reorganization while friendly elements move into a defense behind the platoon.

OBSTACLE RECONNAISSANCE

3-61. How the reconnaissance platoon approaches reconnaissance of an obstacle or restriction depends on whether or not it is covered by enemy fire or observation. (Refer to FM 3-20.98 for more information.) The five following steps outline the process of conducting an obstacle reconnaissance:

- Detection.
- Local security and reconnaissance.
- Reconnaissance of obstacles and restrictions.

Chapter 3

- Selection of a COA.
- Recommendation/execution of a COA, including bypass.

AREA RECONNAISSANCE

3-62. An area reconnaissance is the directed effort of obtaining detailed information concerning the terrain or enemy activity within a prescribed area. The tasks accomplished by the platoon as part of an area reconnaissance are generally the same as those for a zone reconnaissance. In fact, area reconnaissance is often employed during a zone reconnaissance for small towns, dead zones, and NAIs. The primary difference that identifies an area reconnaissance is the reduced size of the area compared to a zone reconnaissance.

3-63. Also, an area has a continuous boundary. Before moving forces into or near a specified area, the commander may call on the reconnaissance platoon to conduct an area inspection to avoid being surprised by unsuitable terrain conditions or unexpected enemy forces. The area can be a town, ridgeline, woods, intervisibility (IV) line/dead space, or another feature that friendly forces intend to occupy, pass through, or avoid.

3-64. Area reconnaissance is frequently employed to gain information on specified areas, objectives, or danger areas (to confirm IPB templates), and provide detailed information regarding enemy compositions and dispositions. Within a designated zone, area reconnaissance can be used to focus the platoon on a specific vicinity that is critical to the commander. Figure 3-1 is an example of area reconnaissance. They include the following:

- Dismounted reconnaissance patrols move ahead of their forward edge of the battle area (FEBA) to locate enemy obstacles that influence the BCT's axis of attack, fighting positions on dominant terrain, and reserve forces hidden prior to a deliberate attack.
- Combined arms battalion reconnaissance platoons are able to focus on dominant terrain locations that influence the CAB movement after brigade reconnaissance has cleared the area of potential enemy forces.

3-65. Area reconnaissance can be a stand-alone mission or a task to a section or platoon within a zone reconnaissance mission. The employment of the UAS can reduce the amount of time reconnaissance platoons need to move through the area by confirming or denying PIR, or clearing danger area/dead space templated during the platoon analysis process. Area reconnaissance can be terrain-oriented, force-oriented (threat/enemy), society-oriented, infrastructure-oriented, or a combination of these factors. The platoon leader analyzes the mission using METT-TC to determine whether to conduct one of these factors of reconnaissance separately, or conduct them in conjunction with each other.

3-66. A platoon augmented with the appropriate assets can conduct the multidimensional aspect of area reconnaissance, if directed, to gain detailed information about the civilian population and infrastructure in a particular area.

Reconnaissance

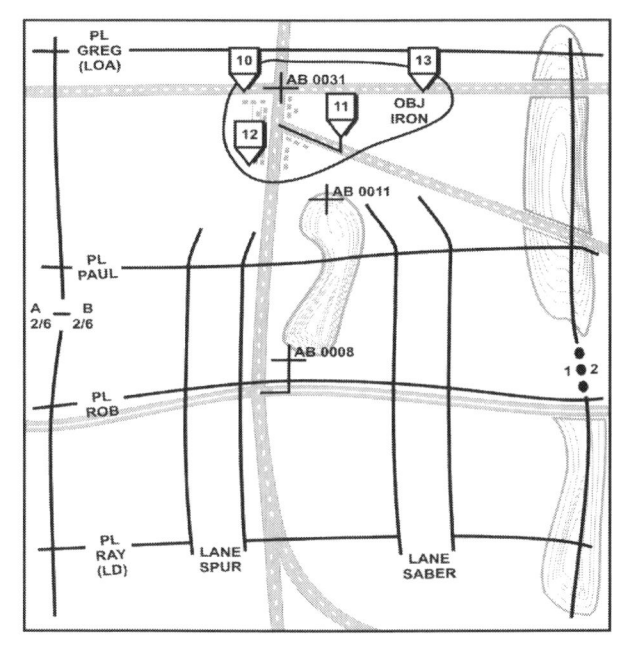

Figure 3-1. Area reconnaissance

PLANNING

3-67. The critical tasks for an area reconnaissance are the same as a zone reconnaissance, except they are now modified for an area. Unless the commander directs otherwise, the reconnaissance platoon's primary critical tasks in the area include:

- Finding and reporting all enemy forces.
- Reconnoitering and determining trafficability of all terrain.
- Inspecting and classifying all bridges.
- Locating fords or crossing sites near all bridges.
- Inspecting and classifying all overpasses, underpasses, and culverts.
- Within capability, locating all minefields and other obstacles, reducing or breaching them, and clearing and marking lanes.
- Locating and identifying bypasses around built-up areas, obstacles, and contaminated areas.
- Reporting information.

3-68. Like a zone reconnaissance, the platoon is prepared to conduct other tasks deemed critical by the higher commander. Additional tasks for the area reconnaissance may include:

- Identifying threat activities (which include insurgent and opposition leaders), countermeasures, and probable COAs.

Chapter 3

- Determining the size, location, and composition of society/human demographics. Examples include race, sex, age, religion, language, tribe, clan, class, education, history, government, and factions.
- Establishing and maintaining contact with local civilian and military leadership.
- Conducting a reconnaissance of the society with HUMINT teams to determine the needs of the citizens, the regional, local, and neighborhood situations, the organizations and methods of operation for terrorists, transnational groups, and ethnic centers of gravity, the financial and economic systems, and the media activities (local, U.S., international).
- Identifying key municipal infrastructure that can affect military operations, including SWEAT-MSO.
- Identifying the allegiances of the local population to factions, religious groups, or other organizations.

3-69. To conduct an area reconnaissance mission, the platoon leader first identifies the area to be reconnoitered within a continuous boundary, such as an inspection objective or NAI. The platoon leader analyzes the mission, threat/enemy, and terrain, and completes TLPs. Movement plans to (and if necessary, from) the area may be specified for the reconnaissance platoon in the operation order/fragmentary order (FRAGORD). In addition, the platoon leader plans for conducting mission command during the execution phase of the area reconnaissance. Platoon leadership conducts mission command in one of two ways:

- Accompanying the section leaders forward in their assigned sectors with a skeleton crew protecting the vehicles in hide sites. This requires support from the higher command.
- Situating themselves with the vehicles in hide sites where they receive and forward reports, update the situational picture, conduct casualty evacuation (CASEVAC), and other support missions for the sections as required. This allows an additional smaller patrol to be deployed if the enemy situation worsens.

PREPARATION

3-70. Preparations for an area reconnaissance are essentially the same as a zone reconnaissance. See the information starting at paragraph 3-49 for further reading.

3-71. The reconnaissance platoon's primary concern during movement to the proposed area is security rather than reconnaissance. If the platoon leader feels there may be enemy forces along the route to the area, the platoon should employ the principles of tactical movement based on METT-TC. If used, the platoon leader also incorporates information from UAS and ground sensor assets into the mission. During movement to the area, it may be appropriate (depending upon the commander's intent) for the reconnaissance platoon to avoid contact. The platoon leader may also choose to orient and focus sections or squads on checkpoints as the platoon moves to the area.

Reconnaissance

EXECUTION

3-72. The platoon leader encloses the given vicinity within a platoon's designated area, if the area size allows. Using boundaries, the LD, LOA, and dividing the area into section zones by placing boundaries on identifiable terrain ensures that each section has responsibility for specific pieces of terrain. The platoon leader ensures cross-talk among the sections to improve SA and target identification, and carefully controls section movement to reduce the risk of fratricide.

3-73. The platoon leader places contact points at the intersections of phase lines and boundaries, and at any other location needed for physical contact and coordination between the sections. For directions, GIRS/TIRS is used as necessary. The platoon leader works with the FSO to plan indirect fires that sustain the reconnaissance platoon's scheme of maneuver. In addition, section leaders have the ability to request targets in their assigned zone.

3-74. The platoon can conduct area reconnaissance using any of the section formations. Platoon leaders consider the location of the PSG during possible contact. Organization of the reconnaissance platoon is in accordance with METT-TC, while allowing the PSG the flexibility to conduct CASEVAC, resupply, and vehicle recovery during extended time periods. The platoon leader deploys the sections across the LD to best accomplish the reconnaissance tasks. Leaders adjust formations in accordance with the factors of METT-TC and the AO.

3-75. The reconnaissance platoon moves methodically through the area based on terrain and section boundaries. Sections/teams ensure that all of the area within a boundary is explored. If obstacles or restrictions are discovered, the proper actions are taken to continue the mission. Upon completion of the area reconnaissance, the platoon leader reports the results of the reconnaissance to the commander.

ROUTE RECONNAISSANCE

3-76. Platoons conduct route reconnaissance to gain detailed information about a specific road or axis. This includes the terrain on both sides of the route that the enemy could use to influence movement. The platoon is usually tasked with this form of reconnaissance when the commander wants to use a certain direction but first wants to make sure that the route is free of obstacles and enemy forces, and that it supports the movement of vehicles. Because of the large number of critical tasks associated with route reconnaissance, the platoon normally can conduct a detailed inspection of only one route. Deliberate reconnaissance is inherently slower than rapid reconnaissance due to more tasks and the detail of search needed to confirm or deny an enemy presence.

3-77. The ABCT reconnaissance platoons are better suited to fight for route information when contact is made with a heavier or armored enemy. For the IBCT reconnaissance troop, anything above individual enemy troops and light wheeled vehicles requires augmentation such as the Mobile Ground System (MGS) or antitank guided missile (ATGM) vehicles, CFVs, and tanks. Engineer attachments

Chapter 3

are desirable during a detailed route reconnaissance when information about the routes, roads, and bridges must include exact weight classifications or structural information. Engineer attachments also increase the flexibility of the platoon by allowing more than one route to be covered. When augmentation is not available, the IBCT reconnaissance platoon may still conduct a route reconnaissance which continues to clear lateral routes with limitations based on protective fire capabilities.

CRITICAL TASKS

3-78. During a route reconnaissance, the platoon is prepared to accomplish a wide range of tasks. Based on the time available and the commander's intent, the platoon may be directed to conduct the reconnaissance to acquire specific information. To be ready for either type of situation along the route, the platoon leader clearly understands the following critical tasks that may have to be accomplished in a route reconnaissance:

- Determine trafficability.
- Find and report all enemy forces that can influence movement; and terrain the enemy can use to dominate movement.
- Reconnoiter all built-up areas.
- Reconnoiter all lateral routes to the limit of direct fire range.
- Inspect and classify all bridges.
- Locate fords or crossing sites near all bridges.
- Inspect and classify all overpasses, underpasses, and culverts.
- Reconnoiter all defiles.
- Locate minefields and other obstacles.
- Locate a bypass around built-up areas, obstacles, restrictions, and contaminated areas.
- Determine the type and volume of traffic.
- Report route information.

PLANNING

3-79. The order the platoon leader receives specifies the route the platoon reconnoiters, defines the start time, and the route from the SP to the RP. Additional control measures specify how much terrain on both sides of the route the reconnaissance platoon explores, and where the mission begins and ends. Additionally, the order may specify:

- Platoon boundaries.
- Phase lines.
- Contact points.
- Limit of advance.
- Reconnaissance objective.

Reconnaissance

PREPARATION

3-80. A route reconnaissance is much like a zone reconnaissance only smaller. Boundaries are drawn on both sides that include the terrain along the route. This usually extends out to include terrain that an enemy force may use to influence movement. The LD is drawn from one boundary to another behind the SP, allowing the reconnaissance and platoon to be fully deployed as they cross the LD and before reaching the route. The LOA or objective is placed beyond the RP on the last terrain feature that dominates the route, or at a location about 3 kms further out.

3-81. The platoon leader may add additional phase lines, contact points, and checkpoints to the graphics received from the commander. Phase lines are used to help control the maneuver of the reconnaissance platoon, and contact points ensure the sections or squads maintain contact at particular critical points. Checkpoints are used along the route or on specific terrain to control movement or designate areas to be explored. Leaders should limit control measures to the minimum number required to accomplish the mission while allowing subordinates maximum freedom to maneuver.

3-82. In coordination with the FSO, the platoon leader plans artillery targets on known or suspected enemy positions, and on dominant terrain throughout the AO.

3-83. Evaluating the factors of METT-TC helps the platoon leader select a reconnaissance organization best suited for the mission, and ensures that at least one section has responsibility for reconnoitering the route. A three-section organization is usually best suited for scouting one route. One section explores the terrain on the left side of the route, another covers the terrain on the right side, and the third section reconnoiters the route and controls the movement of the other two. Using this method, the platoon leader's section has specific responsibility to survey the route. If contact is likely, the platoon leader should not organize the PSG into a maneuvering section since this could interfere with CASEVAC missions.

EXECUTION

3-84. The sections deploy before reaching the LD in order to maximize reconnaissance assets and be prepared for chance contact. This also aligns the sections with their designated section AO, and allows the platoon to be in position early enough to conduct observation of the LD area.

3-85. The platoon executes route reconnaissance using the technique of movement described in the OPORD. The section with route responsibility moves methodically down the specified route based on the movement speed of the flanking sections. Although the center section can usually move faster, terrain and reconnaissance of lateral routes often slows flanking sections. At times the center section may have to halt to conduct evaluations of the route. The platoon leader ensures that the flanking sections do not advance further than is reasonable in order to keep gaps from forming that could allow enemy elements to slip through.

3-86. Route reconnaissance begins when the element on the path reaches the designated SP. This element travels directly on the route whenever possible to verify its stability and trafficability. Usually, the platoon leader's section is in the center and the wingman's vehicle leads the section on the route, allowing the platoon

Chapter 3

leader to focus on controlling maneuvers while verifying the direction. As the sections move along the route, the platoon leader directs the flanking sections by using graphic control measures to verify location and the rate of advance.

RECONNAISSANCE OVERLAY SYMBOLS

3-87. Figure 3-2 shows an example of how graphics are used in overlays. At a minimum, the following information is included on the route-classification overlay:

- Route-classification formula.
- Name and rank of person in charge of performing the classification.
- Unit conducting the classification.
- Date-time, group (DTG) that the classification was conducted.
- Map name, edition, and scale.
- Any remarks to ensure complete understanding of the information on overlay.

Reconnaissance

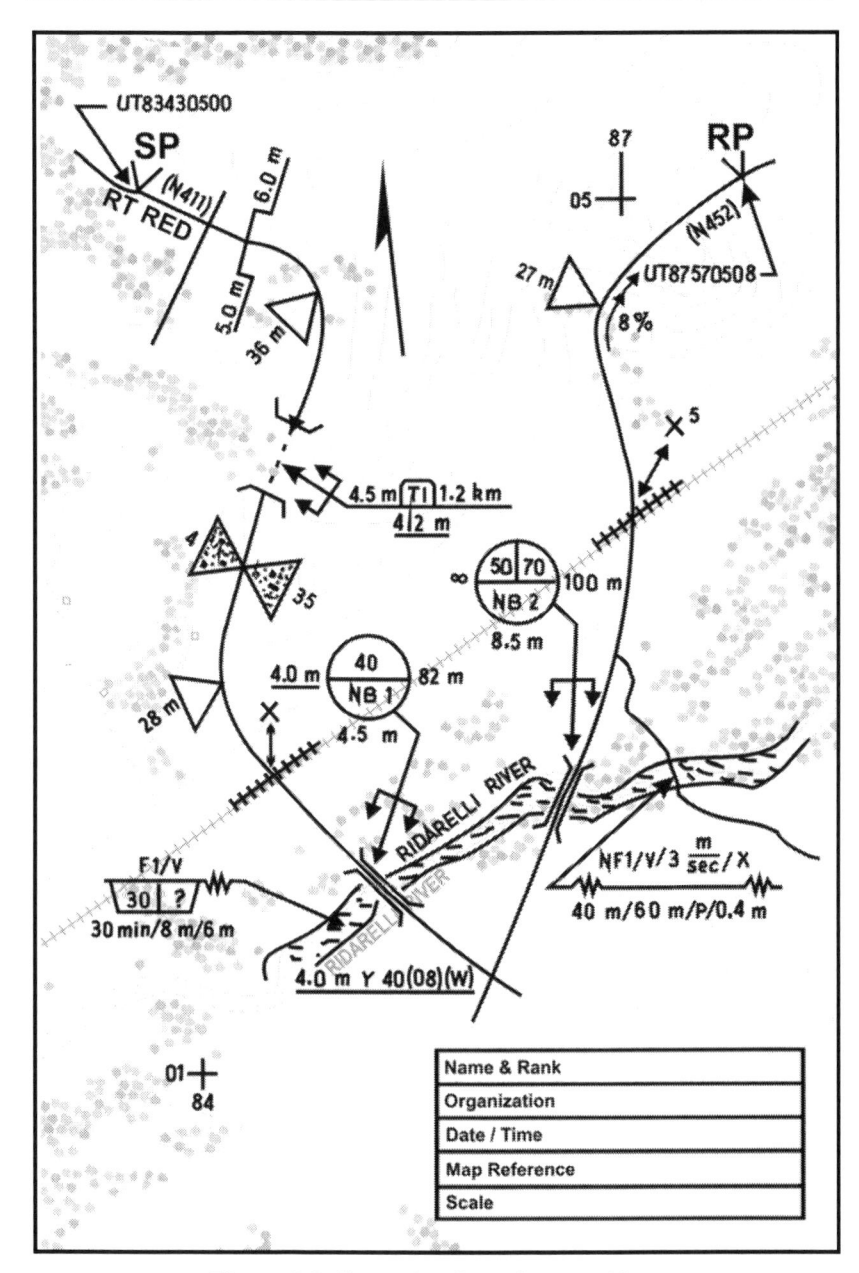

Figure 3-2. Example of overlay graphics

Chapter 3

3-88. Figure 3-3 outlines a variety of symbols that can be used to illustrate reconnaissance data on overlays. These symbols are used in association with route classification formulas discussed in the following paragraphs.

Symbol	Description and criteria
SINGLE CURVE Curve radius → (15 m)	SINGLE CURVE: Any curve with a radius of 25 meters or less is an obstruction. All curves with a radius less than 45 meters are reportable.
MULTIPLE CURVES Number of curves → 3/16 m Sharpest curve radius	SERIES OF SHARP CURVES: The figure to the left indicates the number of curves; that to the right, the minimum radius of curvature in meters.
CRITICAL POINT (3) Number critical points in order and describe them on DA Form 1711-R.	CRITICAL POINT: A key geographic point or position important to the success of an operation; a point in time, a crisis or turning point; or any point along a route of march where interference with troop movement may occur.
CONSTRICTION → 4 120 ← Traveled way width / Total constriction length	CONSTRICTION: (An obstruction.) Any reduction in the traveled way below the minimum required. The figure to the left indicates the width of the constriction; that to the right, the total constricted length, both in meters.
UNDERPASS Minimum traveled way width ↘xx Traveled way width and sidewalks ↘xx Arch type Minimum overhead clearance ↘xx Maximum overhead clearance ↘xx UNDERPASSES: Show shape of structure (obstruction) when overhead clearance is less than 4.3 meters.	
ROUTE DESIGNATION (495)	ROUTE DESIGNATION: Civil or military route designation. Written in parentheses along route.

Figure 3-3. Reconnaissance overlay symbols

Reconnaissance

Symbols for use in the reconnaissance overlay	
Symbol	**Description and criteria**

BRIDGE
Full NATO Bridge Symbol

- Wheel
- Two-way class
- One-way class
- Overhead clearance
- Overall length
- Serial number
- Bypass condition
- Width of traveled way
- Track
- Bridge location

When full NATO bridge symbol is used on an overlay, the additional information column on the DA Form 1249 will not contain bypass length, traveled way width, or overhead clearance.

BRIDGE
Abbreviated Bridge Symbol

- Load classification
- Location
- Serial number

When abbreviated symbol is used, DA Form 1249 must be attached.

TUNNEL

- Serial number
- Minimum and maximum overhead clearance: 5/6
- Tunnel length: 800
- 3.4/5.4
- Bypass conditions
- Traveled way width/plus sidewalk

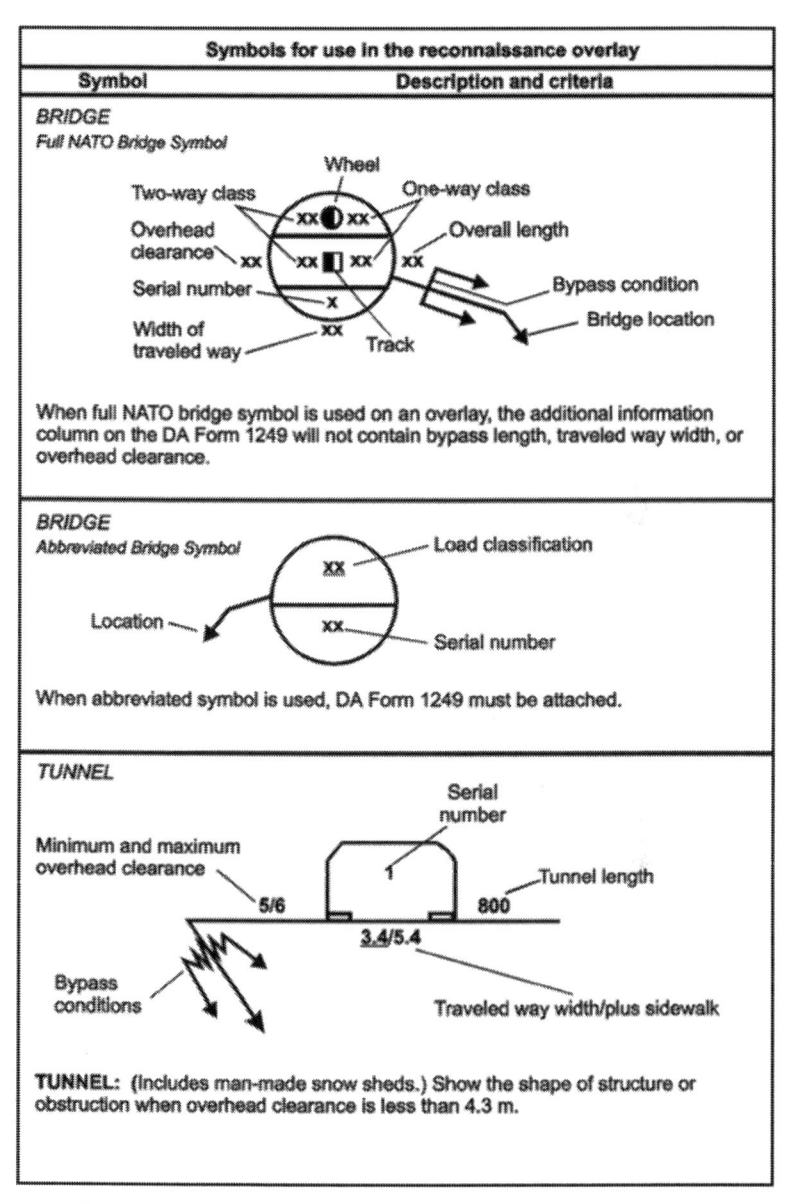

TUNNEL: (Includes man-made snow sheds.) Show the shape of structure or obstruction when overhead clearance is less than 4.3 m.

Figure 3-3. Reconnaissance overlay symbols (continued)

Chapter 3

Symbols for use in the reconnaissance overlay	
Symbol	Description and criteria

FORD

Labels on diagram: Left approach conditions, Serial number, Type of ford, Velocity of stream, Seasonal limiting factors, Right approach conditions, Length, Width, Nature of bottom, Normal depth, Left bank, Direction of flow, Right bank

FORD: All fords are considered as obstructions to traffic.

Type of ford: V— Vehicular
                P— Pedestrian

Seasonal limiting factors:
X— No seasonal limitation except for limited duration sudden flooding.
Y— Significant seasonal limitations.

Approach conditions: ⟿ Difficult
                       ─── Easy

Nature of bottom:
M— Mud   C— Clay   S— Sand
G— Gravel R— rock   P— Artifical paving

FERRY

Labels on diagram: Left approach conditions, Serial number, Type, Right approach conditions, Mil load class, Deadweight capacity, Turnaround time

FERRY: All ferries are considered as obstructions to traffic.

Type of ferry:
  V— Vehicular
  P— Pedestrian

Approach conditions:
  ⟿ Difficult
  ─── Easy

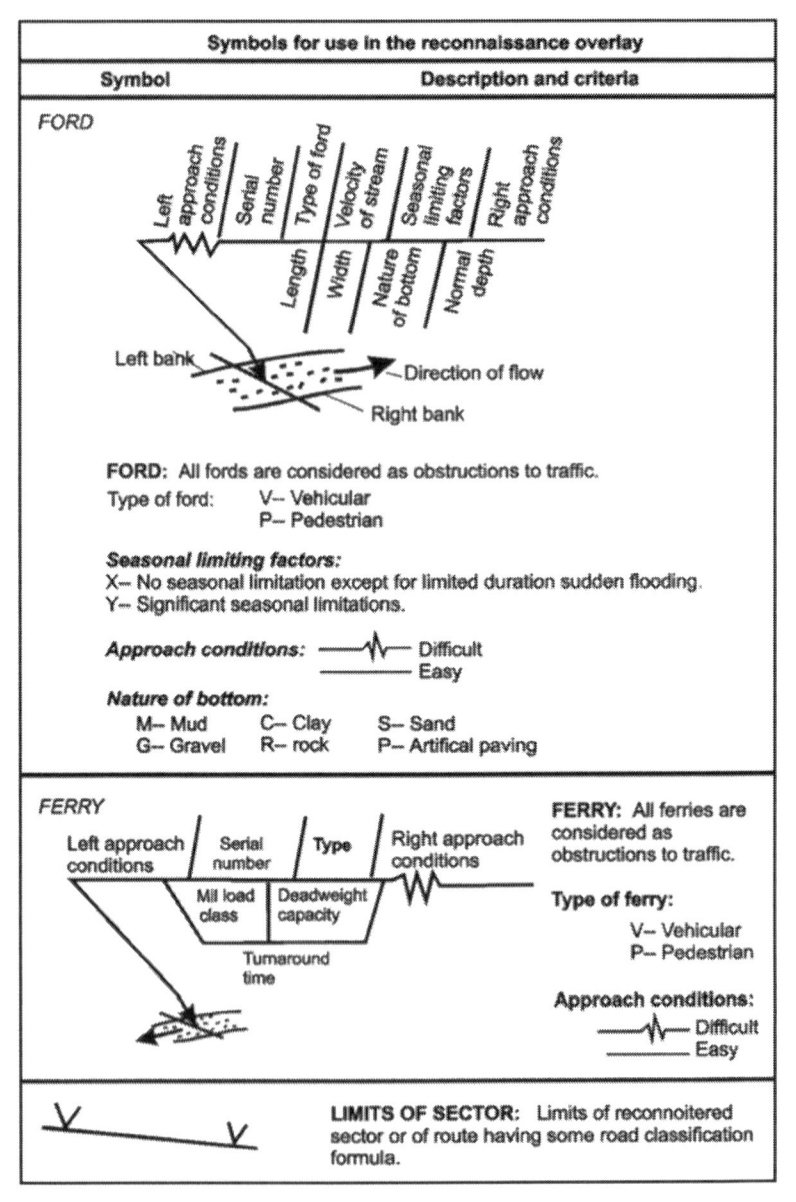

LIMITS OF SECTOR: Limits of reconnoitered sector or of route having some road classification formula.

Figure 3-3. Reconnaissance overlay symbols (continued)

Reconnaissance

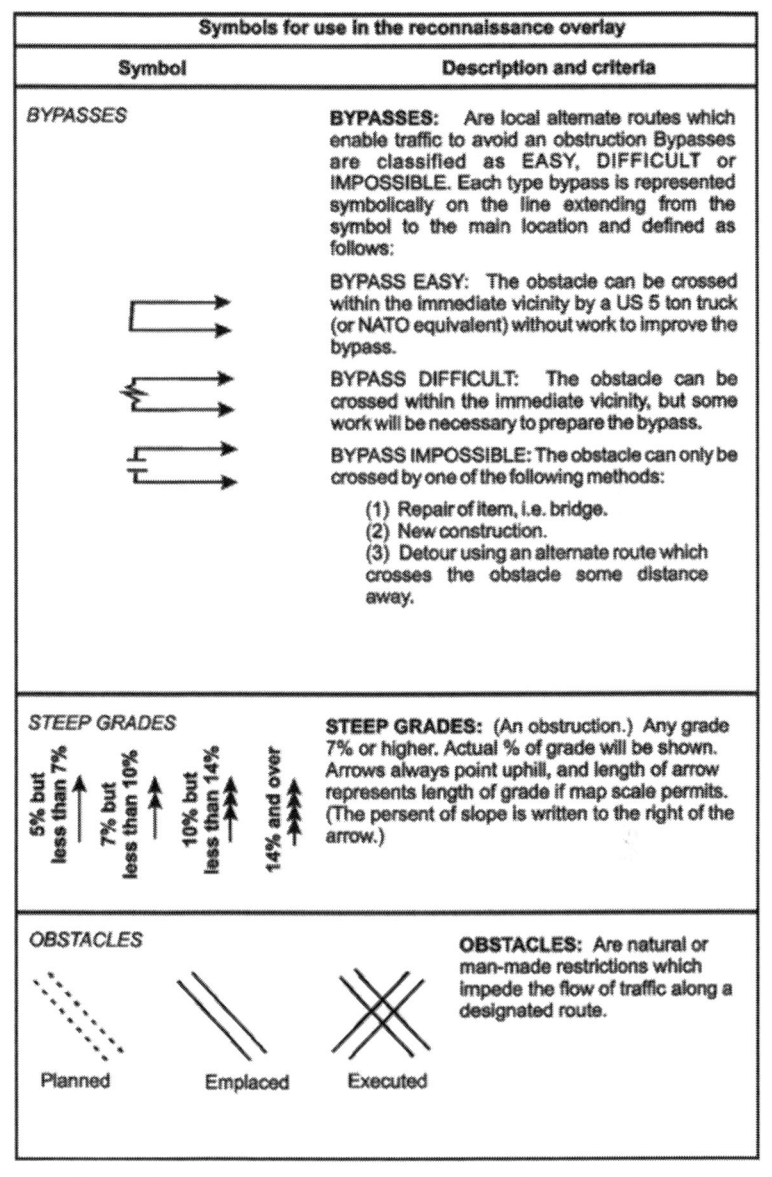

Symbols for use in the reconnaissance overlay	
Symbol	Description and criteria
BYPASSES	**BYPASSES:** Are local alternate routes which enable traffic to avoid an obstruction Bypasses are classified as EASY, DIFFICULT or IMPOSSIBLE. Each type bypass is represented symbolically on the line extending from the symbol to the main location and defined as follows:
	BYPASS EASY: The obstacle can be crossed within the immediate vicinity by a US 5 ton truck (or NATO equivalent) without work to improve the bypass.
	BYPASS DIFFICULT: The obstacle can be crossed within the immediate vicinity, but some work will be necessary to prepare the bypass.
	BYPASS IMPOSSIBLE: The obstacle can only be crossed by one of the following methods: (1) Repair of item, i.e. bridge. (2) New construction. (3) Detour using an alternate route which crosses the obstacle some distance away.
STEEP GRADES 5% but less than 7% 7% but less than 10% 10% but less than 14% 14% and over	**STEEP GRADES:** (An obstruction.) Any grade 7% or higher. Actual % of grade will be shown. Arrows always point uphill, and length of arrow represents length of grade if map scale permits. (The persent of slope is written to the right of the arrow.)
OBSTACLES Planned Emplaced Executed	**OBSTACLES:** Are natural or man-made restrictions which impede the flow of traffic along a designated route.

Figure 3-3. Reconnaissance overlay symbols (continued)

Chapter 3

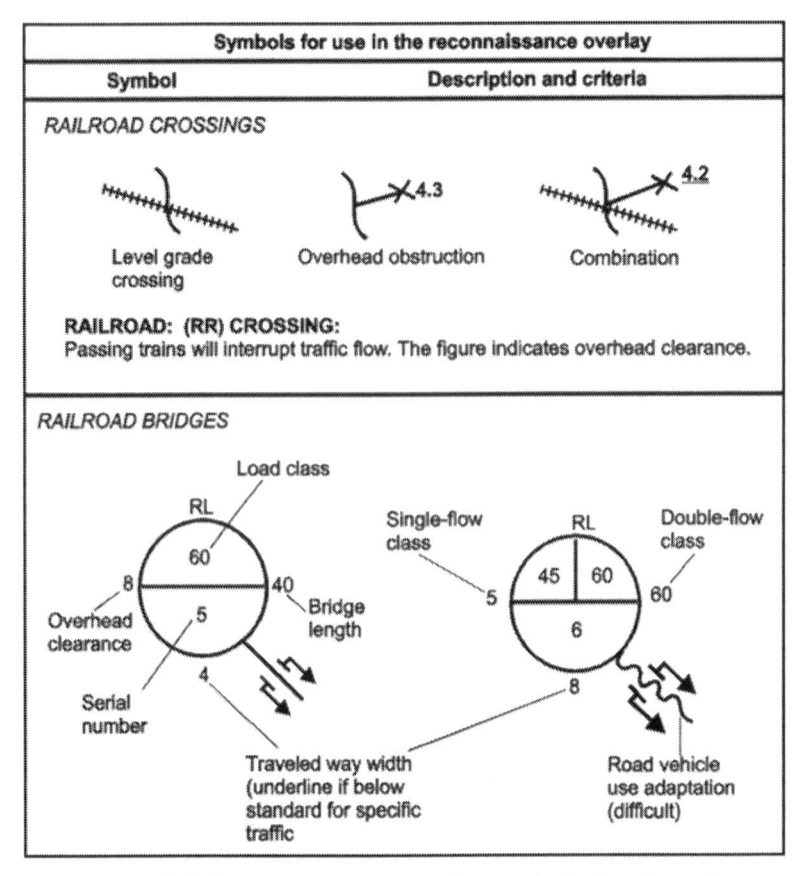

Figure 3-3. Reconnaissance overlay symbols (continued)

ROUTE CLASSIFICATION FORMULAS

3-89. The route classification formula is derived from information gathered during the route reconnaissance. The formula is recorded on the route-classification overlay as, for example, 5.5m / Y / 30 / 4.6 (OB) (W) and consists of the following:

- Route width, in meters.
- Route type (based on ability to withstand weather).
- Lowest military load classification (MLC).
- Lowest overhead clearance, in meters.
- Obstructions to traffic flow (OB), if applicable.
- Special conditions, snow blockage (T) or flooding (W), if applicable.

Reconnaissance

ROUTE WIDTH AND TRAFFIC-FLOW CAPABILITY

3-90. The route width has a direct impact on traffic flow capability. Figure 3-4 outlines the required measurements needed to determine width.

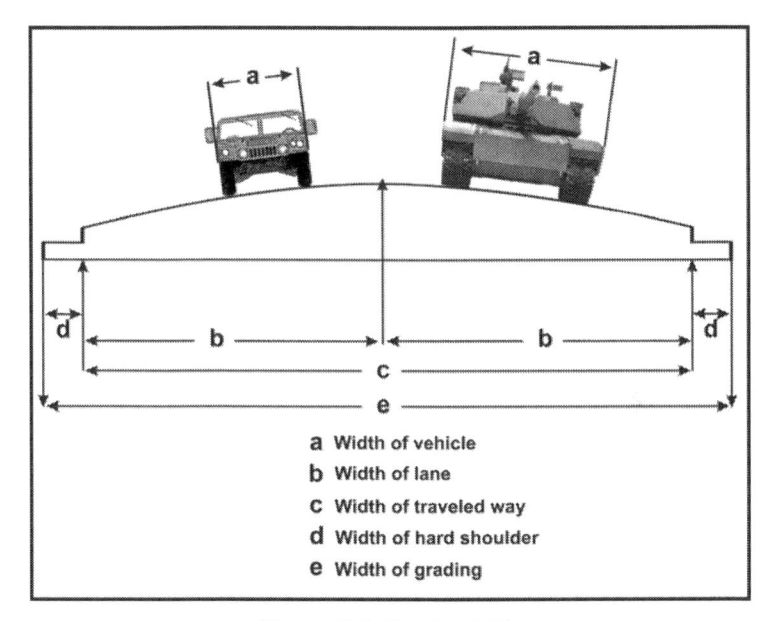

a Width of vehicle
b Width of lane
c Width of traveled way
d Width of hard shoulder
e Width of grading

Figure 3-4. Route width

3-91. Traffic flow capability is directly related to the route width. Table 3-1 contains information to determine traffic flow capability.

Table 3-1. Traffic flow capability based on route width

	Limited Access	Single Lane	Single Flow	Double Flow
Wheeled	At least 3.5 m	3.5 to 5.5 m	5.5 to 7.3 m	Over 7.3 m
Tracked and combination vehicles	At least 4.0 m	4.0 to 6.0 m	6.0 to 8.0 m	Over 8 m

Route Type

3-92. Route type is classified as one of three types of road surfaces. They are:
- **Type X**—An all-weather route that, with reasonable maintenance, is passable throughout the year. This route is normally formed of roads having waterproof surfaces and is never closed due to weather effects other than snow or flood blockage.
- **Type Y**—A limited, all-weather route that, with reasonable maintenance, is passable throughout the year. This route is normally formed of roads

Chapter 3

that do not have waterproof surfaces and is closed for short periods (up to one day at a time) by adverse weather conditions.
- **Type Z**—A fair-weather route passable only when the weather is good. This type of route is so seriously affected by adverse weather conditions that it can remain closed for long periods of time. Improvement of such a route can only be achieved by construction or realignment.

Military Load Classifications

3-93. The basis for MLC is the load, vehicle speed, tire width, or other effect that a vehicle has on a bridge when crossing. Heavy loads such as artillery and tanks make vehicle classification a very important factor when determining what can travel down a route.

Requirements for Classification Numbers

3-94. Classification numbers are mandatory for all self-propelled vehicles having a total weight of 3 tons or more, and all trailers with a payload of 1.5 tons or greater. (Refer to Standardization Agreements [STANAGs] 2010 and 2021.) Trailers with a rated capacity of less than 1.5 tons are usually combined with their towing vehicles for classification. During the classification process, vehicles are divided into two further groups—those with trailers (vehicle combination class number [CCN]) and those without (single vehicle classification number)—and calculated for vehicle classification

Procedures for Vehicle Classification

3-95. The actual mathematical computation of a vehicle's MLC is beyond the capability of route reconnaissance teams. However, temporary procedures are described below. MLC information is found in the vehicle's technical manual or on the dash's dataplate.

Temporary Procedure for Vehicle Classification

3-96. When a single vehicle tows another vehicle at a distance less than 30.5 meters and the vehicles are not designed to operate as one unit, the temporary vehicle MLC number may be assigned to this combination. The classification number assigned is nine-tenths the sum of the normal vehicle classification numbers if the total of both classifications is less than 60. If the sum of the two military classification numbers is 60 or over, then the total becomes the MLC number for the nonstandard combination.

Reconnaissance

> CCN = 0.9 (A + B) if A + B < 60
>
> CCN = A + B if A + B > 60
>
> where—
>
>   A = class of first vehicle
>
>   B = class of second vehicle

Expedient Procedure—Wheeled Vehicle Classification

3-97. On occasions when a vehicle needs to be classified in the field, observe and compare the unclassified vehicle to a vehicle that is similar. Compare the axle loads, gross weight, and dimensions of the unclassified vehicle with those of a similar classification.

> Example: The expedient classification for a wheeled vehicle is estimated to be 85 percent of its total weight. Determine the vehicle's gross weight; multiply the air pressure in the tires (in pounds per square inch [psi]) by the total area (in square inches) of the tires in contact with the ground. If a gage is not available, use 75 psi as an average value. This yields an approximate weight of the vehicle in pounds. Convert this figure to tons and find 85 percent of the weight in tons. The resulting figure is the expedient classification.

Expedient Procedure—Tracked Vehicle Classification

3-98. Tracked vehicles weigh about one ton per square foot of track contact with the ground. By determining the area of track in contact with the ground, the vehicle's gross weight can be assigned. When vehicles weigh a fraction over whole tonnage, the next higher classification number is assigned.

Obstructions

3-99. Several route characteristics are considered obstructions. The following obstructions are annotated on the overlay with graphics and be included in the route classification formula as *OB*:

- Overhead obstructions with a clearance of less than 4.3 meters.
- Reductions in traveled-way widths that are below the standard minimums.
- Curves with a radius of 25 meters and less. (See Figure 3-5.)
- Slopes (gradients) of 7 percent or greater. (See Figures 3-6, 3-7, and 3-8.)

Special Conditions

3-100. When snow blocks traffic on a regular and recurrent basis, the symbol following the route-classification formula is *T*. When flooding blocks traffic on a regular and recurrent basis, the symbol following the route-classification formula is *W*.

Chapter 3

Curves

3-101. Figure 3-5 follows the method of determining a curve's radius based upon the formula R = (C2/8M) + (M/2) (all measurements are in meters):

- **R** = radius of the curve.
- **C** = the distance from the centerline of the road to the centerline of the road at the outer extremities of the curve.
- **M** = the perpendicular distance from the center of the tape to the centerline of the road.

> Example: If C is 15 meters and M is fixed at 2 meters, the formula becomes R = (152/16) + 2/2 = 15.0625. The result of this calculation (a radius of slightly more than 15 meters) would be an obstruction to traffic flow, and *OB* would be entered in the route classification formula.

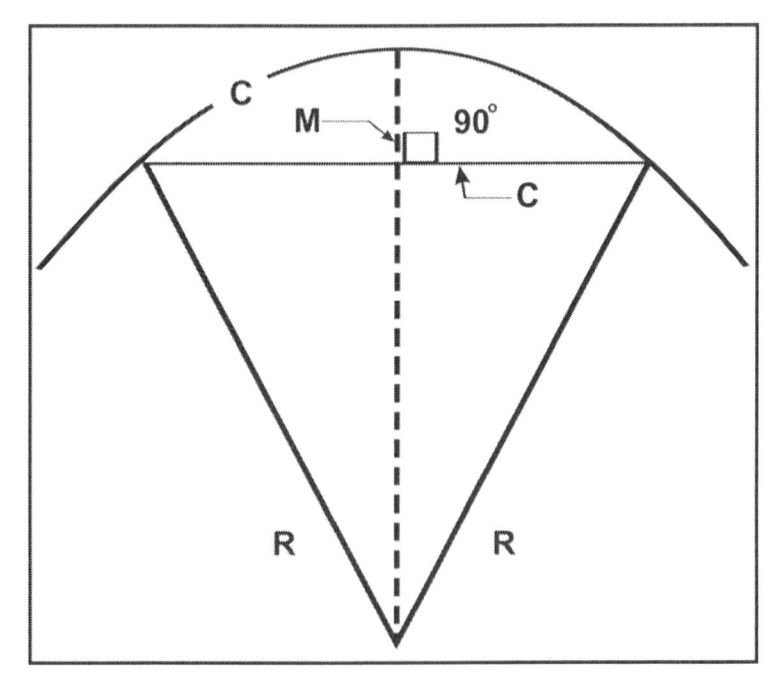

Figure 3-5. Formula method for determining curve radius

Slope

3-102. There are several formulas and methods to determine the gradient of slope, as shown in Figures 3-6, 3-7, and 3-8:

Reconnaissance

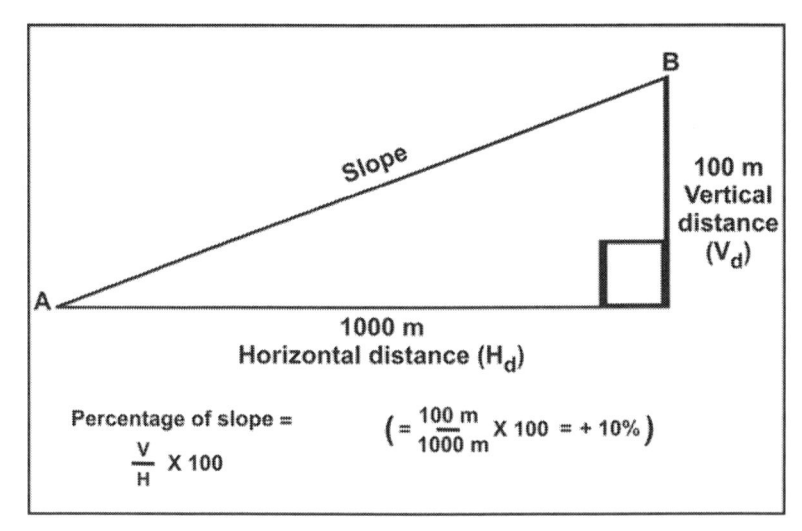

Percentage of slope = $\frac{V}{H} \times 100$ $\left(= \frac{100 \text{ m}}{1000 \text{ m}} \times 100 = +10\% \right)$

Figure 3-6. Formula for slope percentage

Percentage of Slope

Given: Eye-level height = 1.75 m
        Pace = .75 m

Answer: Vertical distance = 2 x 1.75 m = 3.5 m
        Horizontal distance = (75 paces + 125 paces x .75) = 150 m

Percentage of Slope formula

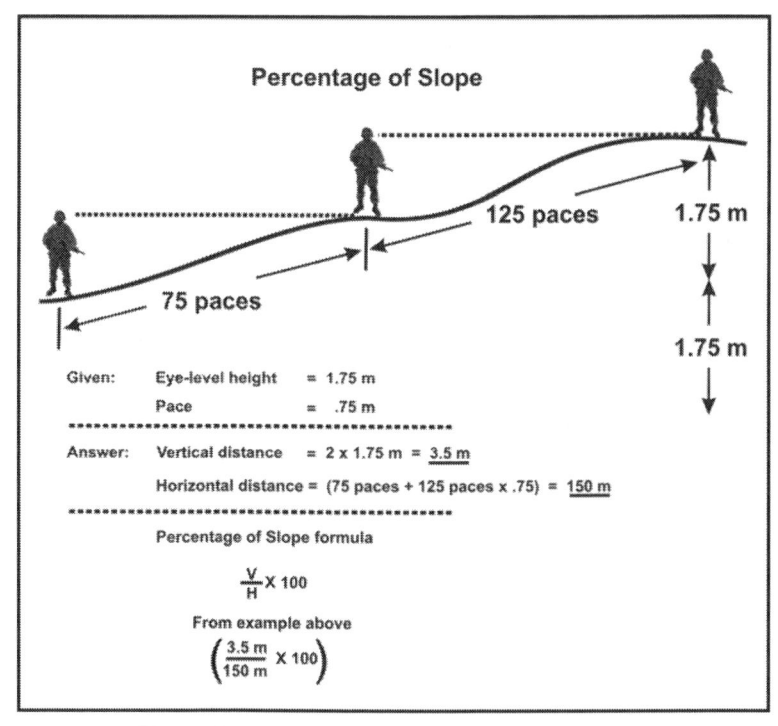

$$\frac{V}{H} \times 100$$

From example above

$$\left(\frac{3.5 \text{ m}}{150 \text{ m}} \times 100\right)$$

Figure 3-7. Pace method for percentage slope

Chapter 3

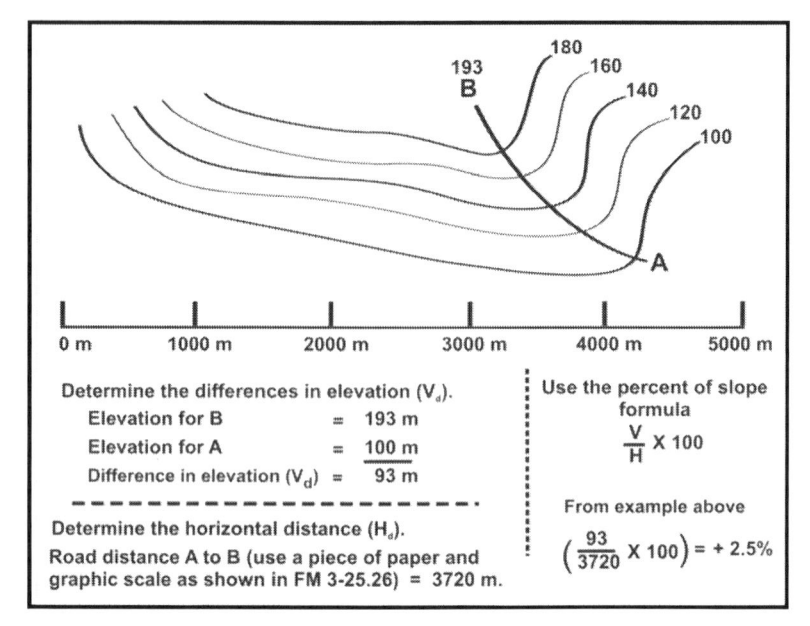

Figure 3-8. Map method for percentage slope

Determine the differences in elevation (V_d).
- Elevation for B = 193 m
- Elevation for A = 100 m
- Difference in elevation (V_d) = 93 m

Determine the horizontal distance (H_d).
Road distance A to B (use a piece of paper and graphic scale as shown in FM 3-25.26) = 3720 m.

Use the percent of slope formula

$$\frac{V}{H} \times 100$$

From example above

$$\left(\frac{93}{3720} \times 100\right) = +2.5\%$$

3-103. The platoon leader captures route reconnaissance information as it is collected. The collection team that actually conducts the reconnaissance disseminates this information to the platoon and team leaders. All information is entered into the appropriate report formats on FBCB2 and forwarded to the troop CP for collection.

3-104. Route reconnaissance continues until the section reaches the RP. The platoon continues to move in their assigned section boundaries to a distance of 2-3 km beyond the RP for security purposes. The platoon then transitions to its follow-on mission as dictated in the OPORD. Upon completion of the expedition, the platoon leader reports the results of the reconnaissance to the commander. If a route overlay developed by the platoon leader or engineer assets is used, it is included in the report.

RECONNAISSANCE IN FORCE

3-105. A reconnaissance in force is a squadron-level mission. The investigating platoon conducts area, zone, and route reconnaissance in support of the unit conducting the mission. (Refer to FM 3-20.96 for more information.)

SECTION IV - RECONNAISSANCE HANDOVER

3-106. Coordinating the transfer of an assigned area from one element to another is known as reconnaissance handover (RHO). The term "element" refers to all echelons involved in the RHO, from OPs to squadron/battalion-sized components. Information and responsibility for reconnaissance and surveillance of potential enemy contact are shared. Assets such as ground sensors and the UAS are also transferred.

3-107. Reconnaissance handover is similar to battle handover (BHO) in that it may be conducted in conjunction with other tasks such as relief in place, linkup, and passage of lines. However, it does not imply the assumption of a fight or being within enemy direct fire range, but focuses on planning, preparing, and executing information of enemy contact and the responsibility of an assigned area passing from one element to another.

3-108. This task provides continuous surveillance, FBCB2 connectivity, and overlapping communications for the commander's focus. The focus may differ for each echelon when planning and executing layered reconnaissance and surveillance with multiple assets. Reconnaissance handover is normally associated with a designated coordination point (RHOCP) or reconnaissance handover line (RHOL), and may entail handover of a sector/zone, named area of interest (NAI), target area of interest (TAI), or enemy contact. Visual, electronic, digital, and analog information sources are exchanged during the RHO. (Refer to FM 3-20.971 or ATTP 3-20.97 for more information.)

OPERATIONAL CONSIDERATIONS FOR RECONNAISSANCE HANDOVER

3-109. Reconnaissance and surveillance tasks require the platoon conducting the handover to effectively coordinate with higher, lower, and adjacent units. Planning for these tasks requires the RHO coordination to start at the higher echelons and be executed to the lowest element.

PLANNING

3-110. Planning for RHO takes place as part of a change of mission before or during missions. When planning is conducted before a mission, the completed plan is reviewed for layered, redundant reconnaissance and surveillance using all available assets. If appropriate, locations and criteria for RHO are coordinated with higher headquarters and relevant control measures such as RHOL (phase line) between units or potential RHOCP to facilitate ground linkup, are added with other graphic control measures that aid in mission command.

3-111. Reconnaissance platoons follow the control measures and criteria specified by higher headquarters. The unit commander directs how handover is transferred to other elements, and the platoon leader recommends additional measures that support

Chapter 3

mission command. Platoon leadership coordinates and executes RHO tasks using planning steps such as—

- Coordinating for redundant surveillance to assist in maintaining enemy contact.
- Determining location and criteria for RHO with the platoon.
- Creating a communications plan between platoon elements.
- Synchronizing indirect fires and exchanging fire support (FS) information.
- Exchanging plans.
- Identifying and coordinating for target handover, as necessary.
- Coordinating graphic control measures to facilitate RHO.
- Selecting contact points or linkup points to collocate reconnaissance platoon CPs.
- Coordinating transfer and acceptance of mission command between units.
- Planning for integration of non-digital elements.

PREPARATION

3-112. The platoon leader finds handover criteria in the platoon order and begins coordination as RHO requirements between units are identified. This includes establishment of a communications plan between the units, along with radio frequencies, net identifications (IDs), enhanced position location reporting system (EPLRS), host files required to conduct the linkup (if units are from different maneuver control systems), and communications security (COMSEC) variables. Recognition signals are established or confirmed to prevent fratricide.

3-113. While remaining focused on the platoon or BCT requirements, the reconnaissance platoon exchanges information requirements to understand how to answer or support the follow-on unit's information requirements. This understanding assists in the transfer of vital information collected by the platoon to the squadron/battalion during critical moments, such as identifying a security element along the higher command axis of advance that is not included in the BCTs PIR.

3-114. If necessary, the reconnaissance platoon coordinates indirect fires and FSCMs, critical friendly zones, preplanned targets, final protective fires (FPFs), and obscuration missions. This includes criteria for preplanned RHO and high-payoff target (HPT) handover.

3-115. Coordination is conducted to identify the transfer or acceptance of mission command of elements between units, as necessary. An example is for the reconnaissance platoon to leave a section in contact with an enemy security element while the rest of the platoon continues reconnaissance further into the AO. As the BCT shifts the handoff between units, the follow-on unit may accept mission command of the platoon's section until one of the follow-on sections is able to relieve the reconnaissance platoon section in observing the enemy element.

Reconnaissance

Additionally, the platoon may issue on-order missions to other collection assets to assist in the handover. An example of this is a UAS tasked with establishing and maintaining contact with a moving force while RHO is being conducted from the platoon to a follow-on unit. As RHO becomes imminent and final coordination begins, this level of synchronization supports the RHO by allowing the UAS maximum time on station and ensuring redundant observation during handover.

3-116. Rehearsals are of paramount importance before executing any plan. During practice, elements involved in the RHO confirm coordination to ensure clarity and understanding.

EXECUTION

3-117. Reconnaissance platoons may conduct RHO with follow-on or security (stationary) forces, accept RHO from a forward force, or provide mission command for the handover.

3-118. During execution of RHO, liaison with a unit may consist of collocating both units' mission command nodes, attaching the reconnaissance platoon to the forward maneuver units to facilitate movement of elements into positions, and control of platoon elements. The reconnaissance platoon leader should execute the following actions:

- Use reliable digital and radio voice linkup to exchange critical information.
- Use recognition signals as the distance closes between the forces to prevent fratricide.
- Exchange information and positions in a face-to-face linkup.

3-119. This information is exchanged with the gaining unit to ensure continuous operations and SA during RHO. When handing over targets to the gaining unit, the reconnaissance platoon leader and squad leaders:

- Use a laser, if available, to designate targets and cue gaining unit observers to aid target acquisition and identification for the RHO gaining unit. Target handover is not complete until the accepting unit can acquire the targets.
- Receive FBCB2 updates and properly account for vehicles and crews to prevent being confused with enemy elements.
- Facilitate the follow-on force's attack by conducting reconnaissance pull and executing targeting, including previously coordinated indirect fires, for the passing unit.

Examples of Reconnaissance Handover

3-120. Figures 3-9, 3-10, and 3-11 depict an example RHO from a BCT reconnaissance platoon during a zone reconnaissance.

Chapter 3

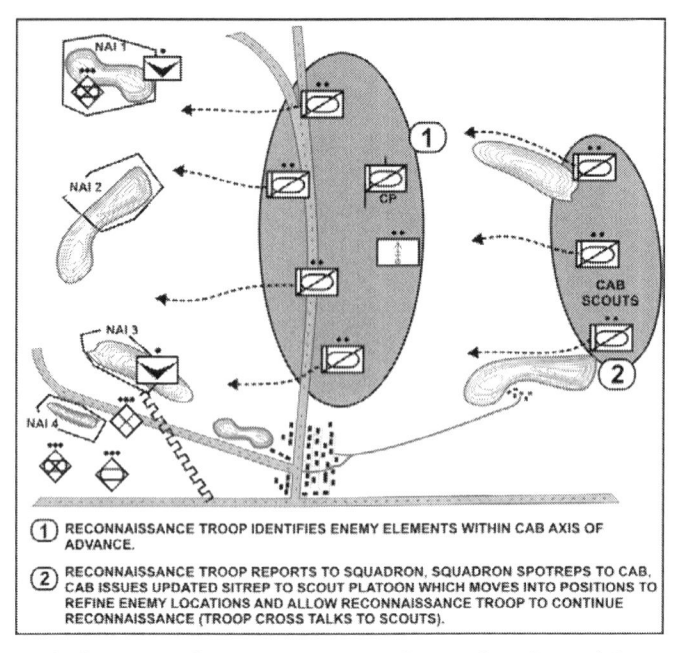

① RECONNAISSANCE TROOP IDENTIFIES ENEMY ELEMENTS WITHIN CAB AXIS OF ADVANCE.

② RECONNAISSANCE TROOP REPORTS TO SQUADRON, SQUADRON SPOTREPS TO CAB, CAB ISSUES UPDATED SITREP TO SCOUT PLATOON WHICH MOVES INTO POSITIONS TO REFINE ENEMY LOCATIONS AND ALLOW RECONNAISSANCE TROOP TO CONTINUE RECONNAISSANCE (TROOP CROSS TALKS TO SCOUTS).

Figure 3-9. Example of reconnaissance platoon handover (phase one)

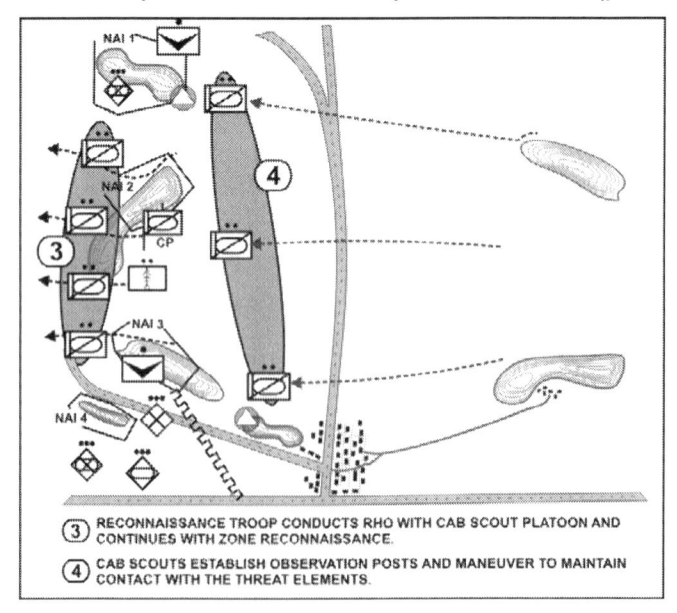

③ RECONNAISSANCE TROOP CONDUCTS RHO WITH CAB SCOUT PLATOON AND CONTINUES WITH ZONE RECONNAISSANCE.

④ CAB SCOUTS ESTABLISH OBSERVATION POSTS AND MANEUVER TO MAINTAIN CONTACT WITH THE THREAT ELEMENTS.

Figure 3-10. Example of reconnaissance platoon handover (phase two)

3-36 ATP 3-20.98 5 April 2013

Reconnaissance

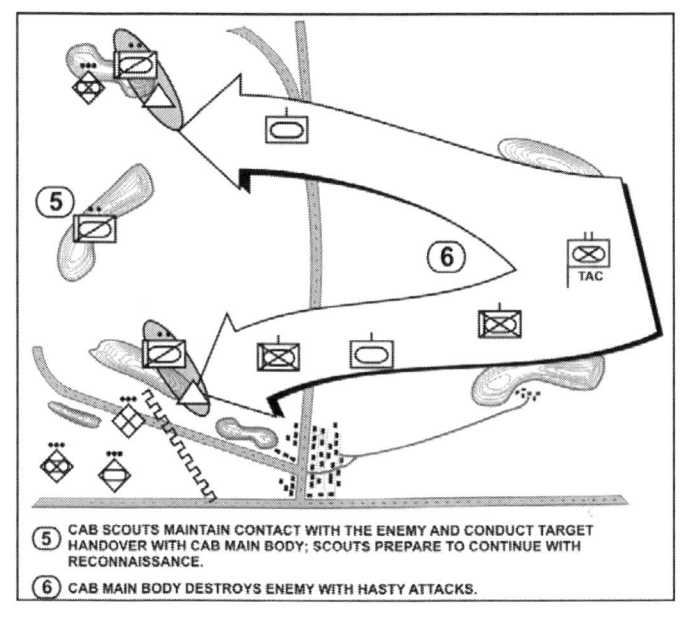

Figure 3-11. Example of reconnaissance platoon handover (phase three)

SECTION V – DISMOUNTED RECONNAISSANCE PATROLS

3-121. Dismounted tasks are a critical element in virtually every reconnaissance platoon mission. The best reconnaissance is done dismounted. It is critical that all leaders understand how and when to employ dismounted scouts to enhance the platoon's effectiveness in reconnaissance and security tasks.

3-122. Patrols are missions to gather information or conduct combat. The platoon is proficient at conducting three types of patrols:

- Reconnaissance.
- Security.
- Combat.

3-123. A mission to conduct a patrol may be given to a team, section, squad, or the entire platoon. Reconnaissance patrols are dismounted versions of zone, area, and route reconnaissance. Routes and patrol organization are planned to facilitate the information collection requirements of each type of reconnaissance. Security patrols are specifically conducted to provide security for an element or location and are discussed in Chapter 4 of this reference. Combat patrols are conducted primarily by platoons organized to perform combat oriented missions. (Refer to FM 3-21.8 for more information.)

Chapter 3

3-124. The following considerations are basic to the platoon's understanding, planning, and execution for every patrol mission:

- Plan and conduct the patrol in accordance with the fundamentals of reconnaissance and patrolling.
- Based on the higher commander's guidance and intent, the platoon leader specifies the following aspects of the patrol:
  - Focus of the patrol. In most cases, this is the reconnaissance objective.
  - Tracking methods.
  - Tempo. This includes the level of planning and preparation (deliberate or hasty).
  - Engagement criteria, including applicable ROE.
- The correct movement technique to prevent compromise of any patrol element is used. It always maintains local security by using separate reconnaissance and protection elements.
- Available resources (including IPB products, UAS, ground surveillance systems, FBCB2, and other enablers) are used to develop the situation prior to enemy contact.
- Enemy contact is avoided unless specifically directed by the platoon leader. In such a situation, the platoon gains contact with its smallest element. Unexpected contact by reconnaissance elements is absolutely minimized.
- Based on the higher commander's intent and the platoon order, all information requirements (IRs), including CCIR, are rapidly and accurately reported by radio or FBCB2.
- Ensure the security of OPs and the integrity of the platoon AO. For example, a section can send out a reconnaissance patrol after establishing an OP to check all locations from which the enemy can observe the OP. This ensures the position was not detected as it was occupied. When executed as part of a screen or other security mission, this type of watch is known as a security patrol.
- Accomplish the assigned patrol mission within the timeline specified by the higher commander.

PLANNING

3-125. When ordered to lead a patrol, the platoon or patrol leader follows the troop-leading procedures outlined in Chapter 2. The following discussion focuses on planning and preparing for patrols that help leaders make and carry out tactical decisions quickly and effectively during the patrol. (Refer to ADP 5-0 and ADRP 5-0 for more information.)

3-126. Once the order is received, the patrol leader must clearly understand what is required to accomplish the mission. First, look at the order and write down the tasks the commander has ordered, such as conduct reconnaissance of a bridge and other missions. These are called specified tasks. Next, identify the tasks to be done even

Reconnaissance

though the commander did not specify them, such as cross a stream and an open area en route to the patrol objective. These are called implied tasks.

3-127. Do not list tasks that are part of the SOP. Take a hard look at the list of specified and implied tasks, and put a check mark next to the tasks needing to be done for the unit to accomplish its mission. These are called essential tasks. To identify these tasks accurately, the patrol leader thoroughly understands the commander's intent. Restate the patrol mission in terms of who, what, where, when, and why.

3-128. The patrol leader issues the WARNORD to all members whenever possible or, at a minimum, to key members of the patrol. It should include the—

- Elements/personnel to which the WARNORD is issued. This identifies the Soldiers involved in the patrol and allows them to prepare for the mission.
- Time and nature of the mission. This is a brief and clear statement of what the patrol is to accomplish. It may summarize the who, what, where, when, and why of the mission.
- Earliest time of movement. This helps the patrol members prepare, inspect, and organize for movement by a specified time.
- Time and place the OPORD is to be issued.

3-129. The patrol leader also gives instructions to special purpose teams and key personnel so they can get ready for the patrol by taking such actions as preparing explosives, checking radios, and making a map study (point and compass men).

3-130. Once the WARNORD is issued, the patrol leader analyzes METT-TC factors and selects a COA that accomplishes the assigned mission(s). The plan should take into account how each aspect of METT-TC influences the others regarding mission accomplishment. The patrol leader should give special consideration to the terrain the patrol has to traverse, enemy forces it passes near or through en route to its objective, the effects of extensive dismounted work on the scouts, and the amount of time available to conduct the mission.

3-131. The method the patrol leader uses to organize time is reverse or backward planning from mission completion to the present moment. This aids in planning and provides a schedule of events for all patrol members. An example of backward planning a time schedule is illustrated in Table 3-2.

Table 3-2. Example of patrol time schedule (backward planning)

PATROL TIME SCHEDULE	
0200	Return friendly
2330 – 0200	Movement en route
2300 – 2330	Accomplish mission, reorganize

Table 3-2. Example of patrol time schedule (backward planning) (continued)

PATROL TIME SCHEDULE	
2230 – 2300	Reconnaissance of objective area
2000 – 2230	Movement en route
2000	Depart friendly area
1945 – 2000	Movement to departure area
1930 – 1945	Final inspection
1845 – 1930	Night rehearsals
1800 – 1845	Day rehearsals
1745 – 1800	Inspection
1700 – 1745	Supper meal
1515 – 1700	Submit planning and preparation
1445 – 1515	Issue operation order
1400 – 1445	Complete detailed plans
1315 – 1400	Conduct reconnaissance
1300 – 1315	Issue warning order

3-132. Patrols may act independently, move beyond the direct fire support of the parent unit, or operate forward of friendly units. As a consequence, their coordination effort is thorough, detailed, and continuous throughout the planning and preparation phases. The patrol leader may perform coordination personally, or it may be done by his superior. Because the entire platoon may be tasked to patrol, the necessary coordination may be extensive. A checklist is a common tool used to ensure that all items of vital importance are covered. Rehearsals from team level through platoon level are the best method for mission understanding and success.

Reconnaissance

3-133. Times of departure and return are based on the amount of time needed to accomplish the following:

- **Reach the objective.** This is determined by considering the distance, terrain, anticipated speed of movement, friendly and enemy situation, and (if applicable) time the mission is to be accomplished.
- **Accomplish essential tasks in the objective area.** This includes the leader's reconnaissance, movement of elements and teams into position, and the accomplishment of the patrol's mission.
- **Return to a friendly area.** This may be difficult to determine because casualties, enemy prisoners of war (EPWs), or captured equipment may slow the patrol.

3-134. Whenever possible, patrols should be executed and synchronized based on triggers (events) such as confirmation of PIR or an element reaching a specific terrain feature. This method provides more tactical flexibility than the use of a rigid preplanned timeline.

Primary and Alternate Routes

3-135. The patrol leader selects a primary route to and from the objective. The return route should be different from the route to the objective. The patrol leader also selects an alternate route that may be used either to or from the objective. This is used if the patrol makes contact with the enemy on the primary route and can also be used when the patrol leader knows or suspects that the patrol has been detected. (See Figure 3-12.)

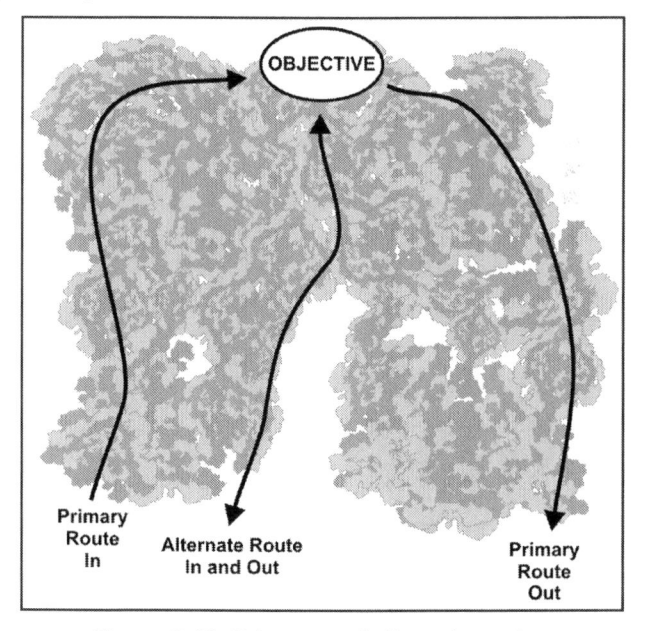

Figure 3-12. Primary and alternate routes

3-136. Routes are divided into legs with each leg starting, if possible, at a point that can be recognized on the ground. When it is not possible to start and stop legs at recognizable points, a continuous pace count and azimuth may be used to stay oriented on the route. If the patrol leader requests the use of a sniper for overwatch on the legs, careful planning of the sniper coverage in relation to the patrol route improves opportunities for clear engagements. Overflights of the legs by the UAS can provide current information about the terrain and enemy presence before the patrol moves through it. Alternate routes require the same consideration as the primary ones.

Rally Points

3-137. A rally point is a place where a patrol can conduct these actions:
- Temporarily halt to prepare departure from friendly lines.
- Reassemble and reorganize if dispersed during movement.
- Temporarily halt to reorganize and prepare for actions at an objective.
- Disseminate reconnaissance information after the objective.
- Temporarily halt to prepare to reenter friendly lines.

3-138. The most common types of rally points are initial, en route, objective, reentry, and near side or far side. Soldiers know the rally point to which they are moving at each phase of the patrol mission, what actions are required at that point, and how long they are to wait before moving on. Rally point considerations include the following:

- **Initial rally point.** An initial rally point is where a patrol assembles and reorganizes if it makes enemy contact before departing friendly lines or before reaching the first en route rally point, or is dispersed. Located within friendly lines, the initial rally point is normally selected by the commander of the friendly unit.
- **En route rally point.** An en route rally point is where a patrol rallies if dispersed en route to or from its objective. There may be several en route rally points between friendly lines and the objective. They are either planned or designated by the patrol leader every 100 to 400 meters (based on the terrain, vegetation, and visibility). When the leader designates a new en route rally point, the previously designated rally point goes into effect. This prevents uncertainty over which point Soldiers should move to if enemy contact is made immediately after the leader makes the designation. There are three ways to choose an en route rally point:
    - Physically occupy the rally point for a short period. This is the preferred method.
    - Pass by the rally point at a distance and designate it using hand-and-arm signals.
    - Walk through the rally point and select it using hand-and-arm signals.
- **Objective rally point.** An objective rally point (ORP) is where the patrol halts to prepare for actions on its objective. The ORP is located near the objective, and is out of sight and sound range so that the patrol's

Reconnaissance

activities at the ORP are not detected by the enemy. This is normally at least one terrain feature from the objective, out of small arms range of enemy forces, and far enough from the objective that it cannot be overrun if the patrol is forced off the objective. The ORP is tentative until pinpointed, and is used as a base for conducting the following actions:

- Reconnoiter the objective.
- Issue a FRAGORD.
- Disseminate information from reconnaissance if contact was not made.
- Make final preparations before continuing operations, such as applying or replenishing camouflage, preparing demolitions, caching rucksacks for quick recovery, inspecting weapons, and preparing enemy prisoner of war (EPW) bindings, first aid kits, and litters.
- Account for Soldiers and equipment after actions on the objective are complete.
- Reestablish the chain of command after actions on the objective are complete.

- **Reentry rally point.** A reentry rally point is where a patrol halts to prepare to reenter friendly lines. It is located just short of friendly lines and out of sight, sound, and small arms range of friendly OPs. This also means that the reentry rally point should be outside the limit of FPF of the friendly unit. The patrol occupies the rally point as a security perimeter while it awaits reentry.
- **Near side and far side rally points.** These rally points are established on the near and far side of danger areas. If the patrol makes contact while crossing the danger area and control is lost, Soldiers on either side move to the rally point nearest them. They establish security, reestablish the chain of command, and determine their personnel and equipment status. They can then continue the patrol mission, linkup at the ORP, or complete their last instructions.

3-139. The patrol leader should pick rally points during the patrol or by a map study before the patrol. Those selected before the patrol starts are tentative and remain in that status until confirmed on the ground. In selecting rally points, the patrol leader looks for locations with the following characteristics:

- Large enough for the patrol to assemble.
- Easily recognizable.
- Affording adequate cover and concealment.
- Defensible for a short time.
- Away from normal routes of troop movement and natural lines of drift such as streams and ridges.

PREPARATION

3-140. The leader directs the patrol to move once the warning order is issued and plans are made. This movement may involve securing a passage point or moving to the SP.

Chapter 3

3-141. The patrol leader conducts ground or aerial reconnaissance, and makes a map before completing the tentative plan. This allows time to proof the plan and obtain an idea of the ground to be traversed. Patrol leaders keep an open mind during the reconnaissance because not everything experienced during the mission matches the tentative plan.

3-142. Following the WARNORD and reconnaissance, patrol members prepare themselves and their equipment as the leader completes the plan. Essential tasks to be performed in the objective area are assigned, along with tasks that help the patrol reach the objective and return. The following discussion focuses on additional planning considerations.

3-143. Weapons and ammunition considerations apply if the patrol needs to bring additional ammunition (Class V) with its basic load. This includes significant amounts of demolitions or squad weapons requiring additional ammunition to be carried by the patrol.

3-144. Signals used on the patrol are planned and rehearsed. This includes visual and audible signals such as hand and arm gestures, flares, radio voice, and whistles, along with radios and infrared equipment. They are needed to lift or shift supporting fires, order withdrawal from the objective, send an "ALL CLEAR," stop and start movement of the patrol, and to direct linkup of elements. All patrol members need to know the signals.

3-145. Preparations include plans for retransmission sites; correct FBCB2 programming, radio call signs with primary and alternate frequencies, times to report, and codes. The platoon can use the odd-number system as a challenge and password. For example, if the patrol leader specifies 11 as the odd number, the challenge could be any number between 1 and 10. The password would be the number which, when added to the challenge, equals 11 (such as challenge 8, password 3). Another code is to designate a running password to get Soldiers quickly through a compromised passage of lines. This code alerts a unit that friendly Soldiers are approaching in a hasty manner and may be under enemy pressure. The running password is followed by the number of Soldiers approaching (such as Dogwood, 6). This prevents enemy soldiers from joining the group in an attempt to penetrate friendly lines. The patrol leader is not restricted to these two challenge and password methods, but may devise another system. However, the challenge and password from the signal operating instruction (SOI) should not be used by a patrol beyond the FEBA and the patrol leader should devise a separate challenge and password system for use beyond the FEBA.

3-146. The locations of the leader and assistant leader are planned for all phases of the patrol during movement, including danger areas and at the objective. The following considerations apply:
- The patrol leader plans to be present at the pre-designated decisive point for each phase of the mission.
- The assistant patrol leader may have a specific job for each phase of the patrol and may help the leader control the patrol by being in positions to best take charge, if required.

- Everyone on the patrol understands their position or element of the patrol.
- Duties and responsibilities for the assistant patrol leader during actions on the objective area include:
  - Area reconnaissance in the ORP.
  - Zone reconnaissance with a reconnaissance element that has been directed to establish the point at which all elements are to link-up after completing the mission.
  - Combat patrol (raid or ambush). The assistant patrol leader normally controls the support element.

PATROL ORGANIZATION

3-147. To accomplish the patrolling mission, a platoon or squad performs specific tasks such as providing security for itself at danger area crossings or rally points, reconnoitering the patrol objective, and conducting breach, support, or assault tasks. Elements of a platoon are tasked by the leader in accordance with the estimate of the situation. If possible, the patrol leader should maintain squad and fire team integrity when assigning tasks.

3-148. The basic patrol configuration includes a reconnaissance element and security element. These elements are composed of individual Soldiers with specific roles, and subordinate and supporting groups known by the terms "element" and "team." These refer to the squads, fire teams, or buddy teams that perform the common and specific tasks for each type of patrol. Some squads and fire teams may perform more than one task in an assigned sequence. The leader plans carefully to ensure that all required tasks have been identified and assigned in the most efficient way. All patrols include the—

- **Headquarters element** consisting of the patrol leader, assistant patrol leader, radio telephone operator, and other attachments that the patrol or assistant patrol leaders control directly, such as a forward observer.
- **Aid and litter team** for the treatment and evacuation of casualties.
- **Enemy prisoner of war team** for controlling prisoners according to the secure, silence, separate, safeguard, and speed (five-S) principle, and the leader's guidance. This team may also be the search team. If contact results in wounded or killed enemy soldiers, this team searches those individuals for information and materiel they may have been carrying while the rest of the patrol provides security.
- **Surveillance team** that keeps watch on the objective from the time the leader's reconnaissance ends until the unit deploys for actions on the objective. The members of the team then rejoin their elements.
- **Point man** who provides security to the front of the patrol and is guided by the compass man or patrol leader.
- **En route recorder** who writes down and collects all information gathered by the patrol.
- **Compass man** who assists in navigation by ensuring that the point man remains on course at all times. Instructions to the compass man include

an initial azimuth, with subsequent azimuths provided as necessary. The compass man should preset his compass on the initial azimuth before moving out, especially if the move is during limited visibility conditions. The patrol leader should also designate an alternate compass man.
- **Pace man** who maintains an accurate pace at all times. The patrol leader designates how often the pace man is to report, along with reporting the pace at the end of each leg. The leader should designate an alternate pace man.

3-149. The order is issued in standard five-paragraph OPORD format with terrain models or sketches used to illustrate the plan. Sketches to show planned actions can be drawn in the sand, dirt, or snow. The patrol leader considers specific details in planning the patrol using the OPORD format.

3-150. Rehearsals and inspections are vital to proper preparation. They are well planned and conducted at all times. Coordination is made with the commander or S-3 for use of an area resembling the objective area, and inspections before rehearsals guarantee that uniforms and equipment are complete and correct. Each Soldier is questioned to ensure they know—
- The plan (concept and intent).
- What to do and when to do it (task and purpose).
- What others are to do (adjacent elements).
- Challenges and passwords, signals, codes, radio call signs, frequencies, and reporting times.

3-151. Rehearsals help ensure the proficiency of the patrol and let the patrol leader check plans, make any needed changes, and verify the suitability of equipment. It is through well-directed rehearsals that Soldiers become familiar with their actions and responsibilities during the patrol.

3-152. If the patrol is at night, it is advisable to have day and night rehearsals on terrain similar to that which the patrol will operate. When time permits, all actions are rehearsed but when time is short, only the most critical actions are rehearsed. Actions on the objective and actions on contact are the most critical and should always be rehearsed.

3-153. A good way to rehearse is to have the leader walk and talk the whole patrol through each action of elements, teams, and individuals, and then have them perform these actions. In this "dry run," patrol members take their positions in formations at reduced distances so that Soldiers get the "feel" of the patrol. When the different actions are clear, a complete rehearsal at full speed is conducted with the whole patrol. This is called a "wet run." Conduct as many "dry runs" and "wet runs" as necessary to ensure mission proficiency. Element and team leaders rehearse battle drills, actions on contact, and actions at danger areas during troop-leading procedures prior to the final rehearsal. Supervision is continuous by all leaders and a precombat inspection (PCI) after the final rehearsal just before departure ensures that all equipment is working, nothing is left behind, and each member of the patrol is ready.

EXECUTION

3-154. The dismounted patrol begins by departing from friendly lines and conducting a passage of lines, if necessary (refer to section 9 of this chapter). They conduct movement as outlined in the OPORD, with particular attention to danger areas, rally points, and actions at the objective.

3-155. As the patrol progresses, the patrol leader makes decisions to continue or modify the plan based on METT-TC. Any changes to the patrol plan need to be distributed to the entire patrol to ensure understanding and execution.

3-156. The patrol leader reports progress to the platoon leader on a regular basis, with the location and mission status tracked and sent to higher HQ for information purposes.

3-157. Upon completion of the mission objective, the patrol returns to friendly lines via the preplanned route, halts in the reentry rally point, and establishes security. The patrol leader communicates the code word, and advises the friendly unit of the patrol's location and its readiness to return. The friendly unit acknowledges the message and confirms that guides are waiting before the platoon moves from the reentry rally point.

3-158. If digital/radio communications are not possible, the patrol leader, radio-telephone operator (RTO), and a two-man security element (buddy team) move forward and attempt to contact an OP using the challenge and password. The OP notifies the friendly unit that the patrol is ready to return and requests a guide. If an OP cannot be found, the patrol leader moves with the RTO and security element to locate the coordinated reentry point. They move straight forward (or away from) friendly lines, never parallel to them. All lateral movement should be outside small-arms weapons range and the patrol leader should only attempt this procedure during daylight. At night, other backup signals to make contact with friendly units should be used. The preferred method is to wait until daylight if contact with the friendly unit cannot be made as planned.

3-159. Once the friendly unit acknowledges the return of the patrol, the patrol leader issues a five-point contingency plan and moves with the RTO and security element on a determined azimuth and pace to the reentry point. The patrol leader uses far and near recognition signals to establish contact with the guide. The patrol leader signals the platoon forward (radio) or returns and leads it to the reentry point. The security element is posted with the guide at the enemy side of the reentry point and the assistant patrol leader counts and identifies each Soldier passing through the reentry point. The guide leads the patrol to the assembly area.

3-160. The patrol leader reports to the platoon leader and reports everything of tactical value concerning the friendly unit's area of responsibility. After rejoining the patrol in the assembly area, the patrol leader immediately guides the team to a secure area where personnel from higher HQ conduct a thorough debriefing. This may include all members of the patrol and any attached personnel. Although typically conducted orally, a written report is sometimes required.

Chapter 3

Tracking Methods

3-161. The reconnaissance platoon may utilize tracking to follow the trail of a specific enemy force. When operating in a low-intensity conflict environment, the platoon has a greater likelihood of utilizing tracking during a patrol. Tracking is one of the best sources of immediate-use intelligence. Indicators may be so fresh that the tracker becomes an enemy stalker, or they find information that helps the commander plan a successful mission. (Refer to TC 31-34-4 for more information.)

Organization

3-162. When the reconnaissance patrol requires the use of tracking, the patrol leader assigns the task to only one squad. The remaining squads provide security or act as a reserve if contact is made. They are:

- Squad leader—carries the radio, is the primary navigator, and has overall responsibility for accomplishing the mission, organizing the force, and setting each Soldier's load.
- Primary tracker—focuses on following the main trail left by the tracked group.
- Security—observes to the front and flanks of the trail and provides security for the primary tracker. Usually, this is the assistant squad leader.
- Rear security—provides security for the rear by looking back along the trail at irregular intervals to keep from being ambushed from behind. If the squad makes enemy contact to the front or flank, the rear security Soldier is in the best position to support those in contact. Recording the traveled azimuths to assist in navigation is also part of the duties.

CONCEPTS

3-163. A tracker has patience and moves slowly, quietly, and steadily while observing and interpreting available indicators. Reckless speed may result in overlooking important signs, losing the trail completely, or blundering into an enemy force. Attention to detail, common sense, logic, and knowledge of the environment and enemy habits allow Soldiers to obtain valuable information from signs in the area of operation. Any indicator that the tracker discovers can be defined by one or more of the following concepts:

- **Displacement.** This takes place when anything is moved from its original position. A well-defined footprint in soft, moist ground is a good example of displacement. By studying this indicator, the tracker can determine several important facts. The print left by worn footwear or by a barefoot person may indicate lack of proper equipment.
- **Stains.** A stain occurs when any substance from one organism or article is smeared or deposited onto something else. The best example of staining is blood from a profusely bleeding wound. They are often in the form of spatters or drops but are not always on the ground. They can be smeared on leaves, twigs, or bushes. Staining can also occur when muddy footgear is dragged over grass, stones, and shrubs. Staining and displacement combine to indicate movement and direction. Crushed leaves may stain rocky ground that is too hard to leave footprints. Roots,

stones, and vines may be stained where leaves or berries are crushed by moving feet. In some instances, it may be hard to determine the difference between staining and displacement since both terms can be applied to some indicators. For example, water that is muddied may indicate recent movement. Stones in streams may be stained by mud from footwear; algae can be displaced from stones in streams and stain other stones or the bank. Water that collects in footprints in swampy ground is muddy if the tracks are recent. With time, however, the mud settles and the water clears. The tracker can use this information to indicate time. Normally, the mud clears in about one hour. Clearing time, of course, varies with the terrain.

- **Weather.** The natural elements can aid or hinder the tracker. Wind, snow, rain, or sunlight may completely erase indicators. By studying the effects of weather on indicators, the tracker can determine the age of the clue. For example, when bloodstains are fresh, they are bright red. Air and sunlight change the color of blood to a deep ruby red that then turns into a dark brown crust when the moisture evaporates. Scuff marks on trees or bushes darken with time; sap oozes and then hardens when it makes contact with the air. Footprints are greatly affected by weather and by carefully studying this weather process, the tracker can determine the approximate age of the footprint. If particles are just beginning to fall into the print, the tracker should become a stalker. If the edges of the print are dried and crusty, the prints are probably at least an hour old. This varies with the terrain and should be considered as a guide only.

- **Litter.** A poorly trained or poorly disciplined force moving over a piece of terrain is likely to leave a clear trail of litter. Gum or candy wrappers, ration cans, cigarette butts, remains of fires, or even piles of human feces are signs of recent movement. However, the tracker considers weather when estimating the age of such litter. Rain flattens or washes litter away and turns paper into pulp. Ration cans exposed to weather rust first at the exposed edge where it is opened and then moves toward the center. The last rain or strong wind can be the basis for a time frame.

- **Camouflage.** Camouflage applies to tracking when the party being followed employs techniques to confuse or slow down the tracker. Walking backward to leave confusing prints, brushing out trails, and moving over rocky ground or through streams are examples of techniques that may be employed to confuse the tracker. If the party attempts to throw off the tracker by walking backward, the footprints are deepened at the toe, and soil is scuffed or dragged in the direction of movement. By following carefully, the tracker normally finds a turnaround point.

- **Immediate-use intelligence.** The tracker constantly asks questions and finds indicators that help form a picture of the enemy. The tracker avoids reporting interpretations as facts. Including the indications of certain things should also be in the report. Immediate-use intelligence is information concerning the enemy that can be put to use right away. It

Chapter 3

helps gain surprise, and keeps the enemy off balance or from escaping the area entirely.

Footprints

3-164. Footprints may indicate direction and rate of movement, number of persons in the moving party, whether the enemy realizes that they are being followed, or heavy loads are being carried. If footprints are deep and the pace is long, rapid movement is apparent. Extremely long strides and deep prints with toe prints deeper than heel prints indicate running. Prints that are deep, short, and widely spaced with signs of scuffing or shuffling indicate that the person who left the print is carrying a heavy load. If party members realize they are being followed, they may try to hide their tracks. Persons walking backward have a short, irregular stride and the prints have an unnaturally deep toe. Soil is displaced in the direction of movement.

Key Prints

3-165. The last person in a file normally leaves the clearest footprints. These are the key set of prints. The tracker should cut a stick to match the length of the key prints and notch it to indicate the width at the widest part of the sole. After studying the angle of the key prints to the direction of march, the tracker should also look for an identifying mark or feature such as a worn or frayed part of footwear to help identify the key prints. If the trail becomes vague or erased, or merges with another, the tracker can use the stick-measuring device to identify the key prints. This helps the tracker to stay on the trail. A technique used to count the total number of individuals being tracked is the box method. There are two methods the tracker can use to employ the box method:

- The first and most accurate method is using the stride as a unit of measure when key prints are determined. The tracker uses the set of key prints and the edges of the road or trail to box in an area to be analyzed. This method is accurate under the right conditions for counting up to 18 people. Determine the key print (in this case, the key print is the print left by the lug sole boot. This boot made the last print on the trail and it is the easiest print to recognize). Draw a line across the heel of one of the key prints. Move forward to the opposite key print and draw a line across the instep. Add the extra one-half print to determine if a person is making an abnormally long stride. Use the edges of the road or trail as the sides of the box, and the drawn lines as the front and back. Any person walking normally has stepped in the box at least one time. Count each print or partial print in the box. Remember to count the key print only once.
- The second technique a tracker can use to employ the box method is the 36-inch box. It is used where there are no key prints distinguishable. However, this system is not as accurate as the stride measurement. Use the 36-inch box method when no key print is available. Use the edges of the road or trail as the sides of the box. Measure across a section of the area 36 inches in length. The M16 rifle is 39 inches long and can be used as a measuring device. Count each indentation in the box and divide by two. This gives a close estimate of the number of persons who made the prints.

Other Signs of Displacement

3-166. Footprints are only one example of displacement. Anything that has been moved from its original position by a moving person is an example of displacement. Foliage, moss, vines, sticks, or rocks that are scuffed or snagged from their original place form good indicators. Vines may be dragged, dew droplets may be displaced from leaves or stones, and sticks may be turned over to indicate a different color underneath. Grass or other vegetation may be bent or broken in the direction of movement. Bits of clothing, threads, or dirt from boots can be displaced from a person's uniform and left on thorns, snags, or on the ground. The tracker should inspect all areas for bits of cloth or other matter ripped from the uniform of the person being tracked. An enemy entering or exiting a stream creates slide marks, footprints, or scuffed bark off roots or sticks. With many examples and signs of displacement, the tracker needs to carefully analyze those signs that indicate movement.

This page intentionally left blank.

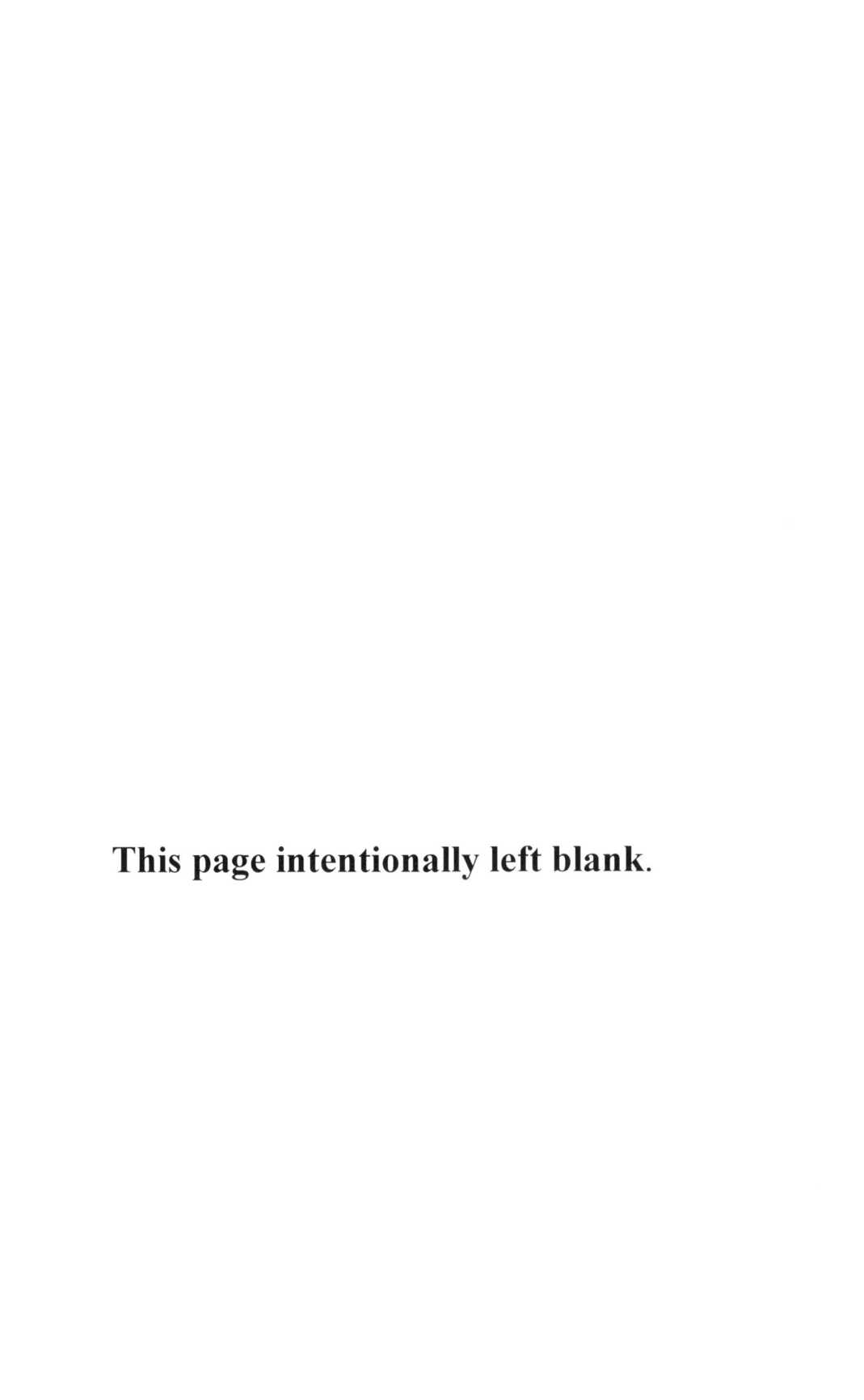

Chapter 4

Security

Security tasks are undertaken to provide early and accurate warning of enemy actions, provide time and maneuver space to react to the enemy, and develop a situation that allows the commander effective use of the protected force. For the reconnaissance platoon, security tasks are conducted in conjunction with reconnaissance and surveillance (R&S) missions. They are characterized by reconnaissance to reduce terrain and threat unknowns, gaining and maintaining contact with the threat to ensure continuous information, and providing early and accurate reporting of information to the commander.

SECTION I – OVERVIEW

4-1. All reconnaissance platoon security tasks protect a specified force from being surprised by the enemy and reduce unknown factors by providing early warning to friendly forces within a given area. The reconnaissance platoon may operate at considerable distances from the friendly elements it is protecting, limited only by communications capabilities and the range of direct fire, close air support (CAS), close combat attack (CCA), and indirect fire support. This provides friendly forces with the time and space to react and position the elements needed to defeat the enemy.

4-2. Reconnaissance platoons can conduct screen and area security tasks independently or as part of a larger force. Due to the requirements associated with conducting guard tasks, the platoon works as part of a larger unit such as a combat aviation brigade, squadron, or battalion. In addition, the platoon may be tasked to conduct screen or reconnaissance tasks in support of the larger unit's guard or cover mission.

SECTION II – FUNDAMENTALS OF SECURITY TASKS

4-3. Security tasks fundamentals are important to the reconnaissance platoon because they provide a direction during maneuvers. (Refer to FM 3-20.96 for more information.)

Chapter 4

PROVIDE EARLY AND ACCURATE WARNING
4-4. Detecting the enemy force quickly and reporting the information provides early, accurate warning to the protected force commander. This allows the time, space, and details needed to retain the tactical initiative, enabling the commander to choose the time and place to concentrate against the enemy.

PROVIDE REACTION TIME AND MANEUVER SPACE
4-5. The security force operates as far from the protected force as possible, consistent with the factors of METT-TC. Greater distances generally yield greater reaction time and maneuver space for the protected force commander. If necessary, the reconnaissance platoon fights to gain time and space for the commander.

ORIENT ON THE FORCE, AREA, OR FACILITY TO BE PROTECTED
4-6. The reconnaissance platoon focuses all of its actions on securing the protected force or facility, and providing maximum early warning of enemy activity. It operates between the protected force and known or suspected enemy elements. The reconnaissance platoon moves as the protected force moves.

PERFORM CONTINUOUS RECONNAISSANCE
4-7. Security comes from detailed knowledge about the enemy and terrain within the assigned AO. This comes from ongoing reconnaissance that supports the overall unit surveillance and reconnaissance plan. As it attempts to determine enemy COAs by focusing on the enemy and key terrain, the platoon uses combinations of OPs, Army aviation, the UAS, patrols, and other intelligence collection assets to perform continuous reconnaissance.

MAINTAIN ENEMY CONTACT
4-8. Contact once gained is not broken unless otherwise directed. Although contact does not have to be maintained by the individual section or team, the reconnaissance platoon stays in contact collectively and continuously by maintaining the capability to use direct and indirect fires, freedom to maneuver, and depth of observers in time and space.

SECTION III – FORMS OF SECURITY

FIVE FORMS OF SECURITY
4-9. Reconnaissance platoons perform or participate in five forms of security tasks:
- Screen.
    - Moving screen.
- Guard.
- Cover.

- Area security.
  - Route security.
  - Convoy security.
- Local security.

SCREEN
4-10. A screen force provides early warning to the main body as it impedes and harasses the enemy with direct and indirect fires. Within its capabilities and based upon the higher commander's guidance, it destroys or repels enemy reconnaissance units in coordination with other combat elements. Screen tasks are defensive in nature and provide the protected force with the lowest level of protection of any security mission.

4-11. Platoons conduct screens to the front, flanks, and rear of a stationary force, and to the flanks and rear of a moving force. The reconnaissance platoon generally accomplishes a screen by establishing a series of OPs and conducting patrols to ensure adequate reconnaissance and surveillance of the assigned sector. Leaders may integrate direct fire assets such as MGS, ATGMs, and M1A2 tanks with the scouts in the screen line to prevent enemy reconnaissance elements from penetrating the screen.

4-12. The commander calls on the reconnaissance platoon to screen when advance warning of when and where the enemy is attacking is needed. Operating over an extended area, the platoon fights only in self-defense or to prevent enemy observation of the protected force.

Planning
4-13. After issuing a WARNORD, the platoon leader analyzes the mission and determines what is to be accomplished by evaluating the following:
- Commander's guidance on focus (screen objective, threat/enemy, terrain, social/human demographics, infrastructure, or a combination of factors).
- Tempo (short, long, or extended duration).
- Engagement and displacement criteria. Establish what situations constitute a platoon fight, which situations the platoon defers the fight to a higher element, and what determines the bypass criteria.
- Information received about the threat in the IPB. This determines what enemy activity can be expected.
- Terrain. Conduct a map reconnaissance and examine any IMINT, SIGINT, HUMINT, or information from other units to determine the types of terrain the reconnaissance platoon operates over.
- Need for requesting and integrating outside assets such as HUMINT, CI, CA, and MPs.

4-14. Once the platoon leader has a thorough understanding of the surveillance requirements, assessment of available assets to execute these requirements occurs.

Availability of assets depends upon how long the screen remains in place and how the platoon is task-organized. If the screen is of short duration (less than 12 hours), individual squads can emplace and man separate OPs. If the duration of the screen is unknown or longer than 12 hours, the platoon leader assigns a two-vehicle section (CFV/RV platoons) or three-vehicle section (HMMWV platoons) for each OP to facilitate continuous operations.

Task Organization
4-15. The platoon leader task-organizes the platoon and any other assigned assets to achieve the most effective surveillance of the NAI or avenue of approach. Planning may include advantages such as engineer or Infantry squads, ground surveillance systems, artillery observers, air defense elements, and UAS assets. The platoon leader ensures these assets complement other forces in the screen, all scouts understand where the assets are, and what role they are playing.

4-16. The platoon leader uses surveillance assets in a number of ways, including adjusting the number of sections or squads in a particular surveillance team, mixing scouts and other assets into the same team, or maintaining elements in pure teams under the platoon leader's control. The platoon leader considers the characteristics of the NAI or avenue of approach when task-organizing for surveillance. These considerations determine whether the platoon needs to call for fire or conduct dismounted patrols. This also affects the field of view, and applicability of ground surveillance systems and tactical UAS. (For more information, refer to Chapter 2.)

Redundancy
4-17. In terms of size, terrain, or importance, the platoon leader may task more than one element to observe a particular assigned NAI or avenue of approach. For example, a very large avenue may require multiple observation assets to ensure all aspects of the avenue are covered. Terrain that is very broken or mixed with areas of thick vegetation may require more than one asset to ensure adequate continuous coverage. If the commander assigns significant priority to a particular NAI, the platoon leader may assign multiple elements to cover it. Redundancy ensures adequate observation and enables the unit to accomplish the mission even if enemy forces compromise some assets. Figure 4-1 illustrates redundancy of observation assets.

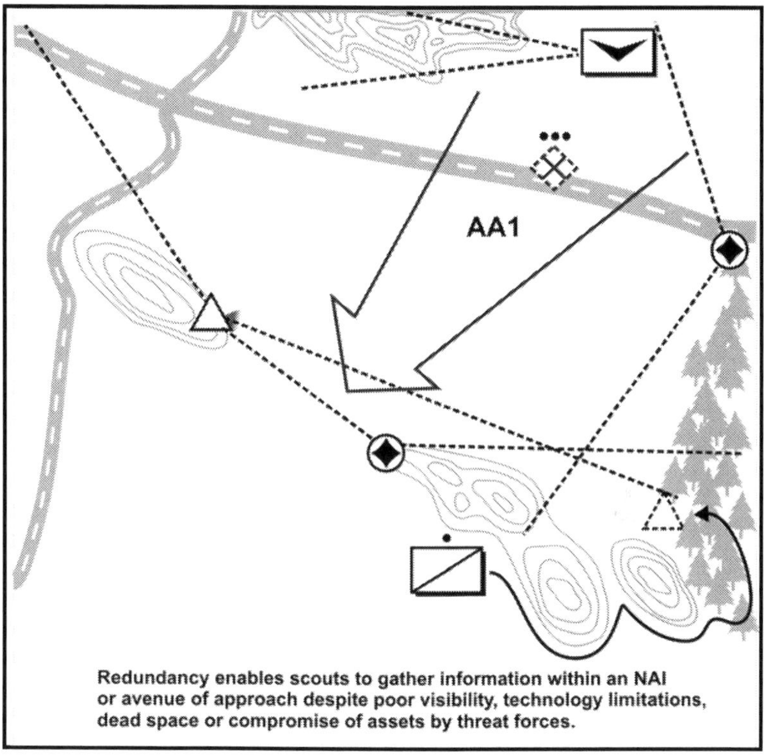

Security

Redundancy enables scouts to gather information within an NAI or avenue of approach despite poor visibility, technology limitations, dead space or compromise of assets by threat forces.

Figure 4-1. Use of redundancy in surveillance tasks

Cueing

4-18. Cueing is a technique the platoon leader uses to cover the NAI or avenue of approach when assets are limited and the capability for redundancy is not available. Contingency tasks by the surveillance teams that increase inspection on a particular NAI are execute tasks when "cued" by activity at that NAI.

4-19. The reconnaissance platoon initially covers the NAI or avenue of approach with a single surveillance team or a remote electronic signaling device such as ground surveillance systems, trip flares, or early warning systems. When scouts detect activity, other teams move into preselected positions and add their capabilities to the surveillance. (See Figure 4-2.)

Chapter 4

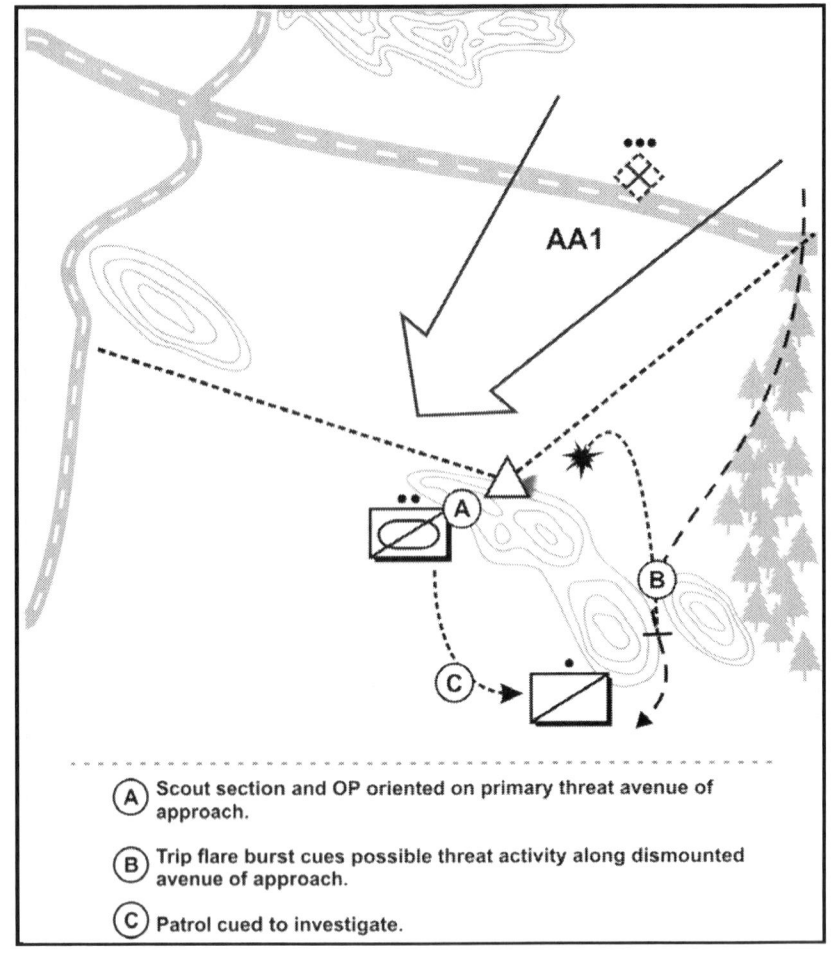

Figure 4-2. Use of cueing in surveillance tasks

- (A) Scout section and OP oriented on primary threat avenue of approach.
- (B) Trip flare burst cues possible threat activity along dismounted avenue of approach.
- (C) Patrol cued to investigate.

4-20. Another critical task of the platoon is providing an early warning of enemy approach. Effective warning requires detailed planning for communications. The platoon leader looks at communications distances and significant terrain features to identify potential problems. If problems are anticipated, they can be addressed by requesting support from higher HQ, or planning for radio relays and directional antennas.

Execution

4-21. The reconnaissance platoon moves toward the screen line as a follow-on or stand-alone mission. It is imperative to approach the screen line with stealth to avoid detection by possible enemy observation. The platoon should deploy in sectors prior

Security

to approaching the screen line so section/team alignment is achieved, and halt short of the proposed screen locations. Dismounted scouts reconnoiter the vehicle positions, OPs, and routes.

4-22. After marking vehicle positions, the dismounted scouts lead the vehicles into hiding positions. Leaders immediately begin developing their fields of observation by emplacing OPs, verifying that all assigned NAIs can be observed, and ensuring observation overlap by adjacent elements. Vehicle movement close to the screen line should be minimized and used to verify hide and battle positions only. Once this is accomplished, vehicle engines are turned off to allow for stealth and sound observation techniques.

4-23. The platoon also verifies the defense plan which entails both direct and indirect fires. Vehicle and OP fields of fire are identified and recorded, the indirect fire template is verified, and additional target reference points are developed and submitted, if needed.

4-24. Surveillance is maintained by a series of OPs that the platoon leader positions to best observe designated NAIs or avenues of approach. These positions are reported to higher HQ and entered in FBCB2 for dissemination within the unit. The screen, normally identified by a phase line on a map, designates the most forward location of the OPs. Commanders carefully weigh time and distance factors in relation to the supported unit when choosing where to place this line. The platoon observes the space between the screen line and the supported/subsequent unit by establishing positions in-depth. The screen line also supports RHO within the platoon and with the supported/subsequent unit by providing knowledge of the area to the gaining unit as it moves forward through the scouts.

4-25. The OP is the preferred means of maintaining surveillance. From OPs, scouts observe enemy movement, direct killer teams, and adjust indirect fires against the enemy. From the OP, scouts send size, activity, location, unit, time, and equipment (SALUTE) reports to their platoon leader to provide early warning of enemy activity. (Refer to FM 3-20.971, FM 3-20.96, and FM 3-21.8 for more information.)

4-26. The platoon can occupy multiple OPs based on the mission's time requirement (short, long, or extended duration), availability of vehicles, and squad strength as shown in Table 4-1.

Chapter 4

Table 4-1. Reconnaissance platoon observation post organization and manning capabilities

Organization	Number of Sections	Scouts per Section	Possible Platoon OPs (up to 12 hours)	Possible Platoon OPs (12+ hours)	Possible OPs (with patrols)
IBCT/BFSB	2 maneuver +HQ	6	3	2	2
SBCT	3 maneuver + HQ	10	4	2	2
ABCT	2 maneuver + HQ	8	4	4	3

4-27. In executing a screen, the platoon conducts combat patrols to extend their observation range, and to observe dead space and the area between OPs. While sensors increase the observation range of the platoon's screen and decrease reaction time for detecting and reporting threats in the area, scouts confirm what the sensors have detected through movement and visual contact. The platoon leader can request to place OPs forward of the LOA if they can more effectively observe the NAI/avenue of approach. A scout's primary means of engaging the enemy is through indirect fire. Unless required, scouts do not fight with their direct fire weapons. Direct fire is generally limited to preventing observation of friendly elements, penetration of the screen line, or self-defense.

POSITIONING THE OBSERVATION POST

4-28. Observation posts can be arrayed in linear or in-depth positions, but in-depth is preferred for maintaining contact with a moving enemy. OPs in-depth can be configured as completely vehicle-mounted, dismounted scouts forward of the vehicle, or a combination of dismounted scouts and wheeled and tracked vehicles. In-depth OP placement allows the reconnaissance platoon to observe the entire sector. This method works well when the platoon is assigned a sector with several avenues of approach or is in heavily vegetated terrain. In-depth placement allows for redundancy in observation and better interlocking coverage of the sector. The ABCT reconnaissance platoon and CAB platoon can place CFVs forward when heavy contact is likely, or HMMWVs forward when stealth is required. Linear placement is effective when the enemy is not moving and provides optimum observation of the enemy. (See Figures 4-3 and 4-4.)

Security

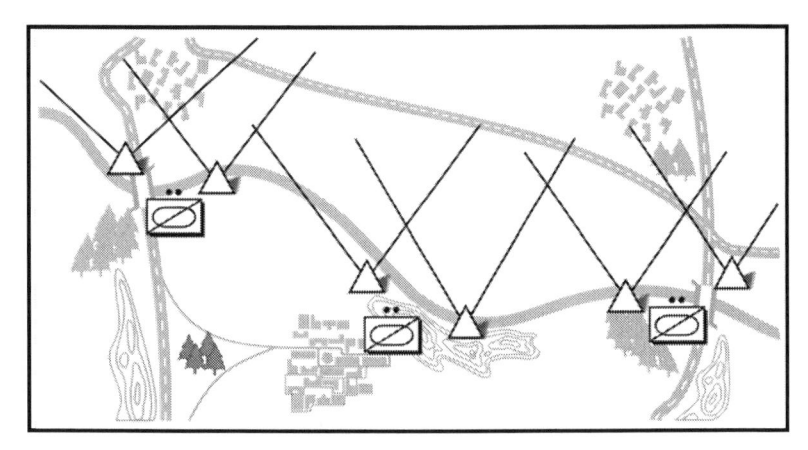

Figure 4-3. Linear positioning of observation posts

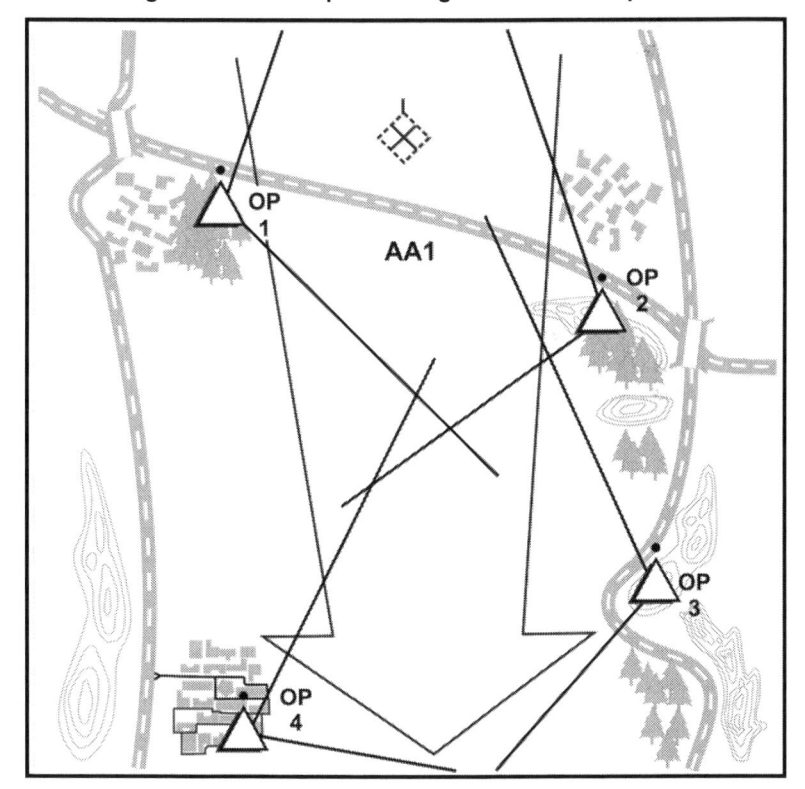

Figure 4-4. In-depth positioning of observation posts

Selecting an Observation Post Site

4-29. Based on the commander's guidance, the platoon leader selects the general location for the OPs after analyzing METT-TC factors. From this analysis, the number of OPs are established, and where they are positioned to allow long-range observation and provide depth through the sector. Digital terrain products may assist commanders and platoon leaders in making the site selection with the line of sight tool in these programs. Section/squad leaders and team leaders then select the exact position for each OP once they are at the planned location. OPs should have the following characteristics:

- Covered and concealed routes to and from the OP. Scouts are able to enter and leave the OP without being seen by the enemy.
- Unobstructed observation of the assigned area or sector. Ideally, the fields of observation of adjacent OPs overlap to ensure full coverage of the sector.
- Effective cover and concealment. Scouts should select positions with cover and concealment to reduce their vulnerability. They may need to pass up a position with favorable observation capability but with no cover and concealment in favor of a position that affords better survivability.
- A location that does not attract attention. OPs should not be established in such locations as a water tower, an isolated grove of trees, or a lone building or tree. These positions draw enemy attention and may be used as enemy artillery target reference points (TRPs). The one exception to this rule is during stability missions where urban emplacement is necessary. The OPs should also be located away from natural lines of drift along which a moving enemy force can be expected to travel. These locations might include a route on the floor of a valley or a site near a major highway.
- A location that does not skyline the observers. Avoid hilltops. Position OPs farther down the slope of the hill or on the side, provided there are covered and concealed routes into and out of the position.

Occupying the Observation Post

4-30. Unless the area has already been cleared, the platoon should conduct a zone reconnaissance to the screen line. This is the most secure method of moving to the screen line, but also the most time-consuming. The following steps provide an example of how a section might occupy an OP:

- The reconnaissance platoon section stops short of its OP site. The section leader directs the drivers into positions to overwatch the general OP site, and any terrain the enemy could use to interfere with movement into or out of the position. (See Figure 4-5.)
- The section leader dismounts with scouts from each vehicle and moves forward to reconnoiter the OP (using the OP site selection characteristics). Drivers and gunners remain in their vehicles to overwatch the dismounted personnel.

Security

- The section leader moves the dismounted scouts to the OP site, establishes security overwatching the far side of the site, and checks the site for mines, booby traps, and enemy personnel. After verifying that the sector or area of responsibility can be observed from this site and determining a position that is best for the OP, the section leader issues a five-point contingency plan and displacement criteria to the OPs before returning to the vehicles.
- The section leader selects hide positions and fighting positions for the vehicles.
- The driver and dismounted Soldiers from each vehicle mark their vehicle position with a ground stake. The stake, which enables a vehicle to reoccupy the fighting position at a later time, is centered on the driver's station. It is tall enough for the driver to see while driving into position. Engineer tape or luminous tape can be placed on the stake so it can be seen during limited visibility tasks. Once the area around the OP is cleared and secure, the section leader signals the vehicles forward to move into their fighting positions.
- The gunner and vehicle commander for each vehicle complete and check their sector sketch. Each vehicle then moves out of its fighting position into a hide position. The section leader checks the sketches to ensure they provide complete coverage of the sector. Sector sketches or range cards are a valuable reference if the vehicle is ordered to fight.

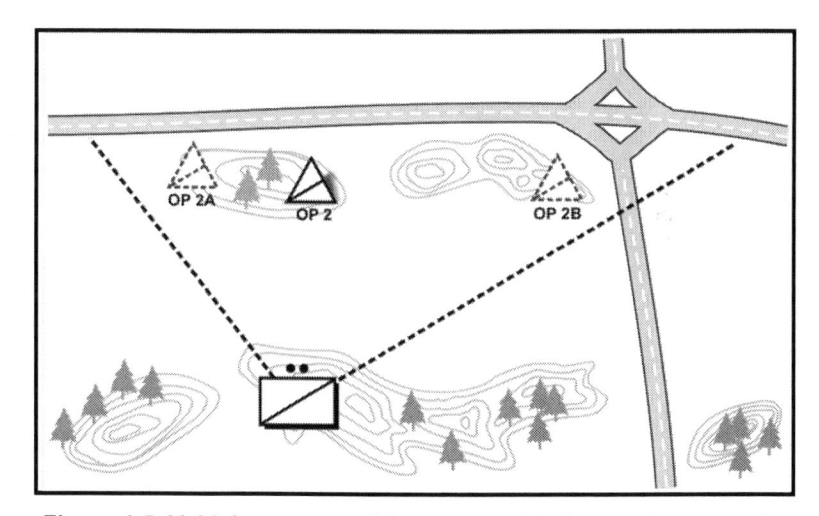

Figure 4-5. Vehicles overwatching a potential observation post site

MANNING THE OBSERVATION POST

4-31. A minimum of two scouts man each OP. They are equipped to observe the area, report information, protect themselves, and call for and adjust fire. One Soldier observes the area while the other provides local security, records information, and

Chapter 4

sends reports to the section/squad leader or platoon leader. The two scouts should switch jobs every 20 to 30 minutes because the observer's effectiveness decreases quickly after that time. Essential equipment for the OP includes the following:
- Map of the area with graphics.
- Compass.
- Communications equipment (wire and radio).
- Observation devices (binoculars, observation telescope, and night observation devices [NODs]).
- Signal operating instructions.
- Report formats.
- Weapons, such as personal and crew-served. This includes AT4 rocket launchers and appropriate mines.
- CBRNE equipment and individual protective equipment to achieve mission-oriented protective posture (MOPP) 4.

Improving the Position

4-32. Once the platoon section leader has established the OP and assigned the scouts their sectors of observation, the section improves the position. The section leader prepares a sector sketch. This sketch is similar to a fighting position sketch but with some important differences. At a minimum, the sketch includes the following:
- Key and significant terrain, including NAIs and avenues of approach.
- Location of the OP.
- Location of the hide position.
- Locations of vehicle fighting and observation positions.
- Alternate positions (hide, fighting, and observation).
- Routes to and from the OP and fighting positions.
- Sectors of observation, with dead space identified.
- Preplanned artillery targets.
- TRPs for direct fire.
- Prepared SPOTREPs and calls for fire based on trigger lines and projected locations where the enemy will first be seen.
- Locations of protective obstacles, such as Claymore mines and trip flares.

4-33. Personnel manning the OP site begin digging-in to provide protection from indirect and direct fires. They also camouflage the position, install wire communications equipment, and emplace hasty obstacles for local protection. As the OP is improved, soil and other materials that have been moved are not disposed of to the front of the OP site. This can give away the scouts' presence when observed from the front. Vehicle commanders (or gunners) and drivers reconnoiter the routes to their fighting/observation positions and alternate positions, perform maintenance, and camouflage vehicles and positions. The section leader's OP sketch is accurate. An azimuth obtained from a hull-down position is attainable and observable from hide and turret-down positions. The same principle applies for dismounted OPs.

When scouts are behind cover, they need to have the same fields of fire for their crew-served weapon as when they expose themselves to engage the enemy.

Observation Post Communications

4-34. The scouts occupying the OP use wire, radio, or both as their primary means of communication. Wire is preferred because it is concealable, secure, and is not vulnerable to enemy direction-finding equipment or jamming. If possible, the scouts in the OP use wire to communicate with their section/squad or team leader, who is located with his vehicle in the hide position behind the OP. As a last resort, messengers may be used to report information if the radio is being jammed or the wire is severed. Scouts moving to and from the OP as messengers ensure their movement is undetected by the enemy.

4-35. The Soldier in the vehicle monitoring OP communications relay reports or information to the platoon leader by FBCB2 or voice radio. The scouts in the OP should carry a radio as a backup means of communications; they can use it to send reports or to talk directly to their fire support team (FIST) or mortar section for indirect fire support.

Observation Post Security

4-36. Scouts are extremely vulnerable in an OP, and their best self-defense is not being seen, heard, or otherwise located by the enemy. They employ active and passive measures to protect themselves from enemy detection, and direct and indirect fires.

4-37. To provide early warning of enemy movement around a screen line or OP position, scouts emplace unattended ground sensors in areas that cannot be directly observed or in the dead spaces around or between OPs. Trip flares and Claymore mines provide additional early warning and protection from enemy personnel. Once these devices are triggered, the enemy has an indication that there is an overwatching element for that device.

4-38. Active patrolling around and between OPs also enhances security. Patrols give the platoon the ability to observe areas that cannot be observed from the OPs and to clear the area around the OP of enemy elements. A patrol can be executed by a minimum of two dismounted crewmen from the vehicles in the hide position. The platoon executes security patrols as soon as possible after occupation of the position to discover enemy elements that might have observed the occupation. The patrol reconnoiters favorable observation positions that might be occupied by the enemy. Route selection is critical when organizing patrols because scouts assume that the OP position is under observation.

4-39. Observation posts cannot always avoid being seen by the enemy, so they take actions to limit their vulnerability. Covered positions provide protection from enemy fires, and vehicle dispersion further reduces the effects of these fires. The vehicles in the fighting positions are used to extract the scouts from the OP when the position has been identified and attacked by the enemy.

5 April 2013   ATP 3-20.98   4-13

Chapter 4

Extended Operations
4-40. Extended OPs are fixed surveillance positions that require the scouts to remain at the site for up to 72 hours without relief, rotation of team, or support from the element's vehicle. Extended OPs minimize the chance of enemy detection. Infiltration and exfiltration, using aerial or dismounted movement, is the primary method of occupying and departing the OP. Once the OP is occupied, movement around the OP ceases until the mission is complete, evacuation is required, or exfiltration begins. During this process, scouts should apply the principles summarized by the acronym BLUES:

- **B** – Blend in with the surrounding area. Does the site look natural? Does it attract unwanted attention?
- **L** – Low-to-the-ground construction techniques are used. Does the site provide protection against small arms and direct weapons fire?
- **U** – Unexpected sites should be used. Do the enemy forces expect Soldiers to look out the window, or out the small hole in the wall?
- **E** – Evacuation routes are planned during site selection. Where is the link-up location with friendly forces?
- **S** – Avoid silhouetting of the site by using the sides of hills, not the crests. Can the sniper see a Soldier silhouetted against the skyline, wall, or other object?

Site Selection
4-41. In choosing where to position extended OPs, the platoon ensures that they meet the following requirements:

- Afford adequate visual and electronic line-of-sight target observation and security for the observers.
- Have a wide a field of view with as little dead space as possible.
- Are not near natural lines of drift or in terrain that would naturally draw the attention of enemy forces, such as on top of a flat rock face on a hill.
- Have covered and concealed exit and entry points.
- Are far enough downwind from the target and inhabited areas to minimize the detection of odors by dogs or people. Remember that wind direction often changes at various times of day.
- Are positioned at a distance from the target in accordance with METT-TC.
- Afford effective side and overhead cover and concealment.
- Are capable of supporting execution of battle drills if the observers break enemy contact.
- Support reliable communication between the observers and their main body, security element, and communications element.
- Are in a location that is not obvious to enemy forces.

4-42. If no single position affords all these features (for example, daytime versus nighttime requirements), it may become necessary to select separate positions suited to the type of surveillance performed. Multiple positions are mutually supporting so that if one position is compromised, observers in the other position are able to continue the surveillance mission and warn the rest of the platoon. If positions are not used during the day, they should be kept under observation. If the positions cannot be secured by observation, they should not be reused the following night. This practice prevents scouts from walking into an ambush while trying to reoccupy a position. Another consideration in the use of separate locations is that observers avoid establishing patterns and trails while moving to and from the different positions.

PERFORM COUNTER RECONNAISSANCE

4-43. Once the platoon leader has planned surveillance of assigned reconnaissance objectives and ensured that early warning can be provided, the enemy's reconnaissance effort and the platoon's assigned role in the conduct of counterreconnaissance is evaluated. These tasks consist of the hunter (who acquires the enemy) and the killer (who engages the enemy). The most appropriate role for the platoon in the counterreconnaissance task is acquiring enemy assets rather than killing them.

4-44. The commander's guidance specifically defines the role of the platoon in counterreconnaissance tasks. The platoon leader considers four factors when planning to acquire enemy reconnaissance elements:

- Enemy avenues of approach (mounted and dismounted).
- When and under what conditions the platoon is likely to encounter enemy reconnaissance forces.
- Likely composition of enemy forces in terms of size, organization, and equipment.
- Identity and location of friendly reconnaissance-killing forces.

4-45. Enemy reconnaissance forces are not likely to use primary avenues of approach to execute their task or mission. To acquire their assigned objectives, the platoon is oriented on reconnaissance avenues of approach which may include trails, rough terrain, and dead space that allows mounted movement, but only for small teams of vehicles. They also realize that enemy reconnaissance is most likely to move during periods of limited visibility. A thorough understanding of the composition of enemy reconnaissance elements allows the reconnaissance platoon to more accurately determine the enemy's likely reconnaissance avenues of approach and how best to acquire them. In other words, reconnaissance platoons war-game how they would move through the area if they were the enemy, and then determine where to find the enemy element.

4-46. Scouts consider the AO, including the enemy, their knowledge of the terrain (including the enemy's view of the terrain), and available systems' capabilities to quickly destroy the adversary. Once initial acquisition of the enemy occurs (by the hunter element), other assets in the CAB, squadron, or brigade are given the specific mission of killing the enemy reconnaissance (the killer element) in or behind the screen line. These assets should have direct communication with the hunter elements and the platoon leader. The reconnaissance platoon rehearses all phases of the

Chapter 4

mission with the augmenting elements to ensure mistakes do not allow the enemy to infiltrate the protected force. (See Figures 4-6 and 4-7.)

(A) OP at position A is oriented on the primary threat avenue of approach.

(B) OPs at positions B are oriented on the the threat reconnaissance avenues of approaches.

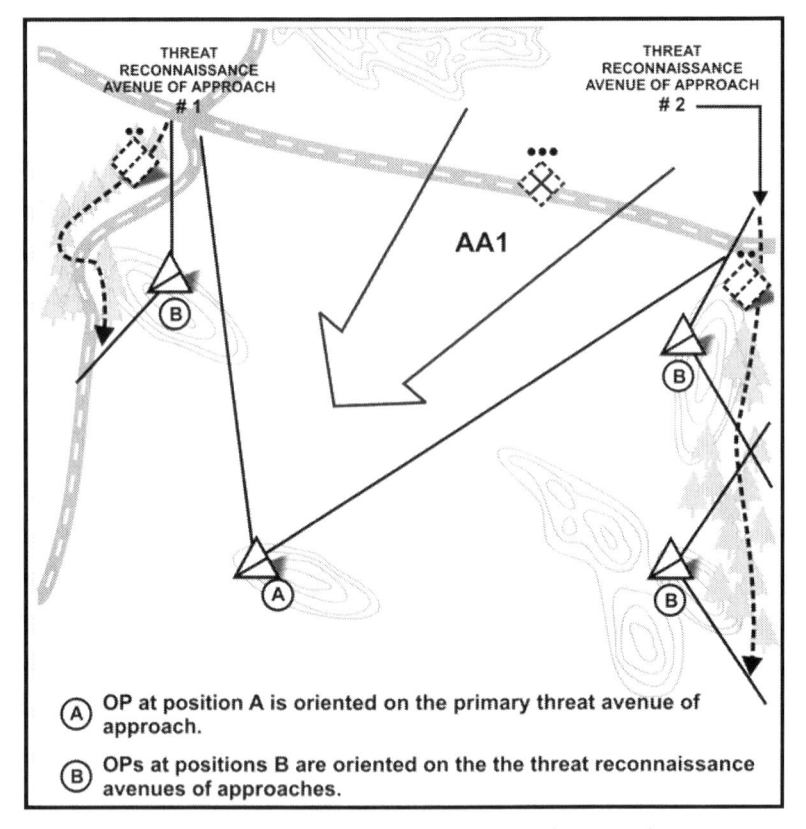

Figure 4-6. Counterreconnaissance (part one)

Security

Upon contact with threat main body OPs previously oriented on reconnaissance avenues of approaches may move to designated positions oriented on the threat primary avenue of approach.

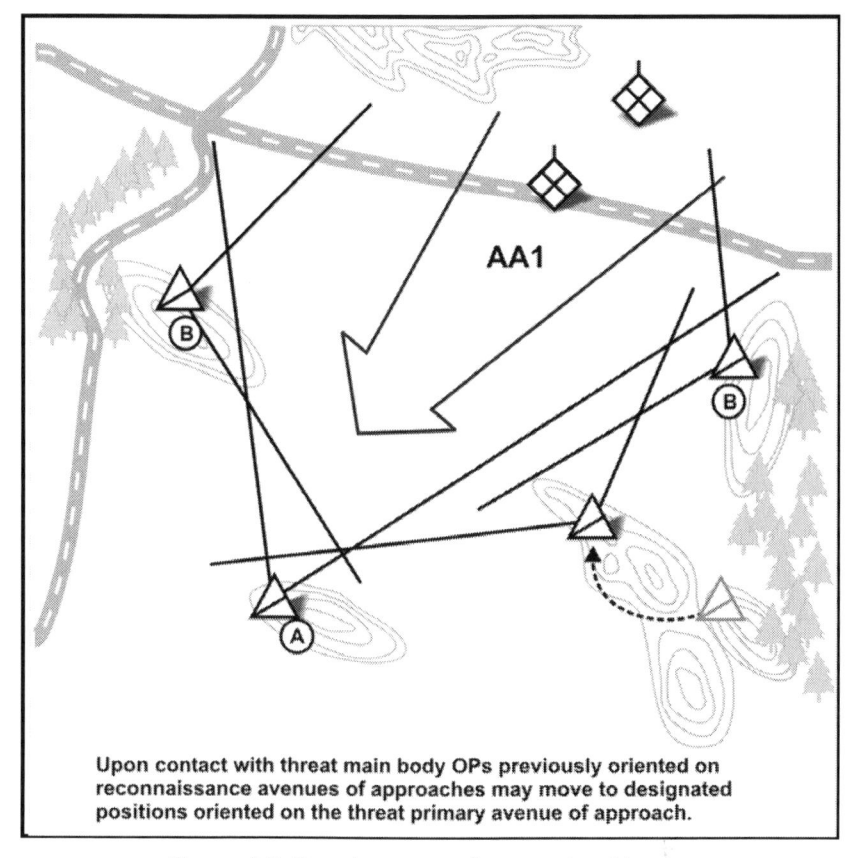

Figure 4-7. Counterreconnaissance (part two)

4-47. To make the hunter-killer team proficient, all elements need to be present to rehearse the following factors in destroying an enemy reconnaissance element:
- Undetected movement into screen positions.
- No fire areas (NFAs) requested through higher HQ.
- Hunter acquisition and reporting of the enemy.
- Hunter tracking and reporting.
- Killing element movement into engagement position.
- Handover to killer element for engagement.
- Exploitation of destroyed enemy element for intelligence, if possible.
- Repositioning of hunter-killer team for acquisition of follow-on threats.

4-48. The counterreconnaissance task is extremely resource-intensive. It is generally most effective when conducted by an element larger than a single platoon, since the platoon by itself does not have sufficient assets to both acquire and kill an enemy. In addition, it may not be able to observe all reconnaissance avenues of approach and still maintain surveillance on the enemy's main avenues of approach. The commander's intent is critical to resolve this dilemma.

4-49. When the platoon has to acquire both enemy elements and the main body, the priority in the early stages of the mission is on the reconnaissance forces focusing on the avenues of approach. The platoon then tracks the echeloned arrival of enemy elements in the AO and shifts priority to the main avenues of approach. This technique permits the platoon leader to time-phase priorities based on conditions in the AO. The platoon leader recognizes when to change priority to the main avenue of approach.

Reconnaissance Platoon (Operating Alone)

4-50. This technique places the responsibility for counterreconnaissance on the platoon. It requires maximum use of any attached enabling assets to acquire the enemy, freeing scouts to perform the killing function of counterreconnaissance. CFV-equipped platoons are best able to perform this task. The platoon leader places acquiring assets along the screen line, which should include the use of dismounts forward of the vehicles. Next, the platoon leader positions his designated killing teams in-depth. The killing assets of the platoon occupy positions on likely enemy reconnaissance routes. Where engineer support is available, killing vehicles should be in hull- or turret-down positions to prevent observation as the enemy moves into their vicinity. Positioning of vehicles is flexible enough to respond to additional enemy elements moving on other routes.

4-51. When the platoon operates with units that commonly have combat observation and lasing teams (COLTs) attached, such as the SBCT, IBCT, and BFSB, the platoon leader may integrate NAIs to support the TAIs positioned in-depth. This places the scouts in the role of acquiring the enemy, with the COLTs as the killer's in-depth employing artillery or CAS.

Reconnaissance Platoon with Attached Killer Element

4-52. This team technique requires the close integration of a reconnaissance platoon and an element capable of defeating the known level of threat. The platoon leaders plan for the employment of an MGS or tank platoon to execute counterreconnaissance tasks. The platoon leader considers using a Bradley section and its associated Infantry squads, especially for a dismounted enemy. The reconnaissance platoon acts as the acquiring element, and the attached MGS, tank, or Bradley sections act as the killing element. The reconnaissance platoon leader, whose element makes first contact, commands the counterreconnaissance effort. The platoon leader pairs the killing force with a platoon's section (at least one reconnaissance section supported by a killing element). During this task, the PSG positions himself to conduct CASEVAC tasks, resupply tasks, and if necessary, guide additional killing elements forward to support the mission.

4-53. The reconnaissance platoon may acquire the enemy with surveillance techniques and sensors. The killing force should occupy a battle position (BP) overlooking likely reconnaissance avenues and wait for orders to occupy their firing positions. They are prepared to move to previously reconnoitered alternate positions based on reports coming from the scouts. The scouts have marked avenues of approach, routes, and lanes to direct the killing force in engaging the enemy.

Reconnaissance Platoon and Company Team

4-54. This technique uses a reconnaissance platoon—either attached or under OPCON—and a company team to execute counterreconnaissance and security tasks. CAB reconnaissance platoons primarily execute this technique. The company team commander controls the security effort. The reconnaissance platoon is the primary acquiring element but it can be supplemented with Infantry assets from the company team, and enabling assets from the battalion. The commander uses all other assets as the killing element.

4-55. This is the most lethal counterreconnaissance technique and has the combat power to be very effective. It also has organic sustainment assets for quicker and more responsive support. Major disadvantages of this technique are the combat power it diverts from the main effort and the execution problems that may result if the scouts and the killing elements have not trained together.

Maintaining Contact

4-56. Another critical task area of security is maintaining contact. After reporting information on enemy reconnaissance elements and locating the enemy main body, the reconnaissance platoon maintains contact until authorized to hand over contact to another friendly element. This is one of the most difficult tasks for the individual section or team to accomplish because of the size of the AO, and the distance the element can move prior to enemy detection. Therefore, maintaining contact is best accomplished through a reconnaissance platoon effort creating interlocking fields of observation.

4-57. The preferred method for maintaining contact with a moving enemy is to position echeloned OPs in-depth along the avenue of approach. As the enemy force reaches the edge of their sector, the OP conducts a handover to another OP without the requirement for the OPs to physically displace. This technique requires the platoon to have interlocking visibility and to pre-position OPs in-depth. OPs rehearse passing contact of the enemy to another element so that if contact is lost, OPs can take action to regain contact.

4-58. Another technique is to displace in front of a moving enemy. This procedure is very difficult because the platoon moves to the rear faster than the enemy is moving forward. This often exposes the platoon to enemy fire. Additionally, if they attempt to use covered and concealed routes only, they risk moving too slowly, having the enemy bypass them, and losing contact. To counter potential problems, scouts conduct detailed map reconnaissance and thorough rehearsals to learn the terrain as they reconnoiter their movement to and around the OP locations.

Chapter 4

4-59. A third technique for maintaining contact is a combination of the two discussed earlier. Leaving the original dismounted OP in position (with a vehicle in support, if possible); the platoon leader repositions the remainder of the section in-depth as a mounted or dismounted OP. This OP can be established or reoriented to maintain contact until the element in contact hands over the enemy to a killing element or a maneuver element positioned behind the screen. The platoon maintains observation of assigned NAIs/avenues of approach. Situations may occur in which the scouts request that other assets maintain the screen while they meet a surveillance coverage requirement such as moving forward for deeper observation. The platoon leader can also request or coordinate handover to maintain the screen. This technique reduces both the time associated with moving OPs, and the likelihood of compromising the platoon's reconnaissance elements.

4-60. No matter how the platoon plans to maintain contact, the platoon leader should attempt to rehearse the method, especially if it requires reconnaissance elements to displace or move to alternate positions. This helps the commander and platoon leader validate the method they have chosen, or to choose another one if it becomes necessary.

Disrupt and Delay
4-61. Reconnaissance platoons should attempt to harass and impede the enemy using indirect fire. They should focus on expected avenues of approach, choke points, the enemy rate of march, and artillery time of flight to determine trigger lines (or points) that allow accurate engagement of the enemy (time of flight information from available weapon systems should be made available to scouts and rehearsed).

4-62. A technique for planning the use of triggers is to have a dismounted OP sited forward of its supporting vehicle observe the triggers and initiate fires, with the vehicle OP observing the impact zone and adjusting the fires. On terrain that offers slower movement, the forward OP may be able to observe the impacts. Leaders may also request available CAS assets and CCA aircraft for interdicting fires. Every scout in the reconnaissance platoon is proficient in planning, coordinating, and calling for indirect fires, such as linear sheaths on main avenues of approach.

Moving Screen
4-63. The planning considerations discussed above for a stationary screen also apply to a moving screen. However, emphasis can shift since the main body is moving. The platoon can conduct a moving flank screen to the side or rear of a moving force as part of the squadron or battalion. Conducting a screen for the rear of a moving force is essentially the same as that for a stationary screen. As the protected force moves, the platoon occupies a series of successive screen lines. Movement is regulated by the requirement to maintain the time and distance factors directed by the main body commander. Small UAS or sensors can support the screen during the maneuver of reconnaissance platoons or sections. They can also work to extend the areas of coverage.

4-64. The moving flank screen poses additional considerations. The width of the screen AO is not as important as maintaining orientation on the force being protected, and maintaining continuous observation of the threat avenues of approach that might affect the protected force's maneuver. The platoon screens forward of the lead combat element in the main body or to the rear of the protected elements, exclusive of front and rear security forces. The trains move with the troop or can travel with the squadron or battalion trains.

GUARD

4-65. Commanders deploy a guard force to protect the main force by fighting to gain time while also observing and reporting information. To prevent enemy ground observation of and direct fire against the protected element, the guard force reconnoiters, attacks, defends, and delays. They normally operate within the range of the main body's indirect fire weapons. Units do not execute guard missions below the reconnaissance squadron (with augmentation) or CAB level. A reconnaissance platoon participating as part of a guard force reconnoiters, screens, attacks, defends, and delays as necessary until the squadron or battalion has accomplished its mission. The reconnaissance platoon operates within the range of direct fire support (MGS, ATGM, and M1A2s) and supporting artillery.

COVER

4-66. Commanders conduct a cover mission to accomplish all the tasks of a screen or guard. The key distinction of the cover is that the force operates apart from the main body to allow early development of the situation. Commanders deploy a covering force at the BCT level. Unlike screen or guard forces, a covering force is tactically self-contained; and is normally a reinforced BCT (the CAB is not equipped to conduct a cover on its own). Leaders organize a covering force with sufficient enabling and sustainment assets to operate independent of the protected force. Because an enemy force can decisively engage the covering force (or a portion of it), it must have sufficient combat power to effectively engage the enemy. A reconnaissance platoon participating as part of a covering force reconnoiters, screens, attacks, defends, and delays as necessary until the BCT has accomplished its mission.

AREA SECURITY

4-67. Area security is a task conducted to protect friendly forces, installations, routes, and actions within a specific area. Platoons conduct area security to deny the enemy the ability to influence friendly actions in a specific area, or to deny that enemy the use of an area for its own purposes such as combat, insurgent infiltration, or information objectives against friendly forces. Area security actions could include area reconnaissance, transitioning to security of designated personnel, equipment, facilities (including point of entry airfields and seaports), and point security for events and locations such as a platoon meeting with a tribal or government leader, main supply routes (MSRs), lines of communications, and critical infrastructure. Route and convoy security fall under area security as additional tasks.

Chapter 4

4-68. Units conduct area security tasks in combat and limited intervention to deny the enemy the ability to influence friendly actions in a specific area, or to deny the enemy use of an area for its own purposes. This may entail occupying and securing an area without the presence of the enemy, or taking actions to destroy enemy forces already present in the area. The area security task may provide protection of designated personnel, airfields, unit convoys, facilities, MSRs, lines of communications (LOCs), equipment, and critical points.

Planning

4-69. Area security involves a variety of techniques and may include tasks related to reconnaissance, security, defense, offense, stability, and civil support tasks. Reconnaissance organizations, including the platoon, may conduct the following maneuvers in support of area security:

- Zone, area, and route reconnaissance.
- Screen.
- Offensive and defensive tasks (within capabilities).
- Convoy security.
- Route security.
- High-value asset security.
- Fixed site security.
- Checkpoint security.
- Downed aircraft recovery team security.

4-70. Other platoon missions or tasks in support of troop area security may include the following:

- Screens along zones of separation or other designated areas.
- Route and convoy security of critical LOCs.
- Checkpoint tasks to monitor or control movement.
- Patrolling between secured perimeters.
- Demonstrations to maintain an observable presence.

4-71. The platoon may conduct or support the following additional tasks in stability tasks and civil support tasks:

- Liaison.
- Leader engagement.
- Compliance inspections.
- Traffic control points.
- Fixed site security.
- Cordon and search.

Preparation

4-72. An area security force neutralizes or defeats enemy operations in a specified area. It screens, reconnoiters, attacks, defends, and delays (within capability) as

Security

necessary to accomplish its mission. The area is delineated by the headquarters assigning the mission and may be offensive or defensive in nature; focus on the threat/enemy, on the force/element being protected, or on a combination of the two. Commanders balance the level of security measures taken with the type and level of threat posed in the specific area to avoid over-tasking resources. However, comprehensive security is an essential consideration at all times.

4-73. Area security tasks are conducted to deny the threat/enemy the ability to influence friendly actions in a specific area, or to deny the enemy use of an area for its own purposes. This may entail occupying and establishing a 360-degree perimeter around the area being secured, or taking actions to destroy or neutralize enemy forces already present. The area to be secured may include specific points (bridges, defiles), defined areas (terrain features such as ridgelines or hills), or large population centers and adjacent areas.

4-74. Proper platoon analysis is vital for providing adequate security in the assigned area. Along with unit capability and the factors of METT-TC, the following considerations established during the platoon analysis determine specific unit operations during area security tasks:
- The natural defensive characteristics of the terrain.
- Existing roads and waterways for military LOCs and civilian commerce.
- Control of land and water areas and avenues of approach surrounding the area to be secured, extending to a range beyond that of enemy artillery, rockets, and mortars.
- Control of airspace.
- Proximity to critical sites such as airfields, power generation plants, and civic buildings.

4-75. Due to the possibility of commanders attaching their forces to fixed installations or sites, area security tasks may become defensive in nature. This is carefully balanced with the need for offensive action. Early warning of enemy activity provides the commander with time to react to any potential threat and is a major consideration in effective area security tasks. It requires thorough reconnaissance and surveillance planning, and employment of dismounted and mounted patrols, aerial reconnaissance, and sensors.

Execution

4-76. A perimeter is established when a unit secures an area where the defense is not tied into an adjacent unit. Perimeters vary in shape depending on METT-TC. If the commander determines a probable direction of enemy attack, an economy of force to mass combat power along the part of the perimeter to cover the approach of enemy forces may be performed. The perimeter shape conforms to the terrain features that afford the most effective observation and fields of fire.

4-77. Perimeters are divided into sectors with boundaries and contact points. Mutual support and coordination between defensive elements (usually combat

Chapter 4

elements within the brigade) require careful planning, positioning, and coordination. A screen line is established integrating OPs, ground sensors, and patrols. Tanks, MGSs, and anti-armor weapon systems are placed on high-speed avenues of approach. Likely threat/enemy drop zones (DZs), landing zones (LZs), or bases are identified and kept under observation. Air assets, if available, are integrated into the intelligence, surveillance, and reconnaissance plan through the commander.

4-78. The reconnaissance platoon may deploy to conduct area security tasks on its own or as part of a larger force. When the platoon conducts area security on its own, it generally moves into a coil formation around the point, area, or asset to be secured. Vehicle positions are adjusted to orient on likely enemy avenues of approach. If engineer support is available, the vehicle positions are dug in or occupy hasty fighting positions. Varying terrain conditions affect the vehicle locations:

- Desert terrain, such as in the Middle East, requires vehicles to be spread out more because of the large amounts of open space.
- Mountainous terrain offers more IV lines and foliage to hide under, but reduced maneuvering room.
- Urban areas often preclude uniform perimeters because of the possibility of infiltration through building windows and rubble.

4-79. To further improve the position, the platoon employs hasty protective minefields, wire, and other available obstacles as appropriate. Wire obstacles should be emplaced outside grenade range of friendly positions. Once vehicle positions and obstacles are established, the platoon develops a fire plan, including integrated indirect fires, and submits it to higher headquarters.

4-80. In addition to setting up its position around the asset to be secured, the platoon also employs patrols and OPs to enhance security. (See Figure 4-8.) The platoon leader may plan for outside resources that can assist the mission. Examples include the use of CA personnel to improve relations with the local populace, and engineer teams to assist in repairing local infrastructure such as water mains or power lines. This type of positive interaction with locals may create favorable conditions for HUMINT assets to gather information. The reconnaissance platoons employ reconnaissance patrols, presence patrols (as a section), and combat patrols (as a platoon) when needed to become familiar with the AO, gain information on enemy forces, and destroy small enemy dismounted reconnaissance elements. OPs and support by fire positions are deployed to observe likely avenues of approach, provide early warning of enemy activity and direct fire on an enemy so the platoon can displace, and assist in controlling indirect fires.

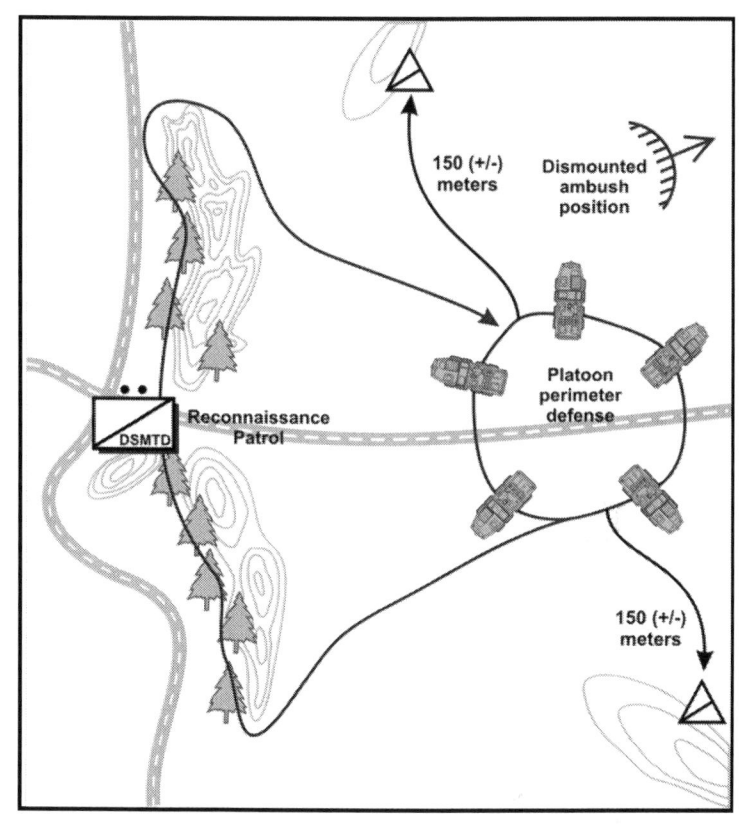

Figure 4-8. Use of patrol, observation post, and ambush site to enhance area security

ROUTE SECURITY TASKS

4-81. Route security is a specialized kind of area security task conducted to protect lines of communications and the friendly forces moving along them. A route security task prevents an enemy from attacking, destroying, seizing, containing, impeding, or harassing traffic along a specific route. It also prevents the enemy from emplacing obstacles on or destroying portions of the route. Route security tasks are defensive in nature and, unlike screen tasks, are terrain-oriented.

4-82. Enemy forces try to interdict supply routes and LOCs by using various methods. Roads, waterways, and railways may be mined or have improvised explosive devices (IEDs) emplaced along them. Ambush sites can be located adjacent to the route being secured. Bridges and tunnels can be destroyed by demolitions. Due to the nature of this mission, very long routes can be extremely difficult to secure. Long routes may also have a number of controlling authorities responsible for tasks along distinct portions of the route.

Chapter 4

Route Security Tasks
4-83. Route security forces operate on and to the flanks of a designated route. A reconnaissance platoon may be tasked to fulfill numerous roles to support route security tasks, which vary widely in scale. To accomplish the route security, the platoon performs some or all of the following functions:

- Conduct mounted and dismounted reconnaissance of the route and key locations along it to ensure the route is trafficable.
- Conduct route clearance (with attached engineers as the main effort) at irregular intervals to prevent emplacement of enemy mines and explosive devices along the route.
- Identify sections of the route to search for suspected enemy locations.
- Establish medical evacuation (MEDEVAC) LZ locations along the route for air evacuation of wounded.
- Establish roadblocks/checkpoints along the route and on lateral routes to stop and search vehicles and persons. The platoon may require augmentation from other units such as an Infantry platoon, engineers, interpreters, or MP elements.
- Occupy key locations and terrain along or near the route.
- Aggressively conduct ground and aerial reconnaissance/surveillance to maintain route security.
- Establish OPs, ambush sites, and reaction force teams to watch for and handle enemy activity.

Route Security Techniques
4-84. The following discussion highlights two techniques that the reconnaissance platoon can execute during route security depending upon the nature of the enemy, purpose of the security mission, and characteristics of the route.

4-85. In the first technique, the platoon is tasked to conduct route security tasks while conducting a route reconnaissance as a part of the mission. The platoon reconnoiters the route at irregular intervals to avoid developing a pattern that the enemy could exploit. This may include conducting reconnaissance to either flank resembling a zone reconnaissance. Organic or attached UAS or supporting aviation assets can reconnoiter in advance of ground troops, or assist in screening the flanks. In addition to reconnaissance, sections or teams may—

- Escort engineers conducting route clearance, improvement, or maintenance to clear terrain at potential ambush sites.
- Repair damage caused by enemy actions.
- Deploy and support HUMINT assets along the route.
- Support the FIST by requesting and registering targets along the route.
- Provide recovery and security for UAS surveillance missions along the route.

4-86. The second technique uses economy of force to protect only critical lengths or locations along the route. The reconnaissance platoon tasks teams to establish mutually supporting platoon combat outposts. These outposts are established at critical choke points to prevent sabotage and defend against or respond to attacks that interdict the route between outposts. Based on METT-TC, a platoon can establish one combat outpost, but this may require augmentation depending upon the enemy situation. The route outside the reach of the combat outposts is not normally secured or patrolled. Patrols are conducted at irregular intervals between the outposts based on enemy trends and recent activities. UAS support may be used to augment the patrols and detect activity along the route. Patrols are organized with sufficient combat power to disrupt or destroy near ambushes and to survive initial enemy contact from far ambushes. Each combat outpost maintains a reaction force that responds to enemy activity or reinforces patrols that come under contact.

Route Security Procedures

4-87. Artillery or mortars may be deployed into firing positions (including collocating with combat outposts) for route security. Indirect fire units and fire support personnel are tasked to support reconnaissance elements operating along the route. Platoon leaders coordinate massing of fires at critical positions or into areas of frequent enemy activity to disrupt the adversary. Platoon and section leaders ensure that they register targets and their fire plans include priority targets supporting convoy or patrol movements, checkpoints, or combat outposts. Augmentation with a FIST allows the platoon to utilize supporting indirect fires and CAS sorties.

4-88. Air, mounted, and dismounted patrols are employed to disrupt enemy forces attempting to create craters or ablatives; emplace IEDs, mines, and demolitions; or establish ambushes or roadblocks to interdict or destroy traffic. Sniper teams can be valuable in support of patrols because of their ability to observe and report enemy activities while remaining undetected. Patrols are organized with sufficient forces to reconnoiter off-route ambush sites, and with enough combat power to survive initial enemy contact. Based on enemy capabilities, reconnaissance patrols should be augmented with engineers, Infantry, MP, and other assets to increase the platoon's combat capability.

4-89. Other techniques to defeat enemy attempts to interdict the route or ambush convoys include—

- Deploying deceptive "mock" convoys under escort to determine enemy reactions.
- Conducting ambushes along known or suspected dismounted approaches to the route.
- Following registered indirect fires triggered by sensor cues—such as ground surveillance systems—with patrols that can perform site exploitation (SE) on successful fire missions.
- Conducting reconnaissance by fire at irregular intervals during limited visibility, prior to sunrise, or before critical convoys to detect and destroy ambushes (ROE dependent).

Chapter 4

4-90. Ground sensors can be used by scouts in an economy of force role to survey key avenues of approach, or areas that require continuous surveillance such as dead space, and areas not considered primary enemy avenues. This reduces the manpower and logistic demands on the higher unit's resources during the mission.

Convoy Security

4-91. Convoy security missions are conducted when insufficient friendly forces are available to continuously secure lines of communication in an AO. They may also be conducted in conjunction with route security. Reconnaissance platoons perform convoy security as part of a larger organization to provide protection for a specific convoy. These missions include numerous tasks for platoons serving as reconnaissance, escort, screen, and reaction forces. Certain organizations are particularly well-suited for convoy security. HMMWV platoons can use speed and optics to screen flanks and perform route reconnaissance ahead of the convoy. Stryker platoons can escort the convoy at highway speeds or perform the role of a reaction force within the convoy. CFV platoons may conduct convoy escort, but they are better-suited as a reaction force positioned in outposts where they respond to enemy actions with overwhelming firepower. DRT and IBCT reconnaissance platoons require tactical vehicle augmentation to execute this mission.

4-92. Depending on the situation, reconnaissance platoons may be reconfigured with tanks, becoming a hunter-killer team that is used as a reaction force operating from a combat outpost. This greatly increases the firepower of the reaction force. The size of the unit performing the convoy security mission is dependent on a number of factors including the size of the convoy, terrain, and the length of the route. (Refer to Figures 4-9 and 4-10 for illustrations of the reconnaissance troop in convoy security tasks.) Depending upon the enemy situation, the ABCT reconnaissance platoon may conduct convoy security in place of an IBCT reconnaissance platoon. This could require upgrading the reaction forces to MGS or tank platoons for increased firepower.

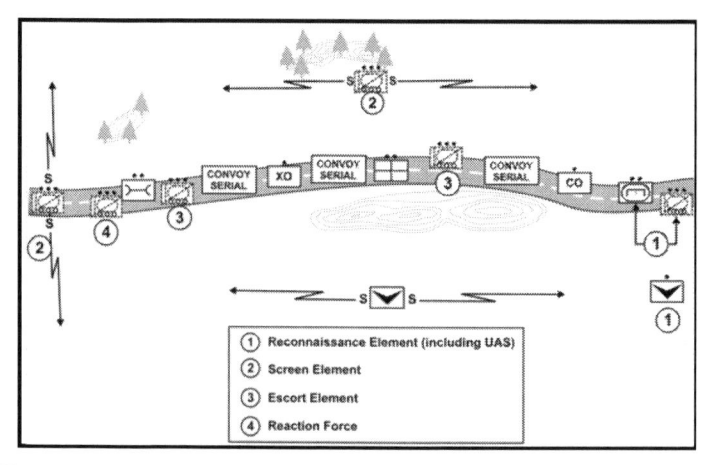

Figure 4-9. Convoy security (possible locations/tasks that can be executed by a reconnaissance platoon within the overall convoy security mission)

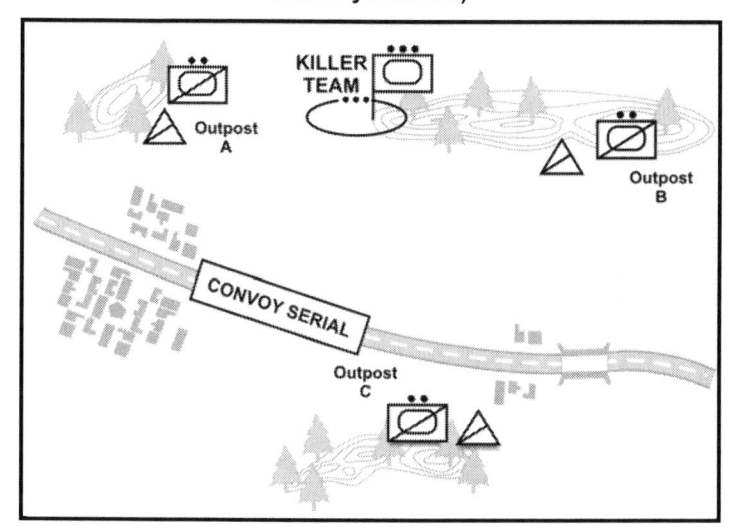

Figure 4-10. Convoy security with combat outposts

Combat Outposts

4-93. Employment of combat outposts is a technique used during convoy security to screen dangerous areas of the route after it has been reconnoitered. The combat outpost is generally performed by the entire platoon in static locations and critical parts of the route, or key avenues of approach to the route. Outposts provide early warning of enemy elements attempting to interdict convoy movement. The outpost may be manned by a section, platoon, or a platoon with augmentation. The enemy

Chapter 4

situation and the area to be covered dictates the size and composition of the combat outpost's force. Combat outposts have the limited ability to destroy small enemy forces attempting to influence the route. Their primary purpose is to acquire enemy elements and then direct the employment of reaction forces or indirect fire to destroy the enemy. The use of HUMINT teams within the sector may gain information on enemy activities and prevent attacks on convoys.

4-94. Combat outposts differ from a conventional screen in that they are oriented on the route, specifically NAIs, rather than on the friendly main body. These NAIs may be found in a designated sector for which the outpost element may be responsible. (See Figure 4-11.) Combat outposts can be established in the following ways:
- The outpost element follows the route reconnaissance element and establishes the combat outpost confirmed to be cleared by the route reconnaissance.
- Move under limited visibility to occupy the outpost unannounced prior to movement on the route.

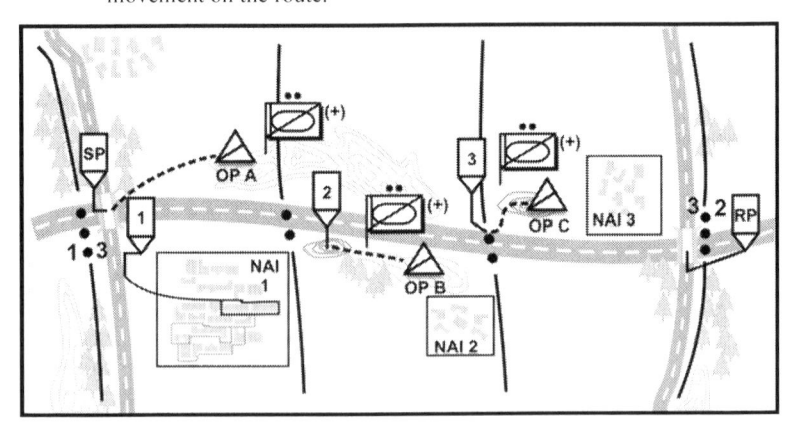

Figure 4-11. Establishing outposts

CONVOY ESCORT

4-95. The reconnaissance platoon may perform a convoy escort mission independently or as part of a larger unit's convoy security mission. They provide close-in protection from direct fire. Normally, a reconnaissance platoon conducts a convoy escort mission for a convoy serial. Escorted vehicles can include military vehicles (sustainment, mission command), civilian trucks, or buses. Among reconnaissance platoons, those equipped with CFVs are best for this mission because of the vehicles' firepower and armor protection against direct fires, indirect fires, and IEDs. Leaders carefully evaluate the enemy before assigning a convoy escort mission to HMMWV or Stryker platoons.

Mission Command

4-96. Mission command is especially critical during convoy escort because of the task organization inherent to the mission. When the reconnaissance platoon is executing the escort mission, it operates under the control of the convoy commander, regardless of the role. The convoy and platoon leaders are familiar with the available weapon systems if they move through different commanders' AOs.

4-97. The platoon leader ensures that a complete OPORD is issued to all vehicle commanders in the convoy prior to execution of the mission. This is vital because the convoy may be task-organized from a variety of units and many of the vehicles may not have tactical radios. The order should follow the standard five-paragraph OPORD format, with special emphasis on the following subjects:

- Order of march.
- Actions on contact.
- Chain of command.
- Communications and signals.
- Actions on vehicle breakdown.
- Actions at a halt.
- Route of march (this should include a sketch for each vehicle commander).
- Casualty evacuation.

Tactical Disposition

4-98. Security during convoy escort mission is in all directions and throughout the length of the convoy. This requires the elements of the platoon and any maneuver or enabling attachments be dispersed throughout the convoy formation. Engineer assets should be located toward the front to respond to obstacles. The FIST or COLT should be located near the platoon leader. The platoon normally uses the column formation because of its inherent speed and ease of mission command. If a HMMWV unit is used as the escort, a tracked, armored engineer vehicle should be attached to the lead elements of the convoy whenever possible because of its superior protection against mines. When engineers are not available, the convoy commander may be able to coordinate the use of tanks, Strykers, or armored personnel carriers (APCs) with rollers and plows. Figure 4-12 illustrates an example of a convoy escort mission. Platoon and section rehearsals are conducted to ensure all elements are proficient in their role and that subordinate leaders are able to move up one position if necessary. Primary control centers and PCIs are critical for success. Platoon members are properly equipped, knowledgeable of their equipment and mission, and able to demonstrate their tasks to the platoon leadership.

Chapter 4

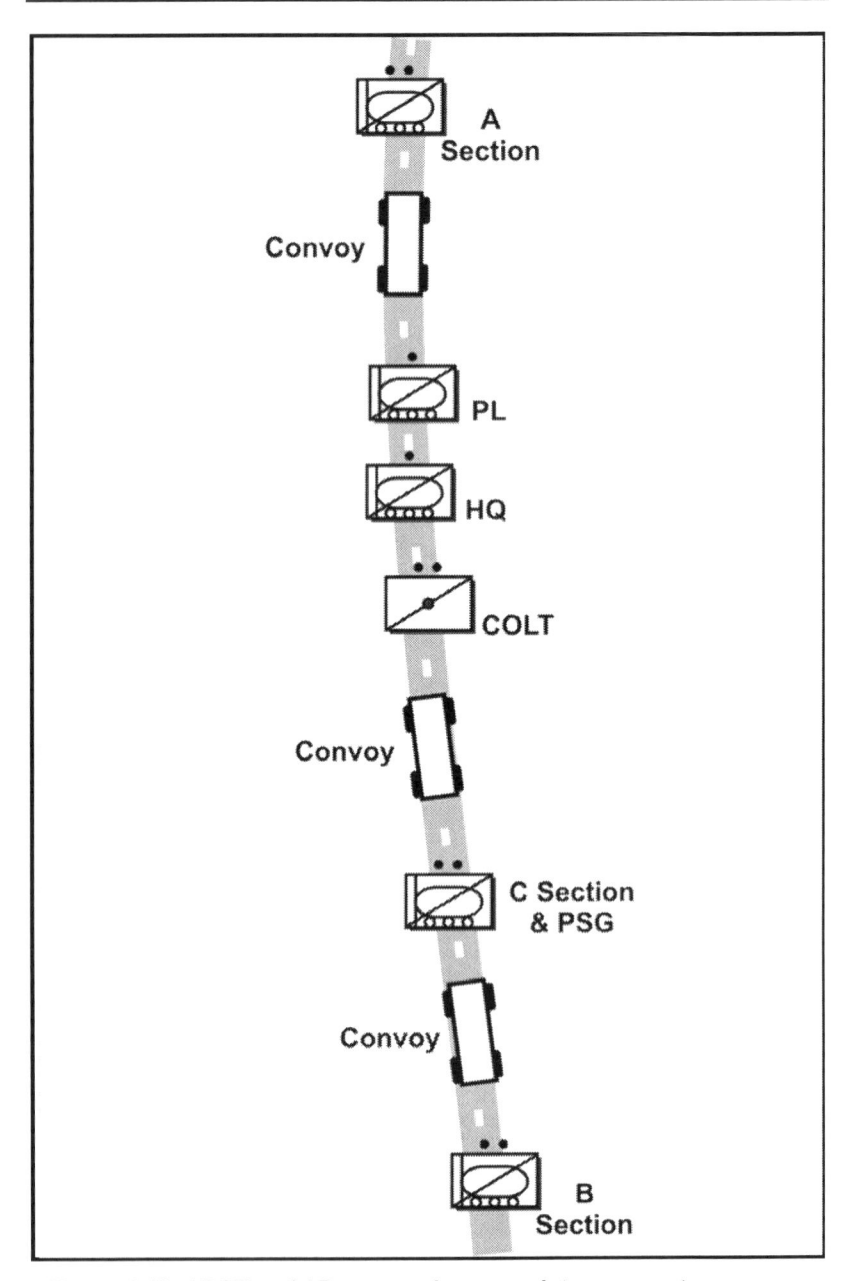

Figure 4-12. ABCT or CAB reconnaissance platoon escorts a convoy

Security

Actions at an Ambush

4-99. Ambush is one of the most effective ways to interdict a convoy. This makes it a priority to conduct ambush reaction training which helps increase the chances of getting the convoy through an ambush with Soldiers and equipment intact. Reaction to an ambush is quick, overwhelming, decisive, and executed as a drill by all escort and convoy elements, with care taken to avoid fratricide.

4-100. The following actions should be included in the convoy escort drill:
- Upon detection of an enemy force, escort vehicles seek covered positions between the convoy and the enemy, and suppress the enemy with the highest possible volume of fire (as shown in Figure 4-13). They send appropriate contact reports to higher HQ.
- Engagement techniques are standardized in the platoon to ensure complete coverage. For example, flank vehicles engage outside targets to inside targets, vehicles in the center of sectors engage center to outside targets, front and rear sections engage far to near targets, and center section vehicles engage near to far threats.

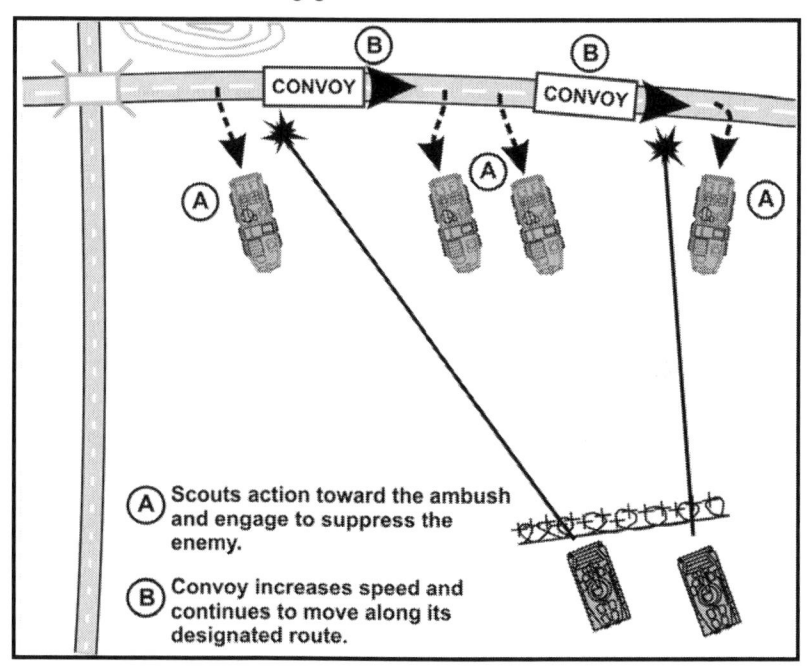

Figure 4-13. Convoy escort takes action toward ambush

4-101. In some situations, elements of the escort force are required to remain with the convoy main body. This is especially true when the convoy is comprised of mainly nonmilitary elements such as NGOs or local civilian agencies. In addition to usually being unarmed, these elements frequently lack communication capabilities,

Chapter 4

making it difficult for escort elements to link back up with the main body. The convoy commander retains control of the convoy vehicles and maintains radio contact with the security force while moving the convoy on the route at the highest possible speed.

4-102. Platoon leaders ensure that the following actions occur during an ambush:
- Convoy vehicles do not return fire when the escort has moved between the convoy and the enemy.
- Elements of the convoy or convoy security, based on the factors of METT-TC, may halt to recover or destroy damaged or disabled vehicles.
- The escort leader (reconnaissance platoon leader) submits SPOTREPs, requests MEDEVAC, requests the reaction force, and calls for and directs indirect fires and CAS, if available.

4-103. Once the convoy is clear of the kill zone, the escort leader chooses one of the following COAs based on the composition of the escort and the strength of the enemy force:
- Continue to suppress the enemy force with direct fire while fire support is requested. (See Figure 4-14.)
- Guide reaction forces into the enemy force if available, and shift fires to interdict the enemy egress route. (See Figure 4-15.)
- Assault the enemy when a reaction force is not practical (near ambush). (See Figure 4-16.)
- Break contact and move out of the kill zone. (See Figure 4-17.)
- Update FBCB2 and the COP with enemy locations throughout the mission.

Security

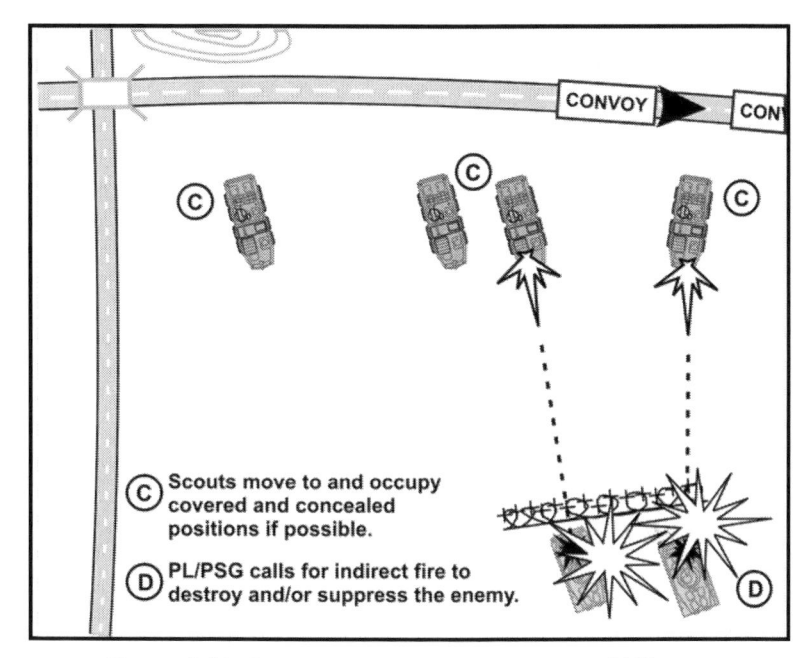

Figure 4-14. Convoy continues to move out of kill zone

4-104. Generally, CFV-equipped platoons continue to suppress the enemy or execute an assault due to their vehicles' capabilities, while HMMWV and Stryker platoons may move out of the kill zone as soon as the convoy is clear. Contact should be broken only with the approval of the platoon's higher commander. If physical contact is broken, platoons can regain visual contact by employing the UAS to maintain SA. (See Figures 4-15, 4-16, and 4-17.)

Chapter 4

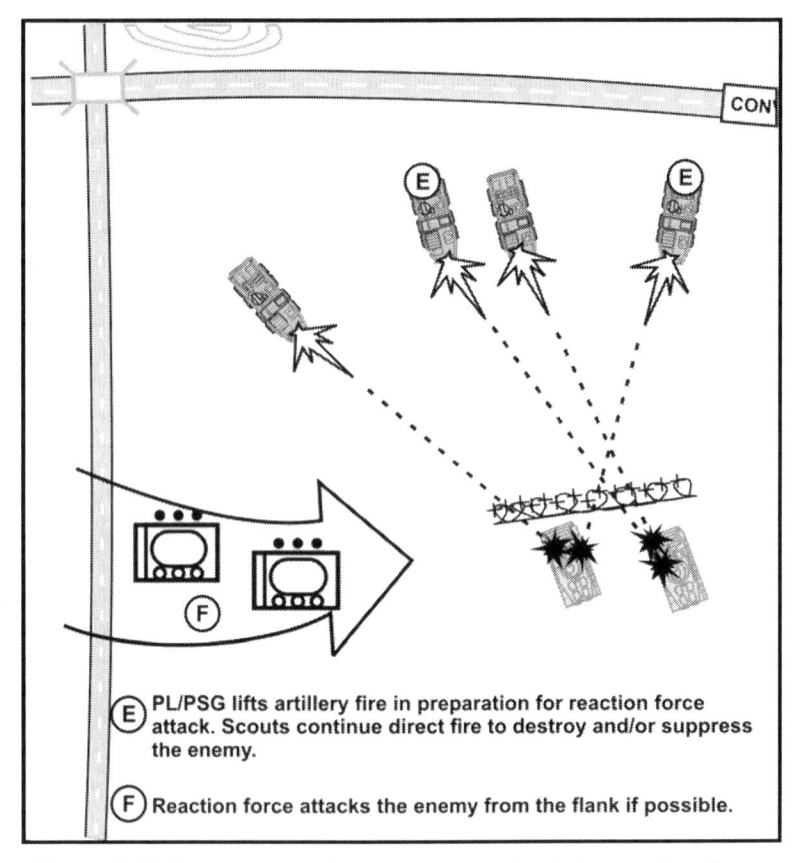

Figure 4-15. Convoy escort suppresses ambush for reaction force

Security

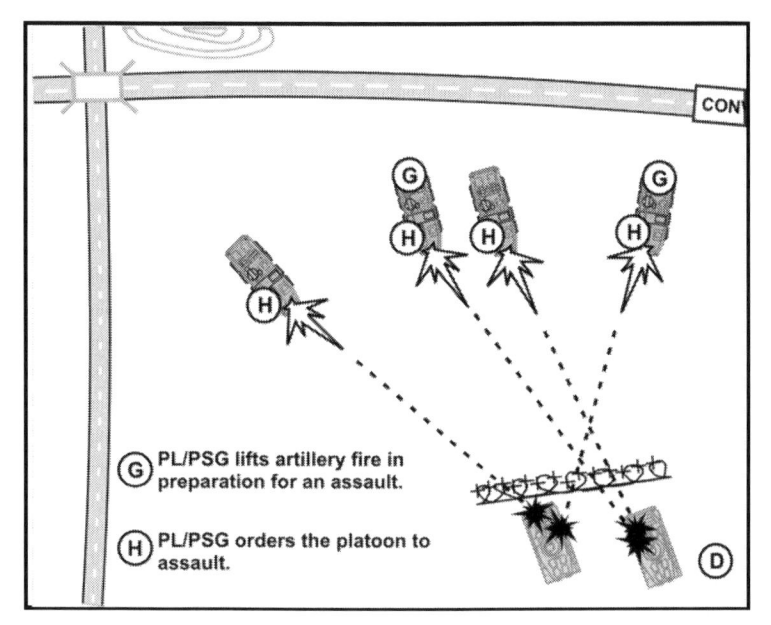

Figure 4-16. Convoy escort vehicles assault ambush position without reaction force

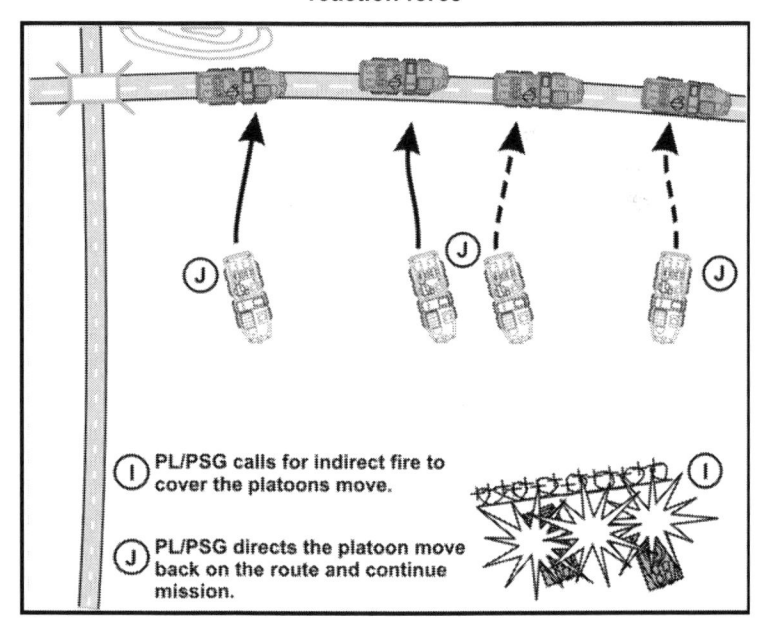

Figure 4-17. Escort vehicles break contact without reaction force

Chapter 4

Actions at a Short Halt
4-105. The convoy may be required to make a short halt for a number of reasons. During the short halt, the escorting unit is at readiness condition-1 (REDCON-1) regardless of what actions the convoy vehicles are taking. If the reconnaissance platoon is the escorting element and the halt is for any reason other than an obstacle, these actions should be taken:

- The convoy commander signals the short halt and transmits the order via tactical radio.
- The convoy assumes a herringbone formation.
- Escort vehicles move to protective positions forward, to the rear, and to the flanks (up to 100 meters beyond the convoy vehicles, as applicable) and orient their weapon systems outward. They remain at REDCON-1, although they establish dismounted local security (as illustrated in Figure 4-18). The vehicles being escorted pull into the protected area in the center of the herringbone between the escort vehicles. Escort vehicles should not leave the roadway if there is a possibility of enemy mines.
- When the order is given to move out, convoy vehicles first reestablish the column formation, leaving space for the escort vehicles. (See Figure 4-19.) Once the convoy is in column, the escort vehicles join the column, leaving local security dismounted. (See Figure 4-20.)
- Once all elements are in column, local security personnel mount and the convoy continues to move.

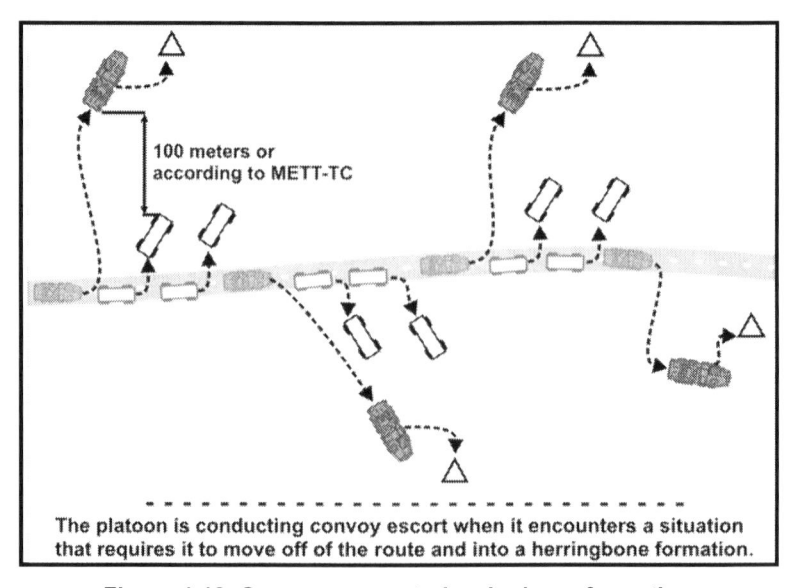

Figure 4-18. Convoy moves to herringbone formation

Security

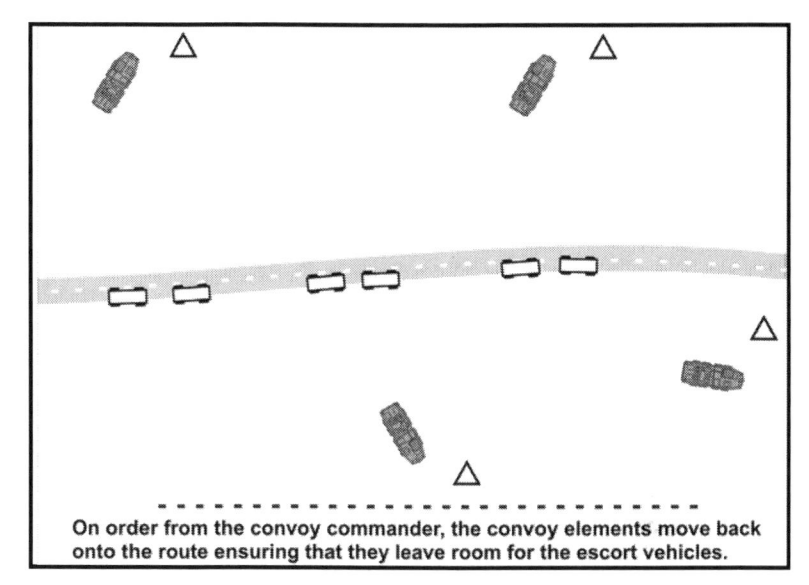

On order from the convoy commander, the convoy elements move back onto the route ensuring that they leave room for the escort vehicles.

Figure 4-19. Convoy moves back into column formation

On order from the convoy commander, the OPs remain at post while the escort vehicles rejoin the column in their assigned locations.

Once the escort vehicles are in place, the convoy commander directs the OPs to rejoin the escort vehicle.

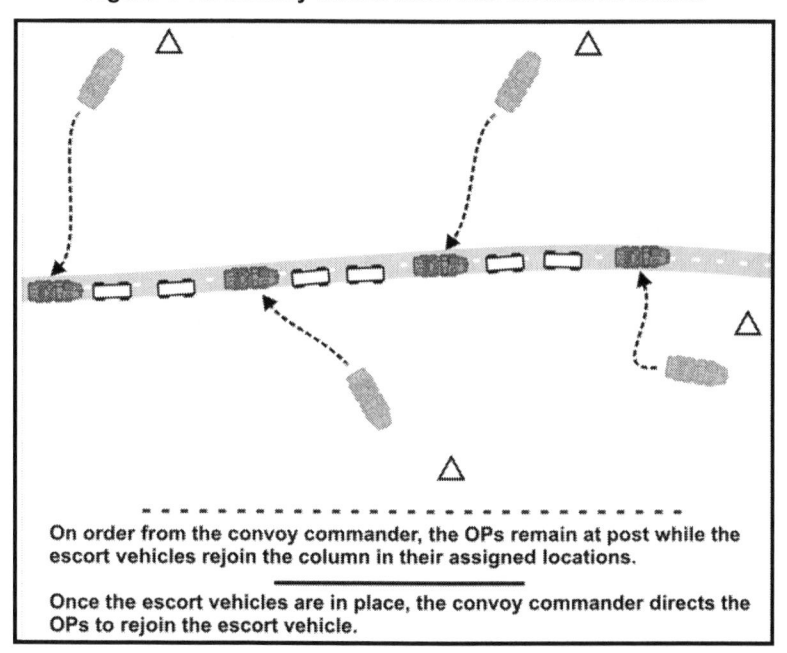

Figure 4-20. Escort vehicles rejoin column

5 April 2013   ATP 3-20.98   4-39

Chapter 4

Actions at an Obstacle
4-106. Obstacles are a major threat to convoys. They can be erected in a matter of minutes and used to delay or stop the convoy. In addition, an obstacle or series of obstacles can be used to fix the convoy within an enemy ambush (which can include well-hidden IEDs in debris). Platoons treat every obstacle as though the enemy is overwatching it with direct or indirect fires. As obstacles or other threats are encountered, the platoon leader or PSG updates the FBCB2 so all units in the AO have knowledge of the threats.

4-107. Enemy elements employing obstacles usually use overwatching units to observe the obstacle encounter, and then employ direct or indirect fires and command-detonated surface and subsurface munitions. This could position the entire convoy in contact with multiple danger areas simultaneously.

4-108. One method to counter obstacles is to employ a route reconnaissance ahead of the convoy to identify obstacles, breach them, or find bypasses. In some cases, it is not possible to conduct a route reconnaissance ahead of the convoy. In other cases, the reconnaissance element may fail to detect the enemy or its obstacles. In either situation, the convoy is prepared to take actions to reduce or bypass the obstacle.

4-109. When a convoy is dealing with an obstacle, it faces a two-sided problem. It is more vulnerable because it is stopped and its escort force is occupied with tasks required to overcome or bypass the obstacle. For these reasons, security becomes critical and actions at the obstacle are accomplished quickly. Reconnaissance platoons in the role of a convoy escort take the following actions upon contact with a point-type obstacle:

- When the lead security element identifies the obstacle, the convoy commander directs a short halt, and establishes dismounted local security and overwatch of the obstacle. Convoy vehicles remain on the road with the escort elements moving to the flanks to provide security. All convoy vehicles are aware that the enemy may have buried mines, IEDs, or explosively formed projectiles in the area, especially on the side of the road.
- The convoy commander relays a SPOTREP from the reconnaissance platoon to higher HQ and requests support from combat reaction forces, engineer assets (if they are not already part of the convoy), and aerial reconnaissance elements. Artillery units are alerted to be prepared to provide fire support. Employment of these assets is designed to reduce the time the convoy is halted and reduce its vulnerability. The convoy commander always assumes the obstacle is overwatched by the enemy.
- The platoon leader tasks the security elements to begin reconnaissance for a bypass while maintaining 360-degree security of the convoy. (See Figure 4-21.)
- Simultaneously, an additional reconnaissance team made up of escort elements and engineer's moves forward to conduct an obstacle

reconnaissance. Far side security is established unless time and physical constraints prevent it.
- Once all reconnaissance is completed and reported, the convoy commander determines which of the following COA is taken:
  - Bypass the obstacle.
  - Breach the obstacle with the assets on hand.
  - Breach the obstacle with reinforcing assets.
- The convoy commander executes the best COA and continues the mission.

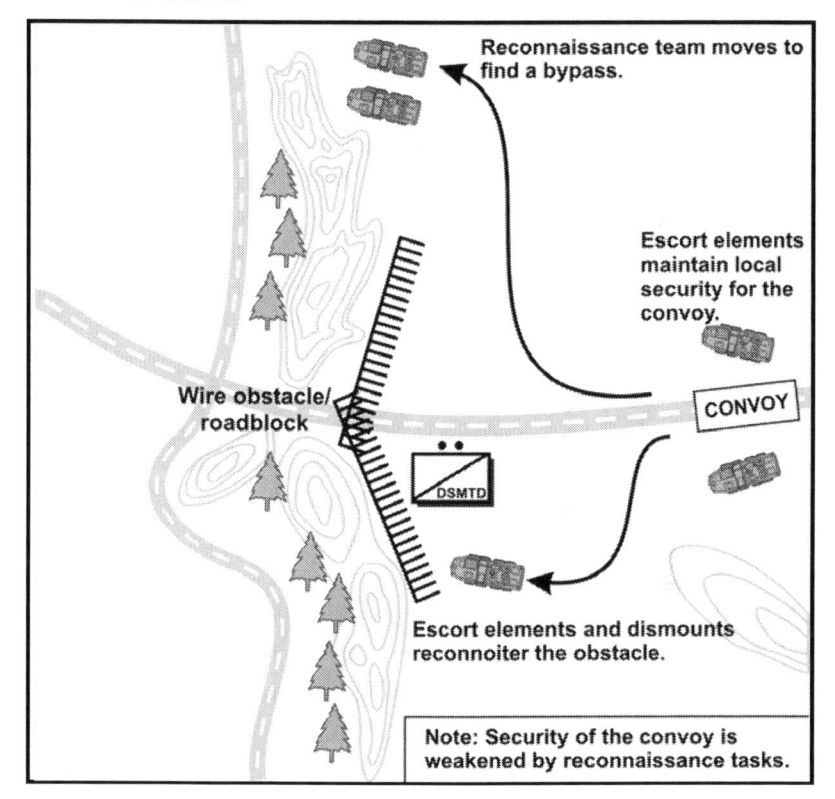

Figure 4-21. Escort teams conduct obstacle reconnaissance and reconnoiter for a bypass

LOCAL SECURITY

4-110. Local security is low-level security tasks conducted near a unit to prevent surprise by the enemy. This is an important part of maintaining the initiative. The requirement for maintaining local security is inherent in all missions. The reconnaissance platoon may support local security as part of a larger unit (such as a

Chapter 4

troop) or maintain local security independently away from friendly elements. In some cases, as when the platoon is part of a CAB or BCT, it maintains its own assembly area and local security within the larger unit's footprint. Local security includes all measures taken to prevent surprise by the enemy, including missions against the platoon's location. It involves avoiding detection by the enemy or deceiving the enemy about friendly positions and intentions.

4-111. Units that come to a halt during missions dismount to provide local security around their vehicles. This prevents surprise and the loss of Soldiers and equipment to dismounted enemy elements. While dismounted, scouts present as small a target as possible while still observing the area and approaches around their location. They are ready to engage the enemy under favorable conditions such as—

- Employing platoon observation posts.
- Employing patrols to cover perimeter and dead space.
- Establishing threat levels and procedures.
- Enforcing stand-to.
- Enforcing proper communications procedures.
- Employing camouflage.
- Enforcing noise and light discipline.
- Employing sensors for surveillance of the area around the unit.

Chapter 5

Stability

Stability tasks encompass various military missions, tasks, and activities conducted outside the United States in coordination with other instruments of national power, such as diplomacy and economics. These maneuvers maintain or reestablish a safe and secure environment, providing essential governmental services, emergency infrastructure reconstruction, and humanitarian relief.

The reconnaissance platoon may also be required to accomplish non-reconnaissance related missions such as conducting negotiations with local leaders, defending a base, and manning checkpoints and observation points. This chapter focuses on planning, preparing, and executing/assessing stability tasks.

SECTION I – FUNDAMENTALS OF STABILITY

5-1. Stability tasks leverage the coercive and constructive capabilities of the military force to establish a safe and secure environment, facilitate reconciliation among local or regional adversaries, assist with the transition of responsibility to a legitimate civil authority, and institute political, legal, social, and economic institutions. Through stability tasks, military forces help set the conditions that enable the actions of the other instruments of national power to succeed in achieving the broad goals of conflict transformation.

5-2. Providing security and control stabilizes the AO, giving a foundation for transition to civilian control and the host nation. Stability tasks are usually conducted to support a host nation government, but may also support the efforts of a transitional civil or military authority when no legitimate government exists. (Refer to FM 3-07 for more information.)

PURPOSE OF STABILITY

5-3. The combination of tasks conducted during stability tasks depends upon the situation. In some operations, the HN can meet some or all of the population's requirements. In these cases, Army forces work with and through HN authorities. Conversely, Army forces operating in a failed state may be responsible for the well-being of the local populace. That situation requires Army forces to work with civilian agencies to restore basic capabilities.

Chapter 5

5-4. Stability tasks complement offensive and defensive tasks, and may be the decisive operation within a phase of a major combat operation. Although military forces set the conditions for success, the other instruments of national power are decisive. Military forces conduct stability tasks to accomplish the five activities listed below. These tasks demonstrate American resolve through the commitment of time, resources, and forces to establish and reinforce diplomatic and military ties. Stability tasks can:

- Provide a safe environment.
- Secure land areas.
- Meet the critical needs of the populace.
- Gain support of the HN government.
- Shape the environment for interagency and host-nation success.

STABILITY TASKS

5-5. Stability tasks include the following five tasks:

- **Establish civil security.** Providing for the security of the host nation and its population, including protection from serious external and internal threats, is essential for a safe environment.
- **Establish civil control.** Establishing civil control is an initial step toward instituting the rule of law and a stable, effective government.
- **Restore essential services.** Military forces restore essential services and protect them until transferring responsibility to a transitional civil authority or the HN.
- **Provide governance support.** Stability tasks establish conditions that enable actions by civilian and HN agencies to succeed.
- **Provide economic support and infrastructure development.** This support helps the HN develop capability and capacity in these areas.

5-6. The platoon's level of involvement in these types of stability tasks is situational dependant. In some missions, the HN is capable of carrying out these types of tasks. The platoon engages in civil-military operations to minimize the impact of the military presence on the populace. (Refer to FM 3-07 for more information.)

ROLE OF THE RECONNAISSANCE PLATOON

5-7. The reconnaissance platoon conducts reconnaissance to complement concurrent operations, or as a separate stability tasks mission directed by the commander. Reconnaissance is planned and executed to support the stability goals of establishing civil security, establishing civil control, and reconstructing or restoring essential services and governance. (Refer to FM 3-20.96 for more information.)

Stability

SECTION II – PLANNING

CONSIDERATIONS

5-8. The most effective plans are clear, concise, and direct. Planning is especially important where experience is lacking. In such situations, creative and adaptive planning is the only viable substitute for experience. With sufficient experience in a given situation, leaders intuitively know what to expect, which goals are feasible, and the actions to take. In situations where experience is lacking, planning enables a systematic approach to problem solving that helps formulate practical solutions to complex situations.

5-9. The platoon uses force within the parameters of the ROE. The force has the proper structure and resources to accomplish the mission and perform its duties swiftly and firmly, leaving no doubt to its will and intensions.

5-10. Food, water, shelter, and medical support are usually the first things the platoon provides until local civil services are restored. Once the immediate needs are satisfied, efforts to restore basic services and transition control to civil authorities typically progresses using lines of effort based on SWEAT-MSO. Military forces, specifically functional units or functional specialists, may support the effort by conducting detailed infrastructure reconnaissance.

ENVIRONMENT

5-11. The environment not only consists of terrain and weather. The cultural, political, and military context is also taken into environmental consideration.

5-12. Stability tasks can take place in any part of the world. To deal effectively with the diverse situations U.S. forces may face, they undergo orientation and training on the complex conditions and factors that exist in a specific region. Each Soldier understands the political and economic situation, as well as the cultures, climates, and terrain of the region. Soldiers understand the military situation, especially the doctrine, tactics, and equipment that belligerent, guerrilla, and terrorist forces employ. Orientation training should clarify certain environmental factors, and the planning and operational considerations discussed in this section.

APPLY FORCE SELECTIVELY AND DISCRIMINATELY

5-13. Leaders make sure their platoon applies force consistent with and adequate to assigned objectives. Leaders employ combat power selectively according to the assigned mission ROE. Soldiers use the ROE to guide the tactical application of combat power. Leaders on the ground are best qualified to estimate the correct degree of force to be used, consistent with the ROE.

INTELLIGENCE

5-14. The platoon leader considers intelligence as a crucial element during the planning, preparation, and execution of stability tasks, understanding that the threats in these missions are more ambiguous than those in other situations. Combatants, guerrillas, and terrorists can easily blend with the civilian population. Before the platoon is committed, intelligence is collected, processed, and focused to support all planning, training, and operational requirements.

DECENTRALIZED OPERATIONS

5-15. The platoon leader understands that stability tasks are normally centrally planned. However, execution takes the form of small-scale, decentralized actions conducted over extended distances. Responsibility for making decisions on the ground falls to junior leaders. Effective command guidance and a thorough understanding of the applicable ROE are critical at each operational level.

FORCE PROTECTION

5-16. The level of force protection required for the mission during the planning phase is understood by the platoon leader. Force protection is a constant priority. Armored forces are commonly deployed in a force protection role. The platoon develops plans to minimize causalities and collateral damage during these missions. Leaders avoid making tactically unsound decisions or exposing the force to unnecessary risks while attempting to limit the level and scope of violence used in stability tasks. An overpowering use of force, correctly employed, can reduce subsequent violence or prevent a response from the opposing force. These considerations are covered in the ROE and the OPORD from the battalion or brigade.

5-17. The platoon leader uses operations security (OPSEC) in conjunction with the ROE to accomplish force protection goals. Security procedures should encompass the full range of antiterrorist activities for every Soldier and leader. Examples include proper radio-telephone procedures; strict noise, light, and litter discipline; the proper wear of the uniform; displaying the proper demeanor for situations; and the effective use of cover and concealment, obstacles, OPs, and early warning.

Media Considerations

5-18. All Soldiers within the platoon understand that news coverage is now broadcast via international television, radio, and the Internet. The presence of the media is a reality that confronts everyone involved in stability. Leaders and Soldiers can be subjects of worldwide scrutiny in an instant. Operating contrary to official U.S. policy may damage the nation's interests and international standing.

5-19. Platoon members learn how to deal with media representatives effectively. Platoon training should thoroughly address any information restrictions that the Armed Forces impose on the media. Soldiers also gain an understanding of what subjects they are authorized to discuss, and which ones they refer to higher authorities.

Stability

Operations with Outside Agencies
5-20. The platoon may be required to conduct certain stability tasks in coordination with a variety of outside organizations. These outside organizations may include other U.S. Armed Services or government agencies, and international organizations (including private volunteer organizations). Some examples of outside organizations are: U.N. military forces or agencies, private volunteer organizations, and Red Cross officials. The platoon leader considers the specific needs of the supported organization when planning for these types of operations.

SOLDIER RESPONSIBILITIES
5-21. Soldiers within the platoon may have extensive contact with civilians during stability tasks. Their personal conduct has a significant impact on the opinions and support of the local population. All Soldiers need to understand that misconduct by U.S. forces can damage the rapport that took years to develop. Soldiers treat local civilians and military personnel as personal and professional equals, affording them the appropriate customs and courtesies.

5-22. Soldiers are continuously updated on changes to operational considerations (rules of engagement/rules of interaction, media, and force protection). Such changes can have an immediate impact on the way to react in any given situation. Leaders disseminate this information quickly and accurately. Soldiers who are informed of changes have an increased SA, enhancing their ability to effectively adapt to change.

5-23. Every Soldier within the platoon is an intelligence-collecting instrument. They collect and report information continuously. Intelligence comes from many sources, including friendly forces, enemy elements, and the local populace. At the same time, enemy soldiers or other countries' intelligence agencies are continuously seeking information on U.S. actions, often blending easily into the civilian population. Soldiers are aware of this and use OPSEC procedures at all times.

INFORM AND INFLUENCE ACTIVITIES
5-24. Inform and influence activities are events that integrate synchronized themes and messages from two lines of effort with actions to support decisive action. When conducting inform and influence, leaders determine how these activities affect the perceptions and actions of the populace.

5-25. Effective decisive action requires commanders to establish synchronized information themes and messages, integrating them with actions to achieve a desired end state. In doing so, commanders personally engage key players to ensure that the themes and messages are transmitted and received as the commander intends. In an information-saturated environment, messages, themes, and actions are inextricably linked. Information as an element of combat power is critical and sometimes a critical factor in decisive action.

Chapter 5

Soldier and Leader Engagement

5-26. Interactions that take place between Soldiers and leaders and their audiences in the area of operations are broadly called Soldier and leader engagement. These engagements can take place as impromptu face-to-face encounters on the street, or in a deliberately scheduled meeting. They can be facilitated by other means such as phone calls or a video-teleconference. These interactions should be as deliberate as possible. However, not all engagements are planned. Soldiers and leaders cannot account for every situation encountered, and should remain flexible, communicating within the bounds of the commander's themes and messages.

5-27. Face-to-face interaction by Soldiers and leaders strongly influences the perceptions of the local populace. Carried out with discipline, professionalism, and cultural sensitivity, day-to-day interaction between Soldiers and the local populace has affirmative effects. Such interaction amplifies positive actions, counters adversary information, and increases goodwill and support for the friendly mission. Actions in keeping with the commander's themes and messages demonstrated during missions among the population also reinforce the commander's message, creating consistency between actions and words.

5-28. Leader engagement meetings may include:
- Key local communicators.
- Civilian leaders.
- Others whose perceptions, decisions, and actions affect mission accomplishment.

5-29. All engagement meetings should be planned and conducted with detailed preparation to ensure that building local support for military operations, providing opportunity for persuasion, and reducing friction and mistrust are met. For the platoon, the keys to leader engagements include:
- Identifying key leaders.
- Preparing intelligence of the AO.
- Identifying desired effects.
- Preparing for the meeting.
- Executing the meeting.
- Preparing debrief/reports.

CIVIL AFFAIRS TASKS

5-30. Civil affairs tasks are those military tasks planned, supported, or executed by civil affairs forces. These tasks are coordinated through, planned with, and supported by the indigenous population, intergovernmental organizations, nongovernmental organizations, or other government agencies.

5-31. The purpose of CA tasks is to modify behaviors and mitigate or defeat threats to civil society. They involve application of CA functional specialty skills in areas that are usually the responsibility of civil government. Civil affairs personnel, other Army forces, or a combination of the two perform these tasks. These activities are fundamental to executing stability tasks.

5-32. Often, CA teams work with or alongside the company team during stability tasks. A framework for evaluating civil considerations is the acronym ASCOPE. ASCOPE stands for:
- **Areas**—determine the geographic variations in the area of responsibility (AOR), the potential military impact, and how it influences the way people live.
- **Structures**—describe the man-made buildings in which the people live and work, and can determine those buildings that have cultural, religious, and economic significance.
- **Capabilities**—determine the ability of various groups to influence the AOR and the rest of the population relative to their possible intent to do so, and determine economic and military potential given the areas and infrastructure.
- **Organizations**—determine what informal and formal social, religious, familial, or political groups exist and what their intent, purpose, and resources are.
- **People**—determine how the population aligns with organizations and one another, and establishes if they are likely to be supportive, detrimental, or neutral to the unit's mission.

RULES OF ENGAGEMENT

5-33. Rules of engagement are directives issued by competent military authority that delineate the circumstances and limitations under which United States forces initiate or continue combat engagement with other encountered forces. (Refer to JP 1-02 for more information.) ROE help commanders accomplish the mission by regulating the use of force in operations. This helps ensure that force is applied in a disciplined, principled manner that complies with law and policy, minimizing collateral damage while facilitating mission accomplishment.

5-34. The platoon leader considers the ROE during the planning and execution of all stability tasks. Understanding, adjusting for, and properly executing the ROE helps achieve success. Unit SOP requires ROE adjustment when restrictions are modified due to changing political and military situations. Updates are continually explained to the troops.

5-35. Due to the unique requirements of stability tasks, the reconnaissance platoon may be task-organized to operate with a variety of units, including Armor or mechanized company teams, or an Infantry rifle company or battalion. In addition, the platoon may also operate in conjunction with linguists, counterintelligence teams, and CA teams.

Chapter 5

SECTION III – PREPARATION

PRECOMBAT CHECKS AND INSPECTIONS

5-36. During stability tasks, leaders conduct precombat checks and inspections of their Soldiers. This emphasizes Soldier responsibilities, knowledge of the environment, and application of the ROE. These checks and inspections should also identify possible OPSEC violations and deficiencies that could place Soldiers or equipment at risk. The key goal is ensuring Soldiers and equipment are fully prepared to execute the upcoming mission.

5-37. Leaders should stress that terrorists and thieves may attempt to mount vehicles or infiltrate positions. Their goal is to steal equipment and supplies, or cause harm to U.S. forces or facilities.

TRAINING FOR STABILITY

5-38. Leaders and Soldiers who are disciplined, well-trained, and combat-ready can adapt to the specialized demands of stability tasks. To achieve this degree of readiness, the platoon is thoroughly trained before deployment on such factors as the operational environment, ROE, force protection, and individual Soldier responsibilities. (A discussion of these operational considerations is included later in this chapter.) After deployment, training is updated continually.

LEADER REQUIREMENTS

5-39. To execute stability tasks effectively, the reconnaissance platoon leader maintains flexibility and SA. The platoon's role and objectives in stability tasks is not always clear, and the platoon leader is sometimes called upon to make on-the-spot decisions that can have immediate and dramatic effects on the strategic or operational situation. In this uniquely tense setting, leaders who disregard the will of belligerent parties and the lethality of their weapons compromise the success of their mission, risking the lives of their Soldiers.

Rehearsal

5-40. Internal coordination and rehearsals increase SA throughout the platoon. The flow of intelligence updates concerning enemy and friendly information is one method to increase awareness. Rehearsals can begin as soon as the platoon receives the company or troop WARNORD.

5-41. The platoon should understand the actions needed to prepare the stability tasks. Initial walk-through rehearsals on a sand table can focus on primary and essential stability task procedures, fire distribution, and specific tasks related to the mission. (Refer to ADP 5-0 and ADRP 5-0 for more information.)

Stability

SECTION IV – EXECUTE AND ASSESS

5-42. Stability tasks are most likely to occur in third-world countries where social, political, economic, and psychological factors contribute to political instability. Each country or region is unique with its own history, culture, goals, and problems. The reconnaissance platoon can be subjected to rapid and dramatic changes in situations and missions, and is prepared to operate in any type of terrain and climate. The platoon leader understands this environment and is constantly prepared to adapt.

5-43. To deal effectively with the diverse situations they may face, the platoon undergoes orientation training on the complex conditions and factors at work in a specific region. All Soldiers need to understand the political and economic situation, and the cultures, climates, and terrain of the region. They should understand the military situation—especially the doctrine, tactics, and equipment—that is being employed by hostile forces or civil unrest.

5-44. The reconnaissance platoon may execute several tasks during stability tasks. This means that occasionally the reconnaissance platoon conducts tasks that are usually handled by specially trained and equipped elements. For example, the platoon could conduct crowd and riot control, if needed.

5-45. The following discussion examines several tasks the platoon could face during stability tasks. The list is not all-inclusive. Assessment of METT-TC factors and the operational considerations applicable in the AO may identify additional mission requirements.

5-46. The platoon leader keeps in mind the ever-changing and often confusing conditions of the tasks. The platoon's flexibility is a key to success under such conditions. The platoon leader should attempt to shape the role or mission to match the platoon's unique characteristics and capabilities.

CONDUCT RESERVE TASKS

5-47. The reconnaissance platoon occupies an assembly area or sets up a perimeter as part of the battalion or company reserve. Potential missions include:
- Linkup with (and relief of) encircled friendly forces.
- Linkup and movement to secure an objective in a mission such as rescuing a downed helicopter or stranded vehicle.
- Tactical movement to destroy enemy forces attacking a convoy.

5-48. In all three scenarios, the platoon conducts tactical movement and tasks in contact. Tasks such as linkup, support by fire, direct fire planning, assault, and consolidation and reorganization are also critical to the reserve mission. (For more information on these tasks, refer to Chapter 6.)

Chapter 5

ESTABLISH A CHECKPOINT
5-49. Checkpoints can be deliberate or hasty and are used to control and direct the maneuver of military traffic/vehicles. They are usually placed on identifiable terrain features such as hilltops, road intersections, or towers.

5-50. The platoon may be directed to establish a checkpoint to achieve one or more of the following purposes:
- Discourage illegal movement.
- Create an instant roadblock.
- Control movement into the area of operations or onto a specific route.
- Demonstrate the presence of peace forces.
- Prevent smuggling of contraband.
- Enforce the terms of peace agreements.
- Serve as an OP, patrol base, or both.

OVERWATCH A BLOCKADE OR ROADBLOCK
5-51. The reconnaissance platoon overwatches a blockade or roadblock from a manned position or a reinforcing obstacle covered by fires. They coordinate with dismounted Infantry from the company for local security (OPs and dismounted patrols) or can provide their own. Positions are improved using procedures for deliberate occupation of a BP. (Refer to FM 3-20.971 for more information.)

CONDUCT CONVOY ESCORT
5-52. Leaders carefully evaluate all situations before assigning convoy escort duties to the reconnaissance platoon. Detailed procedure information is covered in Chapter 4.

IMPROVISED EXPLOSIVE DEVICE DEFEAT
5-53. With a focus on clearing IEDs, the IED-defeat framework is derived from the fundamentals of assured mobility. This encompasses those actions that enable commanders to deploy, move, and maneuver where and when they desire without interruption or delay, and to achieve the mission. (Refer to FM 3-34 for more information.) When properly planned and evaluated, the fundamentals of assured mobility assist in developing SA, allowing the commander to exploit opportunities that defeat the IED prior to its inception.

5-54. Because all IEDs cannot be eliminated, commanders plan to mitigate the impacts by developing SOPs, TTPs, battle drills, and other response actions to lessen the effects of the IED and eliminate the enemy's desired outcome. To effectively diminish the impact of IEDs, the fundamentals of detect, avoid, neutralize, and protect are used in conjunction with the factors of METT-TC to plan and develop coordinated and well-executed responses.

5-55. Platoons conduct clearing tasks in support of an overall IED-defeat mission. The focus of clearing tasks is on the IED or explosive hazard itself. However, the

Stability

device is merely the end product of a complex set of enemy activities. An IED attack is the result of a planned tactical operation with several key elements that work in a coordinated and synchronized manner to attain a desired result.

5-56. Route clearance is a key task in IED defeat. It provides the maneuver commander with the capability to employ a combined arms force of combat engineers, EOD, and other units task-organized, equipped, and trained to neutralize the IED threat. Route clearance is one of several solutions the commander may employ to defeat an IED threat.

AREA SECURITY
5-57. Reconnaissance platoons conduct area security to deny adversaries the ability to influence friendly actions in a specific location. It is also conducted to deny the enemy use of an area for its own purposes such as combat, insurgent infiltration, or actions against friendly forces. Area security is conducted to secure a specific region for the protection of friendly forces, installations, and routes. (Refer to ATTP 3-90.4 for more information.) The platoon may execute one of the following tasks as part of area security:
- Route security.
- Convoy security.
- Check point tasks.
- Fixed site security.
- Combat patrols.
- Cordon and search.
- Cordon and attack.

SUPPORT CORDON AND SEARCH TASKS
5-58. A cordon and search involves isolating and searching the target area; and capturing or destroying possible insurgents and contraband. A cordon and search may be a task during any type of movement based upon the accuracy of intelligence. While the actual mission may fall under any category, the cordon and search is typically oriented at finding insurgents or their caches. (Refer to FM 3-06.20 for more information.)

5-59. Platoon leaders and commanders develop knowledge of enemy organizations based upon intelligence in the area. Once intelligence gathering elements identify and locate important enemy personnel or information, a cordon and search may be conducted to neutralize the enemy or collect more detailed information.

5-60. Leaders account for all identified materiels gained during cordon and search tasks. In some situations, the targeted individuals may escape, leaving behind caches of weapons, equipment, or other materiels. Accurate documentation and cataloging of information and materiel of intelligence value at the site is vital. Once evidence has been moved it becomes more difficult to connect it to the suspected house, incident, or individual.

5-61. Leaders should assess the evidence they discover and then coordinate the resources needed to handle these materials. Examples include situations such as transporting and safeguarding a radio or map, confiscating materiels for making IEDs, or discovering a hidden tunnel storing a long-term cache for an insurgent offensive.

5-62. The reconnaissance platoon occupies overwatch positions to isolate a search area during cordon and search tasks. Employment of OPs and patrols to maintain surveillance of dead space and gaps in the cordoned area, and close coordination and communication with the search team is critical.

5-63. The reconnaissance platoon (or section) is prepared to take immediate action if the search team or OPs identify enemy elements. Enemy contact may require the platoon to execute tactical movement and linkup. The platoon then coordinates with other units to destroy the enemy.

SITE EXPLOITATION

5-64. Primarily, site exploitation is a means of gaining information that supports the intelligence process. As part of a company team, the platoon may execute SE as a tactical task or independent mission to—

- Facilitate subsequent operations by gaining access to personnel or materiel that supports the development of intelligence and the targeting process.
- Answer information requirements.
- Facilitate criminal prosecution by host nation, coalition, or international authorities.

5-65. Site exploitation missions may focus on one fundamental purpose or all three simultaneously. The purpose of the site exploitation should be considered throughout the company team and platoon's TLP. The development of intelligence through immediate analysis or off-site processing can enable the commander to target additional objectives. During stability tasks, the platoon can use SE to gain information that supports criminal prosecution by HN authorities.

5-66. Platoon members identify materiel and personnel of interest, collect, and preserve these items. After the mission is completed, the platoon is debriefed by appropriate intelligence representatives, usually the S-2. The information, materiel, and personnel collected are processed by the appropriate agencies and analyzed to produce intelligence that supports subsequent targeting.

SECURITY FORCES ASSISTANCE

5-67. Security force assistance is the unified action to generate, employ, and sustain local, HN, or regional security forces in support of a legitimate authority. It is integral to successful stability tasks and extends to all security forces. Forces are developed to operate across the range of military operations, combating internal threats such as insurgency, subversion, and lawlessness; defending against external threats; or serving as coalition partners in other areas. (Refer to FM 3-07.1 for more information.)

RESPOND TO CIVIL DISTURBANCE

5-68. The reconnaissance platoon is aware of local civilians that often gather to demonstrate in towns or along strategic locations throughout an AO. Grievances can range from protesting the apprehension of a fellow citizen, policies of U.S. forces, policies of government services, or other causes.

5-69. Civilians have the right to assemble. During spontaneous crowd formations, the platoon provides forces in support of a safe and secure environment, or to assist civilian police in preventing unlawful acts. Aside from the lives of U.S. Soldiers and citizens, rules for the protection of foreign nationals detail who and what may be defended with force. This includes measures that Soldiers can take to prevent crimes in progress or the fleeing of criminals.

5-70. The platoon may be required to respond to civil disturbance in support of company stability tasks. This response may be deliberate or hasty, and the platoon should be prepared to control the local populace. Leaders develop training and conduct rehearsals for responding to civil disturbances. To increase effective responses by all Soldiers, this training should include as many situations as possible.

Conduct Deliberate Operations

5-71. The commander can often be made aware of dates, times, locations, and what groups may assemble before the operation. This allows time to plan, and alert the platoon of potential civil disturbances. Through the effective gathering of information and a working cooperation with local government and police officials, the commander and platoon leader can gain insight on the attitudes of the groups involved. This information assists in determining the size of the control force and the activities that the platoon participates in.

Chapter 5

Conduct Hasty Operations

5-72. It seems to be the norm that platoons are likely to conduct hasty civil disturbance measures rather than deliberate. Unlike deliberate operations, hasty civil disorder tasks are reactionary in nature with little or no time for planning. In these situations, the event of a crowd gathering is already underway. There is often no advance warning of the situation and commanders are usually put in the position of sending their Soldiers into an already volatile, and perhaps hostile, environment.

5-73. Leaders should be in immediate and constant communication between the local civil and police authorities. This helps them gather as much information as possible about who is involved, where they are assembling, what incident promoted the activity, and what seems to be the prevailing attitude of the assembling crowd.

5-74. Responding and controlling civil disturbance training is given to Soldiers at all levels so that they can respond effectively during hasty operations. Crowd control options are often included in the training. Leaders choose their options based on an evaluation of the particular crowd. Using METT-TC, leaders select control techniques and force options that can influence the particular situation. Leaders always try to choose the response that is expected to reduce the intensity of the situation. (Refer to FM 3-19.15 for more information.)

Secure Civilians During Operations

5-75. Always treat civilians with dignity and respect. Leaders cannot assume that noncombatants are predisposed for or against U.S. troops. Use force against civilians only in self-defense or in accordance with the ROE. Civilians are only detained according to command directives.

5-76. The platoon leader plans to move any noncombatants away from firefights and combat areas when conducting stability tasks. Normally, this task is given to the support element after rooms and buildings have been secured. When available, military information support operation (MISO), CA, and MPs can assist with this task.

5-77. The platoon leader should consider a covered and concealed location away from the immediate combat area to secure civilians. Noncombatants should be controlled and not allowed to enter the immediate combat area unless they have been cleared to do so, and do not compromise combat.

5-78. Security is not normally provided for media or NGO personnel if they are permitted in the immediate combat area. Security requirements for civilians should be clarified at the mission briefing. For further information refer to ATTP 3-06.11.

DETAINED PERSONS

5-79. Detained persons and captured equipment often provide excellent combat information and intelligence. This information is of tactical value only if the platoon

Stability

processes, accurately documents, and evacuates detainees and materiel to the rear quickly.

5-80. In any tactical situation, the platoon has specific procedures and guidelines for handling detainees and captured materiel. Soldiers handle detained personnel, including tagging personnel and all captured equipment by using the five-S procedure.

5-81. In addition to initial processing, the capturing unit provides guards and transportation to move detainees to the designated collection points. The capturing unit normally carries detainees on vehicles already heading toward the rear, such as tactical vehicles returning from logistics package missions. The capturing element also feeds, provides medical treatment, and safeguards detainees until they reach the collection point.

5-82. Once the detained personnel arrive at the collection point, the platoon sergeant assumes responsibility for them, providing security and transporting them to the company collection point. The platoon sergeant uses available personnel as guards. This includes the walking wounded, or Soldiers moving to the rear for reassignment.

Handling Detainees

5-83. The basic principles for handling detainees are covered by the five-Ss and T (tag) procedures outlined below.

- **Search:** Remove and tag all weapons and documents. Return all personal items with no military value to the detainee. Detainees are allowed to keep their helmet, protective mask, and other gear that protects them from the immediate dangers of the battle area.
- **Segregate:** Break the chain of command. Separate detainees by rank, sex, and other suitable categories. Keep the staunch fighter away from those who willingly surrender.
- **Silence:** Prevent detainees from giving orders, planning escapes, or developing false "cover stories."
- **Speed:** Speed detainees to the rear to remove them from the battle area, and to quickly obtain and use their information.
- **Safeguard:** Prevent detainees from escaping. Protect them from violence, insults, curiosity, and reprisals of any kind.
- **Tag:** Tag detainees with a DD Form 2745, (Enemy Prisoner of War [EPW] Capture Tag) or a field-expedient capture tag that includes the following information:
    - Date of capture.
    - Location of capture (grid coordinates).
    - Capturing unit.
    - Special circumstances of capture (how the person was captured: if they resisted, gave up, and so forth).

Chapter 5

- **Complete:** The capturing unit completes a capture tag. Failure to do so hinders further processing and disposition.

5-84. Platoon members keep in mind that they should never approach an enemy soldier, even when surrender appears to be certain. They may be booby-trapped or have a weapon hidden nearby. The following procedures apply for taking the prisoner into custody:

- Gesture for the prisoner to come forward, and then wait until it is clear they are honestly surrendering and not trying to lure friendly troops into an ambush.
- Use a thermal sight to locate possible ambushes.
- When searching, always have another friendly Soldier with a weapon cover the prisoner.
- Do not move between the enemy and the Soldier covering the prisoner.

5-85. Crewmen take the detainees to an area designated by the commander under the direction of the platoon leader. The prisoners are then evacuated to the rear for interrogation. If a detainee is wounded and cannot be evacuated through medical channels, the platoon leader notifies the XO or 1SG. The detainee is then escorted to the company or troop trains, or the 1SG comes forward with guards to evacuate him.

Detainee Rights and Responsibilities

5-86. Humane treatment of all detainees is mandatory regardless of their legal status under the Geneva Conventions or U.S. policy (such as DODD 2310.01E). Soldiers treat all detainees in accordance with applicable domestic and international law, national policy, and the law of war. Once an enemy soldier indicates they want to surrender, they are treated humanely. The senior officer or NCO on the scene is responsible for safeguarding detainees. If the unit cannot evacuate a prisoner within a reasonable time, they are provided with food, water, and medical treatment.

CAPTURED ENEMY DOCUMENTS AND EQUIPMENT

5-87. Captured enemy documents (such as maps, orders, records, and photographs) and equipment are excellent sources of intelligence information. If captured items are not handled properly, the information in them may be lost or delayed until it is useless. These items are evacuated to the next level of command as rapidly as possible.

5-88. The platoon tags each captured item. (See Figure 5-1.) If the item is found in the detainee's possession, include the prisoner's name on the tag and give the item to the guard. The guard delivers the item with the detainee to the next higher HQ. Platoons may find themselves in a fast-paced operation where equipment that is not of significant intelligence value may not be transported or recovered. In such cases, the platoon needs to have a plan for destroying the equipment so it does not fall back into the enemy's hands.

Note. Enemy medical equipment is never destroyed.

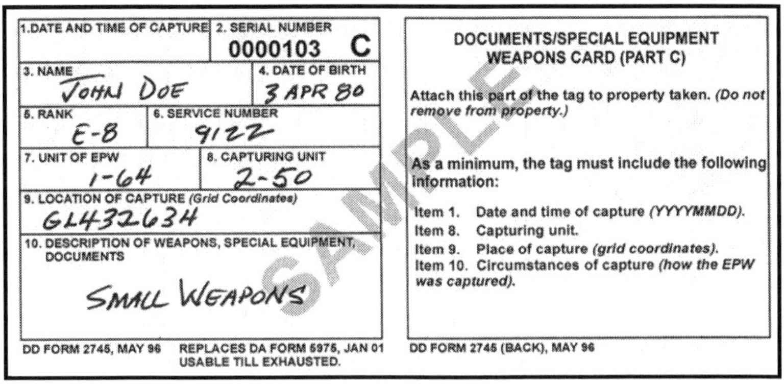

1. DATE AND TIME OF CAPTURE
2. SERIAL NUMBER 0000103 C
3. NAME JOHN DOE
4. DATE OF BIRTH 3 APR 80
5. RANK E-8
6. SERVICE NUMBER 9122
7. UNIT OF EPW 1-64
8. CAPTURING UNIT 2-50
9. LOCATION OF CAPTURE *(Grid Coordinates)* GL432634
10. DESCRIPTION OF WEAPONS, SPECIAL EQUIPMENT, DOCUMENTS SMALL WEAPONS

SAMPLE

DD FORM 2745, MAY 96 REPLACES DA FORM 5976, JAN 01 USABLE TILL EXHAUSTED.

DOCUMENTS/SPECIAL EQUIPMENT WEAPONS CARD (PART C)

Attach this part of the tag to property taken. *(Do not remove from property.)*

As a minimum, the tag must include the following information:

Item 1. Date and time of capture *(YYYYMMDD)*.
Item 8. Capturing unit.
Item 9. Place of capture *(grid coordinates)*.
Item 10. Circumstances of capture *(how the EPW was captured)*.

DD FORM 2745 (BACK), MAY 96

Figure 5-1. Sample tag for captured documents and equipment

CIVIL AFFAIRS UNITS AND PSYCHOLOGICAL TASKS

5-89. Civil affairs units and the military information support operation have essential roles during missions in an urban environment. They are critical force multipliers that can save lives. The battle in urban terrain is won through effective application of necessary combat power, and the CA MISO can help facilitate mission accomplishment.

5-90. CA and MISOs offer the possibility of mission accomplishment in urban terrain without the destruction, suffering, and horror of battle. These units may become key factors in shaping the urban battlefield. They can facilitate movement directly from shaping to transition, and minimize the amount of close combat conducted by companies, platoons, and squads.

This page intentionally left blank.

Chapter 6

Other Tactical Tasks

Reconnaissance units often conduct fundamentals, formations, and techniques known as tactical movement that support the success of the primary reconnaissance or security mission. Tactical tasks are tasks that are accomplished for a unit to carry out or continue its main mission and help achieve or sustain the strategic advantage.

Since platoon reconnaissance tasks are often conducted with stealth while avoiding direct fire, they normally do not perform many of the enabling operations executed by other maneuver units. The tactical tasks most often carried out by the reconnaissance platoon include those that require direct contact with friendly units during infiltration or exfiltration transitions, direct fire planning, assembly area tasks, linkup, and a passage of lines.

SECTION I – PLATOON TACTICAL MOVEMENT

PLANNING AND OPERATIONAL CONSIDERATIONS

6-1. METT-TC, applicable troop-leading procedures, and assets such as FBCB2, ground sensors, UAS, and ground surveillance systems contribute to the planning and operational considerations of other tactical tasks. This section focuses on several critical aspects of tactical movement, including—

- **Movement fundamentals and formations.** In addition to concentrating on their own tactical movement using the operational considerations listed above, ABCT reconnaissance platoons operate with adjacent platoons that follow no more than one terrain feature behind, or one-half the effective range of their primary weapon systems.
- **Movement techniques.** Successfully employed traveling, traveling overwatch, and bounding overwatch movement techniques allow the platoon to conduct reconnaissance without becoming compromised. They also help the platoon leader—
  - Minimize the platoon's exposure to enemy observation and fire.
  - Maximize the number of tactical options available to the platoon.
- **Mission considerations.** Section leaders maintain SA regarding the location of reaction forces, observable areas, and weapon systems capability by conducting stealthy movement and gaining visual contact with enemy forces. This helps support friendly forces in enemy contact.

Chapter 6

- **Chance contact.** The reconnaissance platoon takes steps to minimize chance contact with enemy forces by using detailed platoon analysis, visual clearing of IV lines and templated danger areas, and proper movement techniques (traveling or bounding overwatch). Higher echelon intelligence sources such as the UAS and ground sensors are also used to reduce the possibility of chance contact.
- **Timelines.** Tactical movements are made in accordance with the timelines and operational phases directed by the higher commander.

FUNDAMENTALS OF MOVEMENT

6-2. Sound tactical movement is the essence of all reconnaissance platoon missions. Effectively employed, the guidelines in this section can help scouts see the enemy first and observe them undetected. This helps to achieve a number of tactical goals, including retaining the initiative, confirming or denying the CCIR, and retaining freedom of movement to gain information.

USE TERRAIN FOR COVER AND CONCEALMENT

6-3. Terrain offers concealment from enemy observation and cover from enemy fires. Scouts make maximum use of this natural protection to accomplish their mission and avoid enemy detection. Cover is used whenever possible. When no cover is available, scouts use the concealment offered by trees, shadows, brush, and man-made structures. (See Figure 6-1.)

Figure 6-1. Use of natural terrain for concealment

6-4. During all movement, individual vehicles and personnel should avoid becoming silhouetted against a skyline. Precautions should be taken to avoid moving directly forward from a defilade position as this can enable the enemy to pinpoint the vehicle and engage it as it moves. Instead, vehicles should back up and move left or right around the previous position to get to the next location.

6-5. Despite its obvious advantage, movement along covered and concealed routes is often slower, and leaders face more problems with control of the moving vehicles. The traveling distance may be increased, resulting in the platoon taking

Other Tactical Tasks

longer to get through an area as vehicles move slower and have farther to go. The possibility of being ambushed by enemy forces increases, but can be mitigated through proper movement techniques and increased security measures, if time permits (METT-TC). In most situations, such limitations are accepted because the accuracy and lethality of enemy long-range weapons make unconcealed movement too dangerous. The vehicle commander or dismounted leader carefully balances the required observation and reconnaissance with the need for security.

6-6. Scouts are prepared to take necessary precautions when encountering danger areas. Based on terrain and platoon analysis, the platoon leader considers where enemy reconnaissance assets are focused and determines their fields of observation. The platoon then avoids movement through these areas by combining proper terrain driving techniques with carefully selected routes that maximize security and reduce the signature of the vehicle.

6-7. The platoon should stop short of danger areas and use dismounted scouts away from the vehicles to reconnoiter ahead of them. For example, when encountering an open area, the platoon sends dismounts to a concealed position to observe the area. Scouts carefully check the other side of the open area for enemy positions. Vehicles provide overwatch for the dismounts while using combat identification (CID) techniques to mitigate the risk of fratricide. When clear, the platoon then quickly crosses the open area.

DISMOUNT VEHICLES

6-8. As a general rule, the platoon sends out dismounts in elements no smaller than two scouts. This enhances mission accomplishment and survivability. While vehicles are easily identified by their visual, sound, and exhaust signatures (which increases the possibility of enemy detection), dismounted patrols and OPs are very difficult to notice. Scouts should dismount their vehicles and use optical devices to gain information on objectives or areas of interest.

6-9. For example, during reconnaissance tasks, scouts dismount beyond the direct fire range of suspected enemy positions and weapon systems. They then move in front of their vehicles using the cover and concealment of a dismounted avenue adjacent to the mounted route. Leaving the vehicles in hide or overwatch positions, the dismounted scouts occupy OPs that provide critical information enhancing the unit's survivability.

REDUCE VEHICLE-RELATED SIGNATURES

6-10. The reconnaissance platform's major signatures (audible, thermal, and visual) are reduced by shutting off the vehicle and related systems such as heaters or older thermal sights whenever the vehicle is not moving or the system is not needed. Scouts can further reduce visual and thermal signatures by—

- Erecting camouflage nets. This helps hide a stationary vehicle visually and thermally. Nets tied to the vehicle can reduce dust and exhaust signatures, and reduce the thermal signature while moving.

Chapter 6

- Employing camouflage materiel appropriately on vehicles during movement to break up the color and silhouette.
- Keeping hatches closed and locked with safety pins. This reduces noise and light signatures, as does masking internal lights from outside observation.
- Preventing white light displays at night.
- Conducting external PCIs of vehicles using NODs to spot-check friendly light signatures. This is done by the leaders.
- Reducing vehicle glass reflection from periscopes and windows by removing, covering, or camouflaging them (for example, placing a net over the windshield).

DANGER AREAS

6-11. During the execution of reconnaissance and security missions, the platoon encounters specific types of terrain features or regions that expose them to enemy fire. These danger areas are likely points of enemy contact due to the reconnaissance platoon's inherent vulnerabilities. Enemy cover, concealment, and observation danger areas should be identified and highlighted when the platoon leader performs map reconnaissance and platoon analysis during TLPs.

6-12. Once these areas are identified, the platoon leader plans for specific methods and movement techniques to move through these areas quickly, with maximum security. Danger areas should be included in all phases of the maneuver rehearsal by squads, sections, and the platoon as a whole.

OPEN AREAS

6-13. Open areas frequently allow the reconnaissance platoon to observe the enemy or objectives from long range. Conversely, these areas often expose the platoon to possible enemy observation and fire for long periods of movement. By making maximum use of the terrain and employing powerful optics and effective observation techniques, the platoon avoids exposing itself to the enemy.

6-14. Before moving across a large open area, the platoon makes a thorough mounted and dismounted visual scan of the area. The platoon leader uses all available optics and other assets, including UAS, LRAS3, and ground surveillance systems to reconnoiter the open area and find a bypass. If a bypass cannot be found, the focus is on locating covered and concealed routes to facilitate movement and find potential enemy positions.

6-15. If time and terrain permit, dismounted scouts may be used to move to the far side of the open area and secure it. In very large open areas, use of dismounts may not be feasible because of the distances between covered and concealed positions. Unmanned aircraft systems can perform observation tasks for the dismounts. Many platforms employ integrated sight units that can assist the platoon in scanning for threats at extended ranges and provide accurate fires to protect scouts as they advance.

Other Tactical Tasks

6-16. Once the area has been reconnoitered using visual, digital, and sensor enablers, scouts move across it using a bounding overwatch due to the possibility of enemy contact. If the open area is very large, the overwatch element should only remain stationary until the bounding element has moved a distance equal to half the effective range of the overwatching element's weapon system. When that point is reached, the overwatch element moves out even if the bounding element has not yet reached a position of cover and concealment.

6-17. When the platoon moves across large open areas with limited cover and concealment, indirect fire can provide suppression with obscurant munitions. Concealment with obscurants is limited when the enemy is equipped with thermal sights. Reconnaissance by fire may be an acceptable method of mitigating risk when crossing a danger area. However, leaders adhere to the ROE and take weapons control status into consideration when using this method.

WOODED AREAS

6-18. Wooded areas create opportunities for enemy forces on the ground to attack, disable, and even destroy a vehicle from a blind spot. These areas provide a high degree of concealment for the forces that occupy them, particularly dismounts, and are approached and moved through with extreme caution. Visibility within wooded areas is limited, and reconnaissance is confined primarily to trafficable routes and trails through the forest. In densely wooded areas, mounted scouts are extremely vulnerable to dismounted enemy forces that can close on them undetected.

6-19. Platoon leaders plan for increased security when operating in the restricted environment of a wooded area. Scouts should use available observation devices to scan the wooded area before entering. They should search for movement, reflections, obscurants, thermal images, and any irregular shapes or colors indicating camouflage. Scouts scan the ground to detect signs or patterns indicating enemy movement or activity to prevent chance encounters with obstacles, antitank ambushes, and IEDs. Whenever possible, scouts reconnoiter the entire wood line with dismounts prior to mounted movement into the wooded area. Foliage in wooded areas can conceal the enemy from the UAS.

6-20. The platoon should use a bounding overwatch into the wooded area. Once the vehicles are positioned approximately 100 to 200 meters inside the wood line, the platoon shuts off engines, establishes dismounted security, and conducts a listening/security halt. Combat vehicle crewmen wearing helmets remove them and radio speakers are turned off. The halt should last approximately one to two minutes, with 360-degree security maintained throughout. Similar halts are conducted approximately every kilometer during movement through the wooded area. At the same time, because reconnaissance vehicles are most vulnerable in wooded areas when stopped, halts should be kept to a minimum. Optimally, a hide position should be assumed during short halts to enhance security.

Chapter 6

6-21. During movement through a wooded area, the platoon should move using traveling overwatch. This technique is appropriate because of the extremely short fields of view and the danger of dismounted ambush. Exposed scouts should maintain a minimum silhouette in their vehicles due to danger from snipers and ambush. Adjacent elements overwatching the platoon as it moves are also affected by the shorter engagement distances.

6-22. The reconnaissance platoon may encounter small clearings, buildings, or hills while moving through a wooded area. Each site is treated as a separate danger area. Small clearings may require crossing in the same manner as a large open area, and isolated buildings are secured by dismounted scouts. These areas offer invaluable movement lanes for the enemy to move into cleared areas behind scouts and attack without warning. Hills and curves are approached cautiously, and dismounted scouts clear any dead space.

6-23. Before leaving a wooded area, the platoon clears the open area to the front. Vehicles stop inside the wood line, staying within the shadow line of the woods. Engines are turned off and dismounted scouts move to the edge of the wooded area to observe. If the area is determined to be clear, vehicles move forward to establish OPs. As the dismounts remount, crews use their vehicle optics to visually clear the open area. Once completed, the platoon resumes movement using the appropriate movement technique.

URBAN AREAS

6-24. Detailed reconnaissance of urban areas during a major combat operation is extremely difficult for reconnaissance platoons. Urban areas, including towns and villages, pose numerous dangers, especially if the enemy is occupying the area in strength. Troops can be garrisoned in villages, snipers can dominate approaches, and buildings and roads can be mined with anti-handling devices. Debris can conceal IEDs against buildings and in the street, creating threats and obstacles to mounted and dismounted movement. Cover and concealment is abundant for friendly forces and the enemy creating dire situations. Urban areas are ideal for effective ambush by small numbers of dismounts. The reconnaissance platoon takes steps to counter these dangers and ensure local security.

6-25. Whenever possible, the platoon should initially observe these areas from a distance and from multiple vantage points. The use of the UAS in areas forward of the platoon allows observation beyond the platoon's line of sight.

6-26. The reconnaissance platoon collects tactical information and HUMINT before entering the urban area, looking for movement and evidence of enemy occupation. This includes track marks on pavement, lack of civilian activity, sandbags, stakes, timber, intentional building damage, or any other potential sign of prepared fighting positions and obstacles. In some cases, HUMINT, CA, and military intelligence teams can gather enemy information from the local population before the platoon moves in.

Other Tactical Tasks

6-27. Platoon elements move through the area using traveling or bounding overwatch based on METT-TC factors. This ensures that vehicles remain in mutual support and maintain 360-degree security. Once in the town, all scouts are alert for additional signs of enemy activity. Tactical evidence can include—

- Deliberate markings or signaling devices.
- Evidence of emplaced IEDs or IED explosions.
- Antennas.
- Spent shell casings.
- Spent or emplaced pyrotechnics.
- Intentional damage to buildings and streets.

6-28. Dismounts can reconnoiter major intersections ahead of vehicles and provide security during halts, such as conducting overwatch from building rooftops or windows. Normally, scouts do not have the manpower or time to clear buildings, but they can be employed for limited dismounted search and secure tasks to support a particular reconnaissance mission. Mounted vehicle crews reduce their silhouette to a minimum when moving through a town. Snipers are at an advantage as they can be positioned above the vehicle with the ability to shoot down into vehicle hatch openings.

6-29. As the platoon approaches the far side of the urban area, dismounted scouts are employed to reconnoiter the vicinity for enemy movement. The platoon should stop short, move dismounts to the edge of town, and use assets such as the UAS to observe this location. The dismounts with overwatch responsibilities secure the local area and observe the open region beyond the town. When this reconnaissance is completed, the vehicles move forward and continue to observe from covered and concealed positions while the dismounted elements remount. The platoon then prepares to continue its mission.

LATERAL OR BOUNDARY ROUTES

6-30. As the platoon executes reconnaissance and security missions, routes or mobility corridors that provide access into the terrain between the platoon and friendly elements to its flanks and rear are to be expected. These lateral mobility corridors pose a security threat to the platoon and the other friendly elements by allowing the enemy and scouts to move into the terrain around the platoon flanks unobserved. Leaders coordinate missions with adjacent units to prevent confusion, fratricide, or possible enemy exploitation. Reconnaissance elements should not reconnoiter lateral routes beyond one half the distance of the maximum effective range of overwatching weapon systems.

6-31. It is critical that the platoon maintain continuous surveillance of these mobility corridors to protect against infiltrating enemy forces. If necessary, the platoon uses a series of contact and coordination points to enhance security during movement through the area. The UAS can monitor areas already cleared by

Chapter 6

the reconnaissance platoon and assist in mitigating enemy infiltration between adjacent elements.

6-32. To maintain surveillance of areas along known or suspected paths of enemy travel, the platoon can establish outposts to maximize the reconnaissance effort forward. This security technique uses short duration OPs consisting of two Soldiers with equipment. A section or squad should deploy an outpost when it is at risk of losing observation of a possible enemy approach route that no other element can observe. Once deployed, the outpost maintains surveillance of the avenue of approach until the rest of the reconnaissance element returns. In doing so, this outpost provides security with early warning of enemy activity that the mounted element would not have detected.

PLATOON FORMATIONS

6-33. During mounted or dismounted movement, the reconnaissance platoon employs combat formations when the terrain and enemy situation supports their use, or when the mission or reconnaissance objective is precisely focused, such as in a route reconnaissance.

6-34. There are seven flexible mounted reconnaissance platoon formations:
- Line.
- Vee.
- Column.
- Staggered column.
- Coil.
- Herringbone.
- Wedge.

6-35. These formations do not have exact geometric dimensions and design, so they can be modified to fit the situation, terrain, and combat losses. Transition into and out of the various formations is second nature to each section or team.

LINE FORMATION
6-36. Regardless of the platoon organization, line formation is applicable to most reconnaissance platoon missions. This allows maximum reconnaissance forward and covers a wider AO. It also requires the platoon to have some form of overwatch because vehicles only provide local security.

VEE FORMATION
6-37. The platoon maintains relative positioning based on terrain and combat losses. The vee formation lends itself to immediate mutual support and provides depth due to its flexibility. Using any of the techniques of movement, the two forward vehicles perform most of the information gathering and reporting. The rear vehicles provide overwatch and mission command (the reverse applies when scouts conduct route reconnaissance). In situations where enemy contact is likely with a

Other Tactical Tasks

heavily equipped enemy, CFVs may be the lead element, followed by wheeled components. This alignment provides added security to the wheeled elements, enabling them to displace rapidly, supply early warning, and ascertain enemy composition/disposition.

COLUMN FORMATION AND STAGGERED COLUMN FORMATION

6-38. When speed is essential as it moves on a designated route, the platoon uses the column formation. (See Figures 6-2 and 6-3.) This offers good fields of fire to the flanks but little to the front and rear. Normally, the platoon leader briefs the section leaders on the route and speed, and then allows the lead section to control the column movement. This enables the platoon leader to concentrate on the subsequent mission. However, the platoon leader still has the responsibility of tracking the movement of the platoon.

6-39. The order of march in the column may depend on which organization the platoon uses at the end of the movement. In addition, the lead section may vary based on METT-TC considerations. When conducting movement in a secure area, it is appropriate to specify the order of march by SOP.

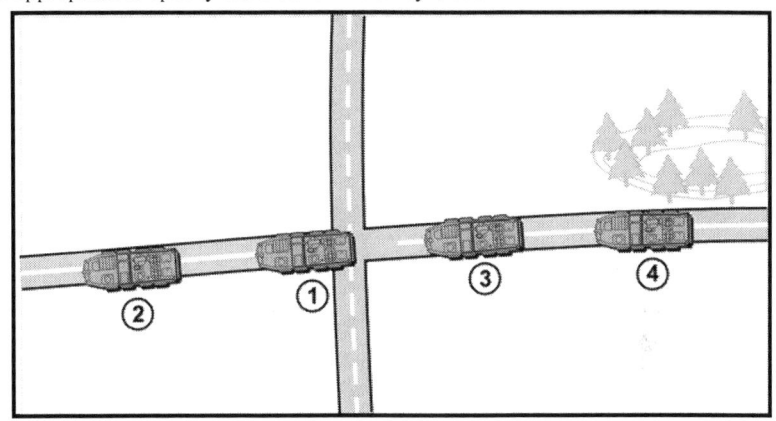

Figure 6-2. Column formation (SBCT reconnaissance platoon)

Chapter 6

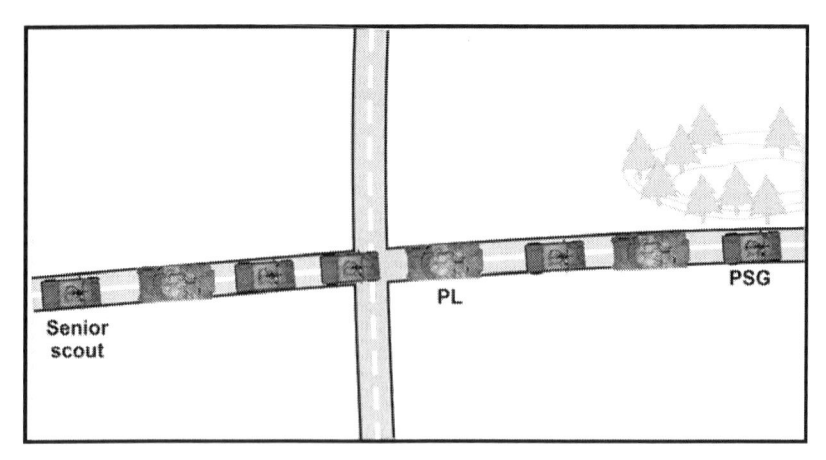

Figure 6-3. Column formation (ABCT reconnaissance platoon)

6-40. The staggered column is used for rapid movement across less restrictive terrain, affording all-around observation and fields of fire. Explosive devices and mines are often positioned just off the roadway, so platoons exercise caution to avoid driving on or just beyond the road shoulder when using this formation. (See Figure 6-4.)

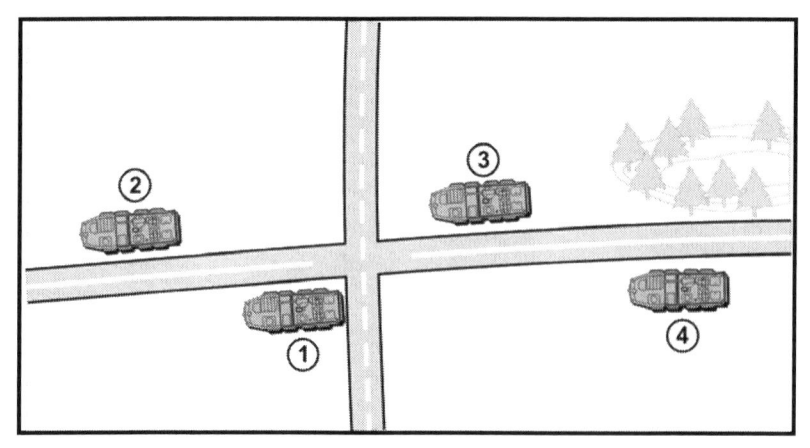

Figure 6-4. Staggered column formation (SBCT reconnaissance platoon)

COIL FORMATION

6-41. The platoon coil is used to provide all-around security during halts. Each vehicle has a particular position to occupy in the coil, and the platoon leader designates the orientation of the coil using a cardinal direction. In the absence of orders, the direction of travel becomes 12 o'clock. The platoon develops a coil SOP

Other Tactical Tasks

based upon its mission-essential task list, war plans, and most frequently used organizations. It should rehearse the SOP as a drill so that correct execution of the coil becomes automatic.

6-42. This formation is usually executed from the column or staggered column, with the lead vehicle occupying the 12 o'clock position. Other vehicles occupy the clock positions in accordance with the order of march. Vehicles are positioned 100 to 150 meters apart. Examples are illustrated in Figures 6-5 and 6-6.

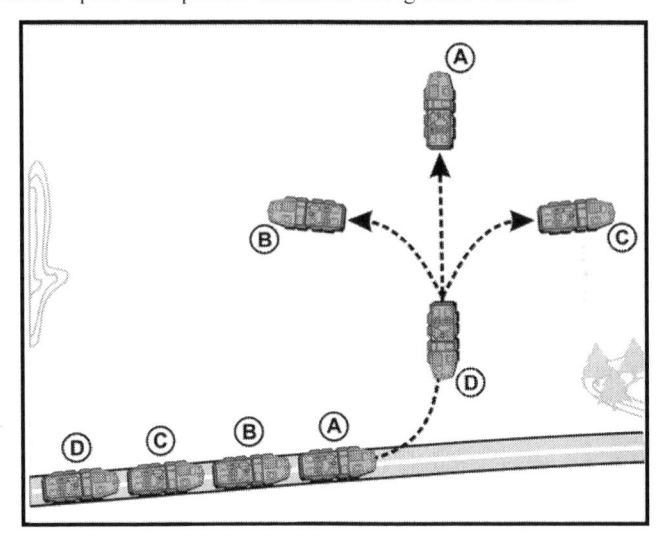

Figure 6-5. Coil formation (SBCT reconnaissance platoon)

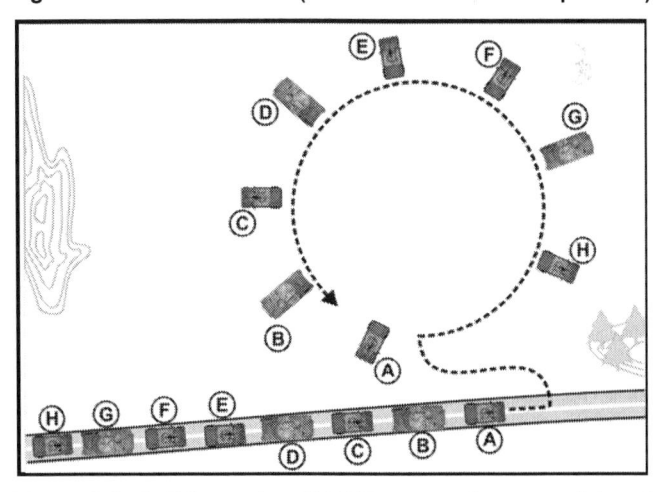

Figure 6-6. Coil formation (ABCT reconnaissance platoon)

Chapter 6

HERRINGBONE FORMATION

6-43. The herringbone provides 360-degree security during a temporary halt from a march column, and scouts should dismount to provide greater security. (See Figure 6-7.) The formation may be widened to permit passage of vehicles down the center of the column. All vehicles should move completely off the road if terrain allows. As with the staggered column formation, platoons exercise caution when they use the herringbone to avoid explosive devices and mines that may be emplaced just off the roadway.

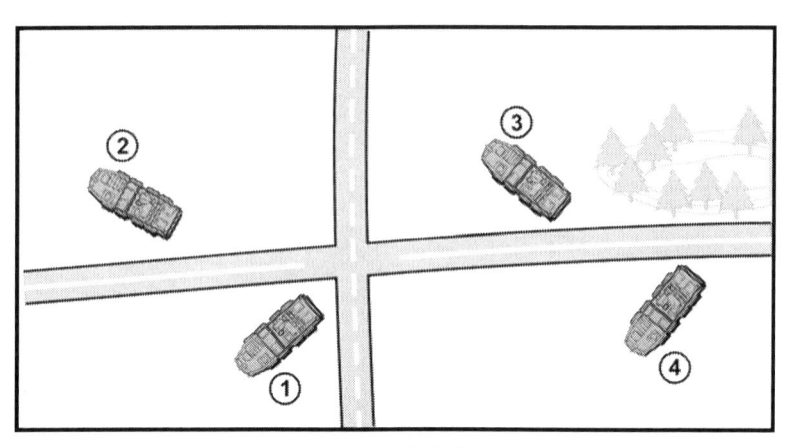

Figure 6-7. Herringbone formation (SBCT reconnaissance platoon)

WEDGE FORMATION

6-44. Non-reconnaissance maneuver platoons primarily use the wedge formation. Although this is not a typical reconnaissance formation, it may be used when enemy contact is likely and the platoon fights for information. The wedge can be formed with six-, three-, or two-vehicle organizations. This formation allows for firepower to be focused forward or shifted to either flank. In the event the platoon makes enemy contact while moving, the wedge formation permits the platoon to gain contact with the smallest possible maneuver element—the section. The wedge formation also greatly improves the reconnaissance platoon's ability to fight when the platoon is augmented with tanks as hunter-killer teams. Hunter-killer teams are generally organized with a three-vehicle CFV section accompanied by a two-tank section.

MOVEMENT TECHNIQUES

6-45. As noted earlier in this section, the reconnaissance platoon employs movement techniques for a number of reasons; minimize exposure, maintain freedom of movement, maximize available tactical options, and react successfully to contact. Effectively employed, movement techniques allow the platoon to find and observe threats without being compromised.

TACTICAL CONSIDERATIONS
6-46. In conducting mounted or dismounted movement in the AO, the reconnaissance platoon uses traveling, traveling overwatch, and bounding overwatch movement techniques. The platoon leader uses common sense in employing these standard methods of movement while performing missions and encountering different situations. Deciding which technique to use is primarily based on the likelihood of enemy contact. Terrain considerations may also affect the choice of movement technique.

6-47. In most tactical missions, the platoon moves as separate sections or teams under the mission command of the platoon leader. Leaders, particularly at the section level, should employ a degree of overwatch when enemy contact is possible. Regardless of which technique is used, the section leader gives the order explaining what each team does. This becomes more critical as the likelihood of enemy contact increases. If possible, the section leader should provide teams with the following information:
- Enemy situation (as known or suspected to be).
- Next overwatch position (the objective for the bounding element).
- Route of the bounding element to that position.
- What the section is to do after the bounding element moves to the next position.

Traveling
6-48. Traveling is usually employed in secured areas when speed is important and enemy contact is not likely. It is the fastest but least secure movement technique because the lead and trail elements move continuously together as a unit. Interval and dispersion are maintained between teams as terrain and weather permit. Weapons orientation is maintained for security, although the platoon does not intend to engage in combat and is dispersed to prevent destruction in case of unexpected air or ground attack. When using this technique, the platoon can be in a column formation or dispersed in other formations. (See Figure 6-8.)

Chapter 6

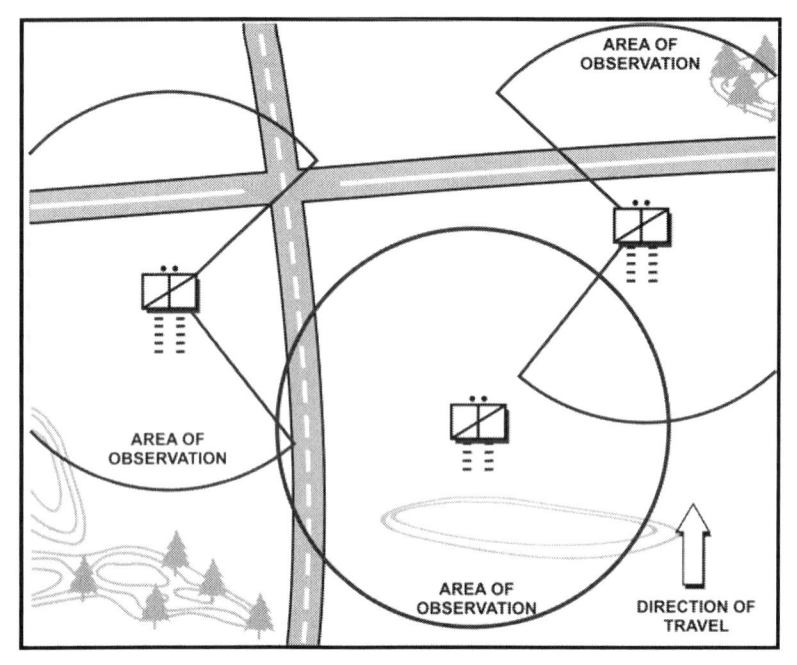

Figure 6-8. SBCT reconnaissance platoon traveling formation

TRAVELING OVERWATCH

6-49. When contact is possible but speed is desirable, traveling overwatch is employed. The lead element moves continuously along covered and concealed routes that afford the best available protection from possible enemy observation and direct fire. The trail element moves at variable speeds, providing continuous overwatch. It normally maintains visual contact with the lead element and may stop periodically for better observation. The trail element remains close enough to provide immediate suppressive fire and to maneuver for support, but be far enough behind the forward element so as not to be decisively engaged by enemy forces. (See Figures 6-9 and 6-10.)

Other Tactical Tasks

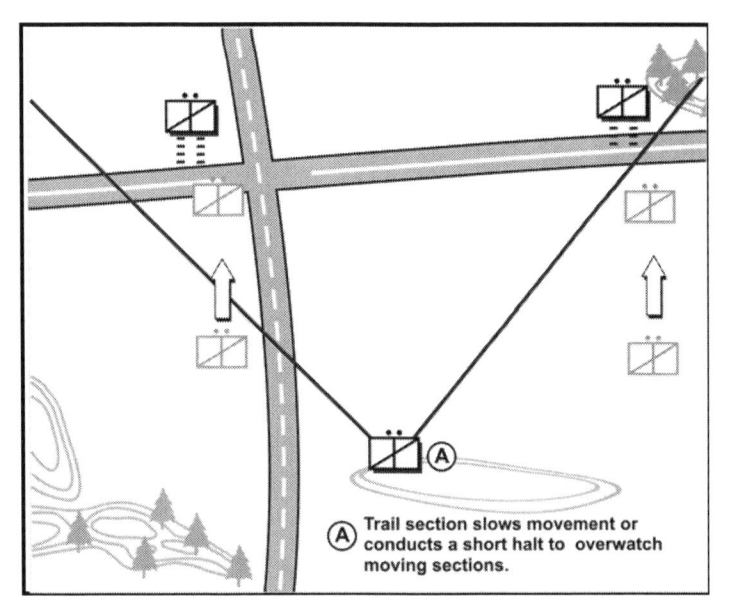

Figure 6-9. ABCT reconnaissance platoon conducts traveling overwatch formation - start

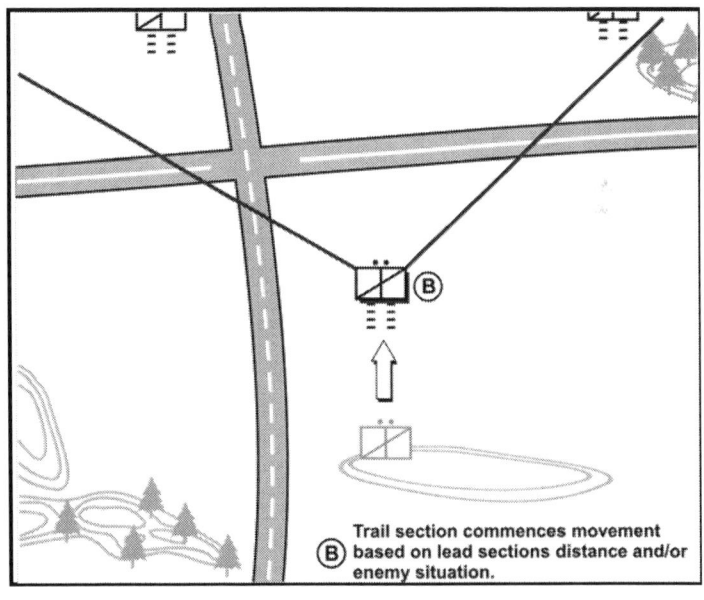

Figure 6-10. ABCT reconnaissance platoon conducts traveling overwatch formation - stop

Chapter 6

BOUNDING OVERWATCH

6-50. Employed when enemy contact is expected, bounding overwatch is the most deliberate and secure movement technique, with one element always stationary to provide overwatch. It provides for immediate direct fire suppression on an enemy force that engages the bounding element with direct fire. The trail element first occupies a covered and concealed position from which it can overwatch the lead element. The lead element, upon completing its movement (bound) occupies a similar covered and concealed position and provides overwatch as the trail element bounds forward to its next position. Bounding overwatch can be executed using one of the following methods:

- **Alternate bounds.** In this method, the trail element advances past the lead element to the next overwatch position. This is usually more rapid than successive bounds and creates a more stable fire platform and better position for the overwatching vehicle.
- **Successive bounds.** In successive bounding, the trail element moves to an overwatch position that is approximately abreast of the lead element. This method is slower but easier to control and more secure.

6-51. The reconnaissance platoon is required to execute bounding overwatch in some missions. METT-TC determines if the platoon uses alternate or successive bounding techniques. When available, CFVs should lead when enemy contact is likely because their increased lethality and survivability enable them to survive chance contact. LRAS3-equipped HMMWVs can enhance security and provide early warning to the CFVs. When enemy contact is unlikely, HMMWVs may lead the bounding. Using stealth, LRAS3, and dismounts to locate the enemy first, HMMWVs can direct the CFVs where to best engage the enemy.

6-52. Reconnaissance patrols can apply the bounding technique by team when enemy contact is likely. Scout sections, if required to move dismounted, may bound by squad. Dismounted scouts should use cover and concealment to remain undetected by enemy elements. If the scouts are bypassed, they can report the contact to the platoon or the overwatching elements. If scouts engage the enemy while dismounted, they break direct fire contact quickly. Dismounted reconnaissance patrols are not equipped for decisive engagements. Once a weapon is fired, the scout presence is known and the element of surprise is lost. Because close-quarter engagements often occur at a fast pace, dismounts ensure positive target identification to prevent fratricide.

6-53. "Move-set" is a mission command procedure to control elements using a bounding overwatch when moving. "Set" means that the element has arrived at its destination and has occupied a position from which it can observe to its front. This procedure triggers the overwatch element to move, allowing for the use of hand and arm signals, or signals via radio. "Move" is announced after "set" and means the overwatch element has transferred the overwatch responsibility to the stationary vehicle as it bounds forward to the next overwatch position. The move-set procedure can be used at all echelons for successive and alternating bounds.

Other Tactical Tasks

SECTION II – INFILTRATION/EXFILTRATION

INFILTRATION

6-54. Infiltration is a form of maneuver that the reconnaissance platoon uses to penetrate the threat security zone or main battle area to accomplish its mission. Infiltration often entails using stealthy forms of movement, including movement by aerial and waterborne platforms. (Refer to ATTP 3-20.97 for more information.) UAS assets may also be employed using infiltration to gain information if this is within system capabilities. Units planning this type of infiltration acknowledge the risk of the UAS being engaged and becoming unrecoverable.

PURPOSE

6-55. The primary focus of infiltration is to move to a designated point without being detected or engaged by the threat. During infiltration, the reconnaissance platoon elements use predesignated lanes to reach their objective. The infiltrating elements employ cover, concealment, and stealth to move through identified or templated gaps in the threat.

6-56. Dismounted reconnaissance elements infiltrate using a variety of movement methods. Infiltration may be conducted as an entire element at once or through movement into the area by echelon at different times.

6-57. Purposes for infiltration include—
- Reconnoitering a specified area and establishing OPs.
- Emplacing remote sensors.
- Establishing communications relay capability for a specific period in support of other reconnaissance tasks.
- Determining threat strengths and weaknesses.
- Locating unobserved routes through threat positions.
- Determining the location of high-payoff targets.
- Emplacing small unit kill teams for interdiction missions.
- Recovering the UAS to protect technologies from the enemy.
- Providing surveillance for follow-on echelons moving into the AO.

PLANNING

6-58. Infiltration imposes a number of distinct and often difficult operational considerations on the reconnaissance platoon. Methods of infiltration, extended operations time, reaction force requirements, CASEVAC resources, and escorted or covert exfiltration methods are taken into account when planning an infiltration.

6-59. The amount of intelligence information available to the commander during the planning process determines the risk involved in conducting the infiltration. Leaders conduct a thorough mission analysis, focusing on enemy activities in the areas of movement, historical locations of attacks, and likely areas of future engagements to prevent accidental contact.

6-60. While planning the mission, the commander conducts platoon analysis that includes selecting appropriate routes and movement techniques based on the mission, terrain and weather, likelihood of threat contact, expected or necessary speed of movement, and the depth to which elements penetrate. The commander's infiltration plan provides elements with enough time for preparation and initial movement. The initial plan should also cover a CASEVAC, evasion, extraction, and reinforcement plan, along with any special equipment requirements.

6-61. When executing infiltration tactics, leaders coordinate and integrate communications, fires, and sustainment activities prior to passing through friendly elements. The squadron also coordinates the activities of adjacent friendly units to ensure they do not compromise the troop and its elements. When possible, coordination should include UAS support, aerial or satellite imagery, and HUMINT briefings.

6-62. The size of the infiltrating elements depends on several factors:
- Mission.
- Time available.
- Cover and concealment.
- Target acquisition capabilities of friendly and threat forces.
- Available communications assets.
- Navigation capabilities and limitations.

6-63. If the troop is tasked to gather information over a wide area, platoons may employ several sections or small teams to cover the complete AO. In most situations, smaller elements are more suitable to take advantage of available cover and concealment. Another consideration is that some elements may not use infiltration. If moving into an AO in echelon, the first to arrive may infiltrate to a specific location, providing surveillance for follow-on echelons that are traveling with more conventional movement techniques. A reconnaissance patrol is typically composed of four scouts but it becomes more difficult for patrols to hide as the patrol size increases.

EXECUTION

6-64. The platoon's higher HQ assigns an infiltration lane or zone. After gathering the necessary information and intelligence to prepare for the mission, the platoon leader decides whether to move the entire platoon along a single lane or assign separate lanes for each section or vehicle.

6-65. Each alternative presents distinct advantages and disadvantages. Moving the entire platoon on a single lane makes navigation and movement easier to control, but also increases the chance that the platoon is detected by threat forces. Moving on

Other Tactical Tasks

multiple lanes can reduce the chances of detection by the threat. This may require the development of additional control measures, make mission command more difficult, and can create navigation problems.

6-66. In choosing infiltration lanes, the platoon leader ensures they afford sufficient width to allow each element to change its planned route to avoid enemy contact. Civilian activity along each lane (and within the infiltration zone as a whole) is also considered. The infiltration route should avoid obstacles, populated areas, and areas occupied or covered by enemy elements. Placing ridgelines, rivers, and other restricted terrain between the platoon and enemy forces provides cover and concealment. The plan should also make use of limited visibility and adverse weather.

6-67. As noted, the focus for the platoon during infiltration is to remain undetected and avoid contact with any enemy elements. In conjunction with IV lines, an IPB modified combined obstacle overlay and TerraBase (if available) can be used on templated enemy positions and dominant terrain to help refine route selection. Using TerraBase at various points of the infiltration route, the platoon leader determines where the route can be observed by the enemy, and identifies potential danger areas prior to moving into the AO. If time permits and assets are available, the UAS or dismounted patrols/observation may be used to proof the route and survey danger areas and influencing terrain. Use of the UAS is weighed carefully against the potential for compromising the infiltration route. If the enemy detects the UAS, it may be able to focus on suspected infiltration routes. On the other hand, information from the UAS can prevent a section moving into a manned outpost or dead space covered by sensors.

6-68. Multiple lane infiltration is the preferred method of infiltration for mounted and dismounted infiltration. The platoon infiltrates through the enemy by sections when multiple lanes have been identified. This method typically has one section moving at any time. Planning and coordination for the multiple lane infiltration is virtually the same as by echelon but increased coordination is required, the platoon execution is decentralized, and the platoon does not move all the sections through the same lane.

6-69. Each section sergeant should personally conduct linkup(s) and plan for specific targets along their route of movement. Platoon leaders plan supporting fires for each infiltration lane in case any sections are detected and engaged. The PSG plans for CASEVAC and possible extractions on more than one lane, to include moving with armor escort. In some instances, the platoon leader can plan to execute a patrol's extraction before it is clear of the infiltration lane. Platoons are careful not to overuse the UAS since excessive activity may give the enemy a hint of possible action, potentially compromising the sections.

Chapter 6

Communications

6-70. Infiltrating elements should maintain radio listening silence except to send critical information directed by the commander, or to report contact with threat forces. Message formats and communications windows should be established according to the unit SOP. When operating out of normal radio communications range, an infiltrating element transmitting required information should move to high ground or set up a long-range expedient antenna. If equipped, units may utilize high frequency and TACSAT for communications during long-range operations.

Fire Support

6-71. Infiltration plans should always include employment of indirect fires that are used only in limited circumstances. Planning includes any necessary restricted fire areas, restrictive fire lines, NFAs, and phase lines coordinated through the unit FIST and the battalion/squadron fire cell. The most common use of indirect fires is when the infiltrating unit makes threat contact. The reconnaissance platoon leader may employ indirect fires in other areas to divert attention away from the infiltration lanes. Indirect fires can also be useful in degrading the threat's acquisition and observation capabilities by forcing them to seek cover. The use of obscurant munitions (such as smoke) can have positive and negative effects. Scouts can employ obscurant to screen their movements through terrain, drawing the attention of observers. Obscuration may also be used to break contact from the enemy during an infiltration. In some cases, the obscurant may hinder the unit's ability to see enemy movements.

Actions on Contact

6-72. Each infiltrating element develops and rehearses a plan that clearly defines actions when faced with one or more of the eight forms of contact. If detected, an infiltrating element usually returns fire, breaks contact, and reports. Fighting through the threat force is the least preferred COA. Direct fire engagements are normally limited to whatever actions are required to break contact. To prevent compromise of their established locations and to retain the ability to report information, elements already established in the AO may choose not to provide direct FS for follow-on echelons in contact.

6-73. During an infiltration using multiple lanes, the detection of one element may alert the threat and compromise other units in the infiltration zone. The OPORD clearly states the criteria under which elements continue the mission or return to friendly lines if they are detected by the threat. If an element makes visual contact but is not detected, the mission should continue once it is certain that observation has not occurred.

EXFILTRATION

6-74. Exfiltration is the removal of personnel or units from areas under enemy control. The reconnaissance platoon and its elements may have to conduct exfiltration in certain tactical situations. Units that infiltrate an AO often have to conduct exfiltration once the required information has been gathered.

Planning

6-75. In all situations, exfiltration is planned as carefully as infiltration. Planning includes identifying casualty collection points (CCPs) and emergency resupply points along exfiltration routes, and providing supporting elements with a more secure, stealthy route into the AO. An effective exfiltration plan is essential in terms of mission accomplishment and morale. In most cases, planning for an exfiltration begins at the same time as planning for the infiltration (or other tactical operation) that precedes it. The platoon leader anticipates contingency measures that may be required if the elements conduct an unplanned exfiltration during a reconnaissance mission. The exfiltration plan should factor in additional time that the platoon may need to react to unforeseen circumstances, such as inadvertent contact with threat forces or unexpected restricted terrain.

6-76. Leaders plan to integrate indirect fire support and direct fires for protection during the exfiltration. The UAS can help locate overwatch or indirect fire positions, from which supporting assets can provide fires. Whether the unit plans to exfiltrate on foot or by another transport method (ground vehicles, aircraft, or watercraft), detailed planning is required to establish criteria for a passage of lines to minimize the chances of fratricide. The exfiltrating force is prepared to plan for contingencies once the mission is under way, particularly if threat contact occurs.

6-77. The exfiltration plan should also cover other types of contingencies that do not require the platoon to exfiltrate. For example, when a section or squad repeatedly misses mandatory radio contact it is assumed that the element has a communications problem, is in trouble, or both. The exfiltration plan might address this situation by calling for a resupply cache drop of new batteries and other means of communication at a predetermined location. The plan would mandate that the resupply location be specially marked to ensure that the equipment does not fall into enemy hands. Getting these supplies in place may require following infiltration methods already used by the platoon.

Movement Considerations

6-78. Urban areas create unique exfiltration challenges for the reconnaissance platoon. Mounted elements negotiating the route to the exfiltration point encounter buildings, narrow streets, scattered rubble, and debris which delays vehicle movement. The principles of route selection, movement formations, movement techniques (overwatch preferred), and movement security are critical to the success of the exfiltration. Plans for extraction by applicable means (ground, air, or water) are developed before the mission, covering procedural contingencies such as the loss of vehicles, evacuation of sick and wounded personnel, and disruption of communications. These plans should address various contingencies for movement, such as evasion. Hazards in the area of movement are avoided to improve the scout's chances of escape. Slow movement on narrow roads by displaced refugees and noncombatants create situations where the exfiltration is compromised.

6-79. Elements may use successful infiltration routes as their exfiltration routes. However, repeated movement in one area increases the likelihood of being detected and ambushed. The more vehicles involved in the extraction, the greater the noise signature.

6-80. The methods used for platoon exfiltration route selection are the same as those discussed for infiltration earlier in this section. The platoon leader ensures that primary and alternate linkup points are not on a single azimuth leading away from the OP or exfiltration route.

6-81. Extraction points for dismounted personnel should be far enough away from the OP to ensure the enemy does not hear vehicle or helicopter noises. The exfiltrating force uses mountains, dense foliage, and other terrain features to screen these noises. Under normal conditions in flat, open terrain on a clear night, rotary-wing aircraft lose most of their audio signature at a distance of approximately five kilometers. Rolling terrain can assist in hiding vehicle sounds as long as they maintain low engine noise. In mountainous terrain, aircraft conducting the extraction can be seen or detected much easier when enemy observers are in place on hilltops offering superior observation. Mounted infiltration faces challenges based on the vehicles used. The larger tracked vehicles used for mounted exfiltration or extraction (such as CFVs and Abrams tanks) encounter more mobility restrictions due to their size, and require dismounts for security at the halt. In the urban areas, exfiltration routes may be down narrow roads and alleys to mask movement. Extraction points may be easily hidden among the materials and debris found in the urban area. While the actual point may be in buildings or in open areas such as an intersection, a patrol may use surface (or below surface) hide locations to avoid detection. This may include inside and outside of buildings. Scouts avoid detection since they are not prepared to fight decisive engagements. Exfiltration in the urban environment requires movement in and around multistory buildings that can conceal movement, and provide advantageous enemy locations with superior fields of view for engaging scouts.

EXECUTION
6-82. Extraction is conducted by air, water, or land. Each alternative presents the platoon with specific operational considerations, and tactical advantages and disadvantages. The exfiltration plan and the OPORD address these factors, and operational contingencies such as actions the reconnaissance unit takes if an unplanned extraction becomes necessary.

6-83. Extraction by air or water is preferred when resources are available and their use does not compromise the mission. These methods are used when long distances are covered, time of return is essential, extraction zone lacks adequate cover and concealment, the enemy does not have air or naval superiority, or ground extraction is obstructed by complex terrain or heavily populated hostile areas.

6-84. Reconnaissance forces normally conduct extraction via land routes when friendly lines are close or no other extraction method is feasible. Ground extraction is preferred when areas along the route are largely uninhabited, and enemy forces

Other Tactical Tasks

are widely dispersed or under such pressure that they cannot conduct counterreconnaissance and security tasks. When terrain is sufficiently restricted to diminish enemy efforts using mobile forces against the exfiltrating/extracting reconnaissance unit, ground extraction is preferred.

6-85. The reconnaissance platoon may have to conduct emergency exfiltration if it is detected or engaged by a threat force. This type of mission requires activation of an escape and evasion plan, or deployment of a reaction or support force to assist with the extraction of friendly elements. Employment of the reaction force and supporting fires is carefully coordinated and rehearsed before the insertion and infiltration (or other tactical mission, if applicable) is initiated. In all situations, the heavier the support, the louder the sound signature becomes. All reconnaissance platoon leaders should be involved in the coordination and rehearsal of these assets since they are most likely to assist in the exfiltration and extraction of their scouts. If possible, exfiltration should be conducted during periods of limited visibility to conceal movement of friendly forces.

SECTION III – PATROL BASES AND COMBAT OUTPOSTS

PATROL BASES

6-86. A patrol base is a position with a security perimeter that is set up when a dismounted team conducting a patrol halts for an extended period. Except in an emergency, patrol bases should be occupied no longer than 24 hours. The platoon or section never uses the same patrol base twice. Platoons and sections use patrol bases to —

- Stop all movement to avoid detection.
- Hide during a long, detailed reconnaissance of an objective area.
- Clean weapons and equipment, perform personal hygiene, eat, and rest.
- Plan and issue orders.
- Reorganize after infiltrating an enemy area.
- Establish a base from which to conduct several consecutive or concurrent tasks such as ambush, raid, reconnaissance, or security.

SITE SELECTION

6-87. The leader selects the tentative site from a map or by aerial reconnaissance. The site's suitability is confirmed and secured before the unit moves into it. Plans to establish a patrol base include selecting an alternate patrol base site. The alternate site is used if the first site is unsuitable or the patrol unexpectedly evacuates the first patrol base. Leaders planning for a patrol base consider the mission and passive and active security measures. Security measures involve selecting terrain that—

- The enemy most likely considers of little tactical value.
- Is off main lines of drift, and affords adequate cover and concealment.

Chapter 6

- Impedes foot movement, such as an area of dense vegetation.
- Is near a source of water.
- Can be defended for a short period of time.
- Avoids ridges and hilltops, except as needed for maintaining communications.

6-88. The leader plans for—
- Observation posts and communication with observation posts.
- Defense of the patrol base.
- Withdrawal from the patrol base, including withdrawal routes and a rally point, rendezvous point, or an alternate patrol base.
- A continuous security system employing passive and active measures completely covering the perimeter all the time, regardless of the percentage of weapons used to cover the entire terrain.
- Enforcement of camouflage, noise, and light discipline.
- The conduct of required activities with minimum movement and noise.

PATROL BASE OCCUPATION

6-89. The patrol base is reconnoitered and established using the same procedures and considerations as an ORP or reentry rally point. The exception is when the platoon finds it necessary to enter the patrol base at a 90-degree turn. This turn is METT-TC dependent. If there is nothing to be gained by doing this step, then the unit does not do it (for example, on flat desert terrain).

6-90. The patrol leader leaves a two-man OP at the turn. The assistant patrol leader and the last patrol element obliterate any tracks from the turn into the patrol base. The patrol moves into the base (see Figure 6-11), and the patrol leader immediately announces the location of the alternate patrol base.

Other Tactical Tasks

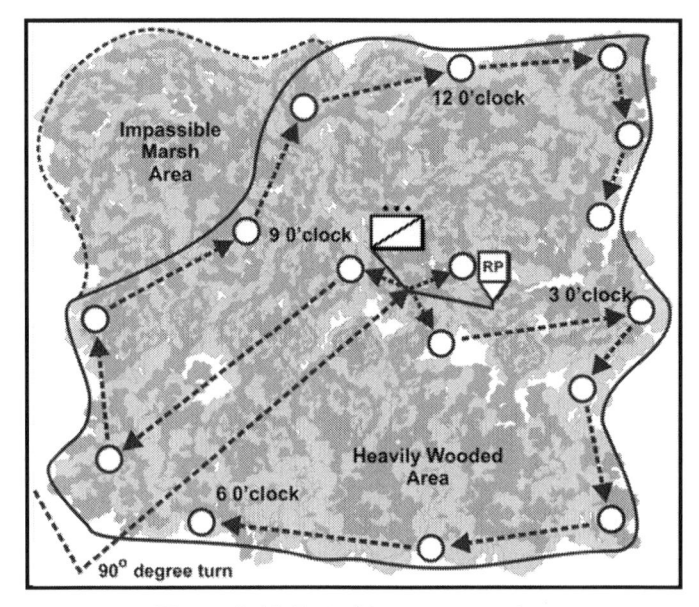

Figure 6-11. Patrol base occupation

6-91. Starting at 6 o'clock, the patrol leader and support element adjust the perimeter by moving clockwise, to meet each element leader at the element's left flank. If the patrol leader and support element leader find a better location for one of the machine guns, they reposition it. Following the sector inspection, all three element leaders plus a patrol member from each element report to the CP as R&S teams. The patrol leader issues a five-point contingency plan reminding the teams they are looking for the enemy, water, built-up areas or human habitat, roads and trails, and any possible rally points.

6-92. If the patrol leader feels the patrol may have been tracked, complete the security procedures and wait in total silence before sending out the R&S teams. The distance the R&S teams move away from the element's sector varies depending upon the terrain and vegetation (anywhere from 200 to 400 meters). All members of the patrol are on 100 percent alert during this time.

6-93. After all element leaders (through their R&S teams) complete their reconnaissance, they report back to the patrol leader at the CP. Information gathered from the R&S teams determines if the patrol is able to use the location as a patrol base.

Patrol Base Activities

6-94. The patrol leader informs the assistant patrol leader and squad/section leaders if the location is a patrol base, and disseminates information such as communication frequencies, call signs, and daily challenge and password. Leaders

Chapter 6

return to their elements, pass along the information, and begin the priorities of work as stated by the patrol leader. Information that is disseminated includes:

- Security.
- Alert plan.
- Withdrawal plan.
- Maintenance plan.
- Sanitation and personal hygiene locations.

Passive (Clandestine) Patrol Base

6-95. The purpose of a passive patrol base is to give a smaller-size element time to rest. A Claymore mine is emplaced on the route entering the patrol base. Teams sit back-to-back facing outward, ensuring that at least one individual per team is alert and providing security.

COMBAT OUTPOSTS

6-96. A reconnaissance platoon may conduct missions from a combat outpost equipped with automatic and crew-served weapons, communications equipment, and sensors supported by indirect fires. Platoons assigned to combat outposts may be augmented with additional combat elements such as UAS teams, Infantry, Armor, and engineers that provide assistance in reconnaissance and offensive actions to counter enemy activities. This is a labor-intensive mission and is used only in response to clearly defined squadron/battalion requirements.

6-97. Combat outposts are also used to protect critical lengths or locations along the route. (Refer to Chapter 3.) Due to the length of some convoy routes, a squadron or troop establishes mutually supporting platoon-size combat outposts, and provides security between them. Combat outposts are established at critical choke points to prevent sabotage and defend against or respond to attacks. While providing continuous surveillance along key points of the route, reconnaissance platoons may be enlarged to supply reaction forces, engineer route clearance assets, and insurgent intervention elements. Patrols are organized with sufficient combat power to destroy near ambushes and survive initial enemy contact from far ambushes. Platoons conduct patrols at irregular intervals between the outposts based on enemy trends and recent activities.

6-98. Each combat outpost maintains a reaction force that responds to enemy activity or reinforces patrols. Based on METT-TC, a troop establishes one or two platoon combat outposts, and a squadron typically establishes up to six platoon-size combat outposts.

SECTION IV – DIRECT FIRE PLANNING

6-99. Reconnaissance platoon leaders plan direct fires in conjunction with estimated development of the situation, completion of the plan, and during actions

Other Tactical Tasks

on contact. Determining where and how the platoon can mass fires is an essential step for the platoon leader developing a concept of the operation.

6-100. After identifying probable enemy locations, the platoon leader determines points or areas to focus combat power. Visualization of where and how the enemy might attack or defend helps determine the volume of fires to focus that have a decisive effect at particular points. If massing the fires of more than one subordinate element is planned, there is an effective means for distributing fires.

6-101. Additionally, the platoon leader evaluates the risk of fratricide and establishes controls to prevent it. These measures include designation of recognition markings, weapons control status, and weapons safety posture.

6-102. After determining where and how fires are massed and distributed, the platoon leader then orients elements so they can rapidly and accurately acquire the enemy. During preparation, the platoon leader plans and conducts rehearsals of direct fires and the fire control process based on the estimated situation.

6-103. The platoon leader continues to apply planning procedures and considerations throughout execution, adjusting direct fires based on a continuously updated estimate of the situation. When necessary, effective direct fire SOPs are applied.

DIRECT FIRE STANDARD OPERATING PROCEDURE

6-104. A well-rehearsed direct fire SOP ensures quick, predictable actions by all members of the platoon. Various elements of the SOP are based on the capabilities of the platoon, and anticipated conditions and situations. SOP topics should include means for focusing fires, distributing their effects, orienting forces, and preventing fratricide. The SOP should be adjusted whenever changes to anticipated and actual METT-TC factors become apparent.

6-105. If the engagement was not initiated by higher HQ, the platoon begins the engagement using this SOP. The platoon leader can subsequently use a fire command to refocus or redistribute fires.

FOCUSING FIRES

6-106. Target reference points are a common means of focusing fires. One technique is to establish TRPs in relation to friendly elements and then consistently number them, such as from left to right. This allows leaders to quickly determine and communicate the locations.

DISTRIBUTING FIRES

6-107. Two useful means of distributing the platoon's fires are engagement priority and target array. An engagement priority assigns each type of friendly weapon system to an enemy vehicle or weapon. The target array technique assists in distribution by assigning specific friendly elements to engage enemy elements with similar capabilities.

ORIENTING FORCES

6-108. A standard means of orienting friendly forces is assigning a primary direction of fire using a TRP that orients each element on a probable enemy position or likely avenue of approach. To provide all-around security, the SOP can supplement the primary direction of fire with sectors using a friendly-based quadrant. The following example of SOP topics illustrate the use of these techniques:

- The center (front) element's primary direction of fire is TRP 2 (center) until otherwise specified. The element is responsible for the front two quadrants.
- The left flank element's primary direction of fire is TRP 1 (left) until otherwise specified. The element is responsible for the left two friendly quadrants (overlapping with the center element).
- The right flank element's primary direction of fire is TRP 3 (right) until otherwise specified. The element is responsible for the right two friendly quadrants (overlapping with the center element).

ENGAGEMENT AREA DEVELOPMENT

6-109. The engagement area is where the platoon leader intends to destroy an enemy force using the massed fires of all available weapons. The success of any engagement depends on how effectively the platoon leader integrates the obstacle plan, indirect fire plan, direct fire plan, and the terrain within the engagement area to achieve the tactical purpose. Beginning with evaluation of METT-TC factors, the development process covers these steps:

- Identify all likely enemy avenues of approach.
- Determine likely enemy schemes of maneuver.
- Determine where to kill the enemy.
- Emplace weapon systems.
- Plan and integrate obstacles.
- Plan and integrate indirect fires.
- Rehearse the execution of tasks in the engagement area.

IDENTIFY LIKELY AREAS OF ENEMY APPROACH

6-110. The following procedures and considerations apply when identifying the enemy's likely avenues of approach:

- Conduct initial reconnaissance along each avenue of approach into the sector or engagement area (from the enemy's perspective, if possible).
- Identify key and decisive terrain, including locations that afford positions of advantage, natural obstacles, and choke points that restrict forward movement.

Other Tactical Tasks

- Determine which avenues provide cover and concealment while maintaining tempo, and what terrain is likely to be used to support each avenue.
- Evaluation of lateral routes adjoining each avenue of approach.

DETERMINE THE ENEMY SCHEME OF MANEUVER

6-111. The platoon leader can use the following considerations to determine the enemy's scheme of maneuver:

- How can the attack be structured? What formation can be used and how can the forces sequence?
- How can reconnaissance assets be used? Can friendly positions be infiltrated?
- Where and when can formations change and support-by-fire positions be established?
- Where, when, and how can assault and breaching tasks take place?
- Where are favorable OP locations and what terrain is likely to be employed for supporting fires?
- Where and when can follow-on forces be committed?
- What is the expected rate of movement?
- What are the effects of combat multipliers?
- What reactions are likely in response to projected friendly actions?

DETERMINE WHERE TO ENGAGE THE ENEMY

6-112. Use the following steps to mark where the company and platoon engages the enemy:

- Find TRPs that match the enemy's scheme of maneuver, allowing the platoon to identify where it engages enemy forces through the depth of the sector.
- Establish and record the exact location of each TRP.
- Determine how many weapon systems focus fires on each TRP to achieve the desired effect.
- Decide which elements conduct mass fires on each TRP.
- Create engagement areas around TRPs.
- Develop the direct fire planning measures necessary to focus fires at each TRP.

EMPLACE WEAPON SYSTEMS

6-113. The following steps apply in selecting and improving BPs, and emplacing crew-served weapon systems and vehicle positions:

- Select tentative BPs. When possible, select these positions while moving in the engagement area. Using the enemy's perspective enables the platoon leader to assess the survivability of positions.
- Conduct a leader's reconnaissance of the tentative BPs.

- Traverse the engagement area to confirm that selected positions are tactically advantageous.
- Confirm and mark the selected BPs.
- Ensure that BPs do not conflict with those of adjacent units, and that they are effectively tied-in with adjacent positions.
- Select primary, alternate, supplementary, and subsequent fighting positions to achieve the desired effect for each TRP.
- Ensure weapon systems are positioned so that the number of weapons effectively covers each TRP.

PLAN AND INTEGRATE OBSTACLES

6-114. The goal of obstacle planning is to support the higher commander's intent through optimum obstacle emplacement and integration with fires. Obstacles allow the enemy into the engagement area and then fix him there. The focus at the squadron/CAB-level and below is the actual integration of fires and obstacles. At the platoon level, obstacle planning deals with the actual sighting and emplacement of individual obstructions within the obstacle groups. The following steps apply in planning and integrating obstacles in the platoon defense:

- Understand obstacle group intent.
- Coordinate with the engineers.
- Site and mark individual obstacle locations.
- Employ combat elements to provide security for the engineers as they emplace obstacles.
- Mark fire control measures such as TRPs and artillery targets in the engagement area (overwatching element).
- Enter the engagement area and move to the far side of the proposed trace of the obstacle group (engineers).
- Collocate in the defensive positions covering the obstacle (engineer squad/platoon leader and reconnaissance platoon leader).
- Move along the proposed trace of the obstacle group (engineer elements).
- Follow the movement of the engineers from the defensive position, ensuring that all points of the obstacle trace can be covered with fires (leaders).
- Maintain communication with the engineers via radio or FBCB2 leaders).
- Refine the obstacle plan, adjusting the position of individual obstacles as necessary (platoon leader and engineer squad leader).
- Refine direct and indirect fire control measures.
- Identify lanes and gaps.
- Report obstacle locations and gaps to higher HQ.

PLAN AND INTEGRATE INDIRECT FIRES

6-115. The following steps apply in planning and integrating indirect fires:
- Determine the purpose of fires and any essential task(s) for fire support.

Other Tactical Tasks

- Determine where the purpose can best be achieved.
- Establish the observation plan, with redundancy for each target. Observers include the FIST, as well as members of maneuver elements with fire support responsibilities such as the PSG and section leaders.
- Establish triggers.
- Obtain accurate target locations.
- Refine target locations to ensure coverage of obstacles.
- Adjust artillery and mortar targets, if the situation permits.
- Plan final protective fires.
- Request close fire zones for protection of maneuver elements and no fire areas for protection of observation posts and forward positions.

SECTION V – ASSEMBLY AREAS

6-116. An assembly area is a site where a parent unit regroups into a complete unit or prepares for future operations. Normally, a reconnaissance platoon occupies a location within an assembly area as part of its parent unit, but it may occupy its own assembly area independently. Once in the assembly area, the platoon prepares and issues orders, conducts resupply tasks, repairs and maintains vehicles and equipment, and feeds and rests its Soldiers. A platoon deployed in training or in an AO may refer to that area as a tactical assembly area. (Refer to FM 3-20.96, FM 3-20.971, and ATTP 3-20.97 for more information.)

CHARACTERISTICS

6-117. The platoon, or a part of it operating within a quartering party, is often directed to find, secure, and occupy an assembly area. There are certain characteristics the scouts look for when selecting the assembly area:

- Concealment from observation.
- Cover from direct fire.
- Passable entrances, exits, and internal roads.
- Enough space for dispersion of vehicles, personnel, and equipment.
- Adequate defensibility and fields of fire.
- Good drainage and a ground surface that supports the platoon's and parent unit's vehicles.

QUARTERING PARTY RESPONSIBILITIES

6-118. Whether the platoon is operating as part of its parent unit or on its own, scouts may have to assume quartering party duties. Understanding these duties makes occupying the assembly area much easier. The quartering party's mission is to reconnoiter the area for enemy presence and booby traps, designate vehicle locations, prepare the area for occupation, and assist incoming units during the occupation. Site selection takes into account activities that occur in the assembly area, including allowing a smaller unit or detachment such as CA, military intelligence, or civilians evacuated by the unit, to move out of the assembly area on short notice.

6-119. The entire platoon may also serve as the unit quartering party, but it is better to draw on elements from each platoon so they are able to lead their own unit into designated vehicle positions. The quartering party for a CAB may require the entire reconnaissance platoon and include some attachments. If the platoon is part of a unit, the quartering party moves to the new assembly area under the control of the unit XO or unit 1SG. The following discussion outlines the primary responsibilities of the quartering party as conducted by a platoon. If the quartering party is comprised of elements from different platoons, the process is the same but individuals report to the XO or 1SG.

RECONNOITER THE AREA

6-120. The first task of the quartering party is to conduct an area reconnaissance of the assembly area to find enemy forces, obstacles, and CBRNE contamination. This is a time-consuming process that is planned by the parent unit. Once the area has been cleared of any possible enemy forces, it is secured to prevent enemy infiltration. To do this, the quartering party establishes OPs and conducts security patrols. The UAS may be employed for covering dead space and avenues of approach beyond the line of sight that allows access to the assembly area to the enemy.

DETERMINE ASSEMBLY AREA SUITABILITY

6-121. Once the area is secure, the platoon leader or platoon sergeant conducts a reconnaissance to verify the region's suitability, and position guides and markings. This task can be conducted in conjunction with the initial area reconnaissance. When checking the position for suitability, the quartering party analyzes cover and concealment, drainage, routes into and out of the locale, internal routes, defensibility, and fields of fire. It designates positions on the ground for the various elements within the assembly area. If the environment is unsatisfactory, the scouts should immediately begin looking for an alternate site to recommend to the platoon leader.

Mark or Remove Obstacles and Mines

6-122. If there is a possibility of mines or cluster bomb units in the assembly area, additional scouts or combat engineers with mine-detection equipment should be requested before the quartering party departs. Obstacle and mine clearance requires prior planning for the proper equipment, including pioneer tools, demolitions, or engineer vehicles. The use of demolitions to neutralize or reduce obstacles or mines is avoided since this alerts enemy sensors that there is activity in the area. Sufficient time is allocated to allow the quartering party to accomplish this mission before the main body arrives.

Organize the Area

6-123. Once the organization of the assembly area is complete, the quartering party marks the positions, entrance and exit, and routes from the RP. Internal routes are marked with materiels such as infrared chem lights, engineer tape, unit tactical signs, flashlights, VS-17 panels, and thermal tape according to the SOP. This helps prevent excessive movement.

Perform Guide Duties

6-124. Guides are thoroughly briefed so they know the proper route from the RP to the new positions. This allows for swift and efficient occupation. Vehicle commanders rely on the guides to reach their designated positions. To reduce their sound signature, vehicles avoid unnecessary movement. Sound is most notable at dusk and dawn.

6-125. The guides are positioned between the RP and the assembly area entrance so they can meet their unit as it crosses the RP and quickly direct the vehicles or personnel to their tentative positions. Once present, all personnel account for their sensitive items, reporting through the platoon leader and PSG. Immediately afterward, the platoon leader briefs the vehicle commanders or section leaders on refining vehicle positions, sectors of fire, location of the CP, adjacent units, alternate assembly area, and any other essential information.

Accomplish Additional Assigned Tasks

6-126. The platoon leader designates a priority of tasks that allows the most important to be accomplished first. These tasks may include providing security for the command group, test-firing weapons, and assisting in traffic control.

OCCUPATION OF AN ASSEMBLY AREA

6-127. When the platoon arrives at an assembly area, all elements move off the route of march without slowing or halting. The platoon leader should keep this in mind as he posts guides, selects routes, and allocates space. After a march serial has cleared the route, it can adjust vehicle positions without holding up traffic. The lead element links up with the guide and follows instructions to the platoon positions. It is important that the lead element pass information such as entrance markings, route information, and vehicle position marking methods to the other elements.

ACTIONS IN THE ASSEMBLY AREA

6-128. Immediately after the platoon occupies its area, it executes the priority of tasks. These should be identified in the unit SOP. Initial tasks may include—

- Positioning vehicles.
- Establishing local security.
- Contacting adjacent elements.
- Developing range cards or sector sketches and submitting them to the platoon leader for inclusion in the platoon fire plan. Scouts may have to adjust their positions accordingly.

Chapter 6

- Camouflaging positions.
- Performing PMCS.
- Initiating and maintaining OPSEC.

6-129. Security is a constant concern in assembly areas. Noise and light discipline are especially important, as is limiting the number of vehicles that enter and exit the assembly area. The initial local security is replaced by OPs once the platoon is in position, and deploy in accordance with procedures outlined in Chapter 4. The platoon leader may require patrols along the perimeter and within the assembly area, especially during periods of limited visibility. Wire and messengers are the primary means of communication. Radio is used only in emergencies when no other means of communication are available. The platoon conducts sensitive item checks prior to departure and requests permission to depart or reenter the assembly area.

DEPARTING THE ASSEMBLY AREA

6-130. Departing an assembly area is a critical and often overlooked task. A well-organized departure sets up the platoon for its next mission, but a poorly organized departure can cause delays and other problems that may adversely affect the mission before it begins. Evidence of the platoon's occupation is removed to deny the enemy any equipment, supplies, or other items (including trash) of tactical or intelligence value. The unit SOP addresses the steps to take that ensures no equipment is forgotten.

SECTION VI – LINKUP

6-131. A linkup is a meeting of friendly ground forces. A reconnaissance platoon may conduct linkup in the following situations:
- Conducting reconnaissance handover.
- Reaching an objective that has been previously seized.
- An encircled element breaks out to rejoin friendly forces.
- Converging forces meet.
- During a passage of lines.

6-132. Linkup can be as simple as a section leader meeting another section leader from a unit on the other side of a lateral boundary, or as complex as a platoon leading a company or CAB to the rear of a unit that requires support and supplies. (Refer to FM 3-20.96, FM 3-20.971, and ATTP 3-20.97 for more information.)

FORMS OF LINKUP

6-133. There are two forms of linkup tasks: a linkup of moving and stationary forces, and a linkup of two moving forces. Both units have a linkup point and other requirements stated in their OPORD and annotated on their graphics. This information can also be posted in the FBCB2 system.

Other Tactical Tasks

LINKUP OF A MOVING FORCE AND A STATIONARY FORCE

6-134. To ensure forces achieve linkup without committing fratricide, linkup points are selected at locations where the advance of the moving force intersects elements of the stationary force. These points are recognizable to both forces, and depend on the terrain and number of routes used by the moving force. Personnel in the moving and stationary forces are familiar with near/far recognition signals, SOPs, and CID procedures. The stationary force supports the linkup by breaching or removing selected obstacles, furnishing guides, and designating assembly areas.

LINKUP OF TWO MOVING UNITS

6-135. Linkup between two moving units is conducted to complete the encirclement of an enemy force. Primary and alternate linkup points are established on boundaries where the two forces are expected to converge. As linkup units move closer, they use fire control measures to prevent fratricide and interdict the enemy to prevent escape.

Planning Considerations

6-136. The headquarters directing the linkup establishes the command relationship between the platoon and the other force, specifies responsibilities of each force, and directs the linkup. If HQ cannot adequately control the mission, responsibility is delegated to one of the forces involved. Often the moving force is placed under control of the stationary force, or the force out of contact is placed under OPCON of the force in contact.

6-137. If the enemy is between the forces conducting a linkup, coordination is accomplished by radio or through digital systems. During the mission, the two forces attempt to maintain continuous radio contact with each other. Before initiating a linkup, the HQ elements of both forces share SA data, including—

- Digital graphic overlays with linkup graphic control measures, obstacles, and fire support coordination measures.
- Manual/digital identification procedures.
- Manual/digital recognition signals.
- Enemy and friendly situations.
- Communications.
- Contingency plans.

6-138. The communications plan includes radio frequencies, digital communications, SOI, and COMSEC variables. The plan establishes recognition signals (day, night, and limited visibility) to prevent fratricide.

6-139. Linkup tasks may require the platoon to resupply the other unit. If sustainment requirements exceed the haul capability of the platoon, the platoon leader may have to request additional vehicles, or resupply by air. It is typically the PSGs responsibility to coordinate and manage these assets.

6-140. Evacuation of equipment, EPWs, or detainees can create problems for reconnaissance platoons. Typically, the 1SG moves forward to a CCP to take on wounded and EPWs, recover inoperable vehicles or equipment, and transfer supplies. When ground routes are not secure, helicopters may be used for evacuation of the wounded. Damaged equipment may be moved forward with the linkup forces until a suitable opportunity for evacuation is available.

6-141. Additional planning considerations for linkup tasks include:
- Distance to the linkup.
- Time the objective area is to be held.
- Planned missions or movement out of the objective area.
- Resupply of the linkup force.
- Movement of fire support and sustainment assets involved in the linkup.
- Whether follow-on forces will secure lines of communication.

Preparation

6-142. Due to the time-sensitive nature of the mission, the platoon leader issues orders and attempts to rehearse the critical events of the mission with subordinate leaders and vehicle commanders. Areas of particular emphasis include movement along the route, reaction to contact, protection of escorted vehicles, contingency planning up to the linkup point, and actions to ensure that linkup coordination is executed without confusion.

6-143. The platoon leader ensures linkup units have the higher unit's fire support plan, current enemy situation, and FBCB2 updates. If any control measures are changed during the mission, updates are sent to both elements.

6-144. Sustainment elements moving with the platoon organize and stay close to combat forces for security. Due to their forward location, the reconnaissance platoon may receive resupply from another company within the squadron/CAB when HHC is not able to move forward to support their sections. The platoon leader thoroughly briefs these elements on movement, actions on contact, and actions at the linkup point.

Execution

6-145. Depending on the enemy situation, the initial conduct of the linkup is similar to a zone reconnaissance. As the platoon begins its maneuver at the SP, the platoon leader establishes long-range communications stating that movement has started. Short-range communications with the other friendly force is set up prior to the near recognition point. Through the use of FBCB2, reports of enemy forces can be monitored throughout the mission, giving the platoon leader time to react to changes.

6-146. As the two forces draw closer, the tempo of the mission slows to help prevent fratricide. Each force uses coordinated signals to identify itself as it

Other Tactical Tasks

approaches the linkup point. The forces should be able to monitor each other's location via FBCB2 and radio, and take the appropriate actions to control the physical linkup. Fire support coordination measures are changed based on the progress of the forces and the enemy situation. If necessary, the linkup point can be moved in accordance with the stated timeline.

6-147. Once the scouts have moved into the urban area undetected, the gaining unit guides the vehicles into a secure position to unload supplies and begin loading wounded, EPWs, and items gathered during site exploitation. Once all requirements for the linkup are met, the reconnaissance platoon acts as a security escort for the returning vehicles, establishing long-range communications with the tactical operations center (TOC), and reporting when the SP has been crossed. FSCMs can also be moved as necessary.

SECTION VII – PASSAGE OF LINES

OVERVIEW

6-148. A passage of lines is the controlled movement of one unit through the positions of a stationary unit. It is conducted so that neither unit interferes with the other's scheme of maneuver, and is often necessary because the combat situation does not permit one unit to bypass another unit's position. (Refer to FM 3-20.96 for more information.)

6-149. The reconnaissance platoon is often tasked with this mission as it begins a zone, area, or route reconnaissance, occupies a screen, or executes a guard mission. These are all examples of the unit moving towards the enemy and are considered a forward passage of lines. When a reconnaissance platoon is conducting a cover mission or displacing from a screen line, they may move away from the enemy and be required to conduct a rearward passage of lines.

6-150. A passage of lines is conducted for the following purposes:
- Continuing an attack or counterattack.
- Enveloping a threat force.
- Pursuing a fleeing threat.
- Withdrawing security or main battle area forces.
- Facilitating route, zone, or area reconnaissance.
- Executing a defense or a delay.
- Executing a screen or guard.

PLANNING

6-151. The platoon may perform screen and reconnaissance tasks independently. Participation in a passage of lines is usually part of the RHO. The three key elements in a passage of lines are the stationary unit, passing unit, and the common commander. (See Figure 6-12.)

Chapter 6

6-152. The reconnaissance platoon, acting independently or as part of a larger element, may be the stationary or passing unit. It normally assists in some portion of the passage of lines and may be required to coordinate the passage. In many cases, the platoon is required to conduct a passage separate from the squadron.

6-153. The platoon leader exercising command authority over the stationary and passing units designates the reconnaissance handover line (RHL) or battle handover line (BHL). This is a phase line forward of the stationary unit that is recognizable on the ground. It is done in coordination with the stationary unit commander, who recommends the position of the RHL/BHL. The line is drawn where elements of the passing unit can be effectively protected by direct fires of the forward combat elements of the stationary unit until the passage of lines is complete. The area between the RHL/BHL and the stationary force is the responsibility of the stationary unit commander, who provides graphic control measures to the unit depicting the RHL/BHL and contact points. This overlay is issued to subordinate units with the OPORD or FRAGORD.

6-154. Reconnaissance/battle handover begins on the common commander's order. Defensive handover is complete when the passing unit is clear and the stationary unit is ready to engage the threat. Offensive handover is complete when the passing unit has deployed and crossed the RHL/BHL. The common commander prescribes specific criteria that marks the completion of handover, and ensures that both subordinate commanders understand the criteria.

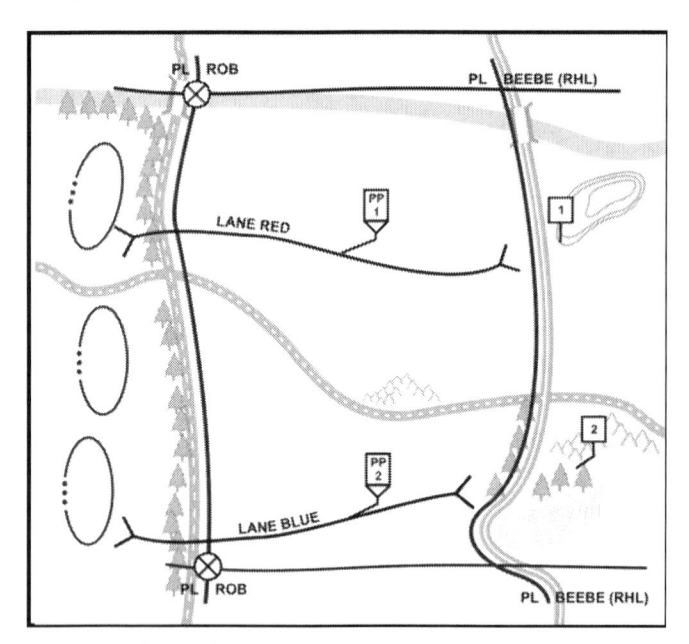

Figure 6-12. Reconnaissance handover

Other Tactical Tasks

PASSING UNIT CRITICAL TASKS

6-155. The passing unit accomplishes several critical tasks during the passage of lines in RHO/BHO, including—

- Establishing communications immediately, entering the command, intelligence, and FS nets of the stationary unit.
- Collocating a unit or vehicle with the tactical air coordinator (TAC) CP or main CP of the stationary unit as soon as possible to enhance communication and unity of effort.
- Continuously reporting to the stationary unit during a rearward passage the location, size, composition, and current activity of all threat forces. If the threat is attacking, the passing unit reports the direction of movement, movement formation, and estimated rate of advance. If the threat is defending, the passing unit reports threat locations, orientation, composition, engagement area reserves (if known), obstacle systems, and flanks.
- Continuously reporting to the stationary unit the location, size, and activity of all parent unit elements, including augmentation, sustainment, and mission command assets.
- Coordinating with the stationary unit based upon the current dispositions of the parent unit to determine contact points for subordinate elements (such as reconnaissance sections) to synchronize handover and passage of lines with representatives of the stationary unit. Once contact points are determined, the passing unit leader sends a FRAGORD to all elements specifying the location for the passage with the stationary unit. The passing unit confirms recognition signals used during passage.
- Ensuring that subordinate elements acknowledge where to coordinate the passage and that representatives are dispatched to the assigned contact points. At the contact points, the representatives confirm recognition signals and exchange required information with their counterparts from the stationary unit.
- Maintaining visual contact with all threat units in a rearward passage, conducting movement back to the RHL/BHL, and avoiding decisive engagement.
- Displaying correct recognition signals and using the correct challenge and password as specified in the SOI during the passage.
- Maintaining proper weapons orientation.

STATIONARY UNIT CRITICAL TASKS

6-156. The stationary unit accomplishes a variety of critical tasks when ordered to conduct a passage of lines during RHO/BHO. These tasks include—

- Establishing communications, coordinating necessary contact points, and directing the passing unit to the contact points based on current dispositions of the designated units.
- Exchanging fire support plans; this also includes target lists and FS contact frequencies.

- Guaranteeing contact points are manned and secured, and that passing elements have established personal communication with their representatives.
- Ensuring representatives at the contact points assign each passing element a passage point into the AO, and a route that extends from the passage points to the rear boundary or assembly area (in a rearward passage) or to the attack position (in a forward passage).
- Exchanging required information, including FBCB2, with the passing unit as outlined in their unit SOP.
- Positioning elements to overwatch the RHL/BHL where they have the best possible observation of threat avenues of approach, adjusting as necessary during limited visibility.
- Ensuring routes through an obstacle system are clearly marked and physically controlled by guides, or escorts are provided to the passing unit.
- Guaranteeing all routes of withdrawal obligated to the passing unit are unobstructed and facilitate rapid movement to the rearward passage.
- Ensuring obligated routes of advance, attack positions, and routes to the RHL/BHL are clear and facilitate rapid movement (forward passage).

PREPARATION

6-157. Units are particularly vulnerable during a passage of lines. Effective preparation is critical because subordinate elements may be concentrated, stationary unit fires may be temporarily masked, and the passing unit may not be disposed properly to react to threat action. To assist in preparing for the passage, the commander may task subordinate units with a number of missions, including detailed reconnaissance and coordination.

GRAPHIC CONTROL MEASURES

6-158. Graphic control measures for passage of lines are illustrated in Figure 6-13 (forward passage) and Figure 6-14 (rearward passage). Graphic control measures include considerations such as—

- **Reconnaissance/battle handover line.** The RHL/BHL is established by the common leader of the unit in consultation with both commanders. The stationary unit leader determines the location of the RHL/BHL and overwatches the line with direct fires.
- **Fire support coordination measures.** If necessary, these are established or identified.
- **Contact points.** These are established on identifiable terrain and are normally in the vicinity of the passage lanes. For rearward passage of lines, the contact points are established forward at the RHL/BHL. For forward passage, the contact points are established in the stationary unit's AO, rearward of the passage lanes.

Other Tactical Tasks

- **Passage points.** The passage point is the location on the passage lane at which the moving unit passes responsibility for the mission to the stationary unit. It is usually placed where the passage lane begins.
- **Passage lanes.** The stationary unit establishes passage lanes to move the passing unit quickly through defending unit positions. This could include passing through gaps in friendly obstacles and moving near or through friendly engagement areas (EAs) and BPs. Lanes are restrictive and ideally should be wide enough to allow the passing unit to move in a tactical formation. The passage lane begins at the passage point and ends at the rear of the stationary unit BPs. The passage is considered complete when the moving unit exits the lane.
- **Routes.** Routes are used to move the passing unit through the stationary unit. The number of routes designated varies based upon METT-TC but as a general rule, multiple lanes/routes should be planned to facilitate rapid passage of moving units and to avoid unnecessary massing of units. The stationary unit may escort or guide the passing unit along the lane/route.
- **Assembly area.** An assembly area in the AO of the stationary unit allows the passing unit to conduct hasty reorganization and emergency sustainment actions. This assembly area is temporary in nature.
- **Exfiltration points.** Leaders should plan infiltration points and lanes for personnel unable to complete the passage with their unit. Passing unit liaison officers may remain located with stationary unit CPs to serve as a point of contact for infiltrating personnel/equipment. Personnel who infiltrate must have some way of contacting the stationary unit before crossing into friendly territory.

Chapter 6

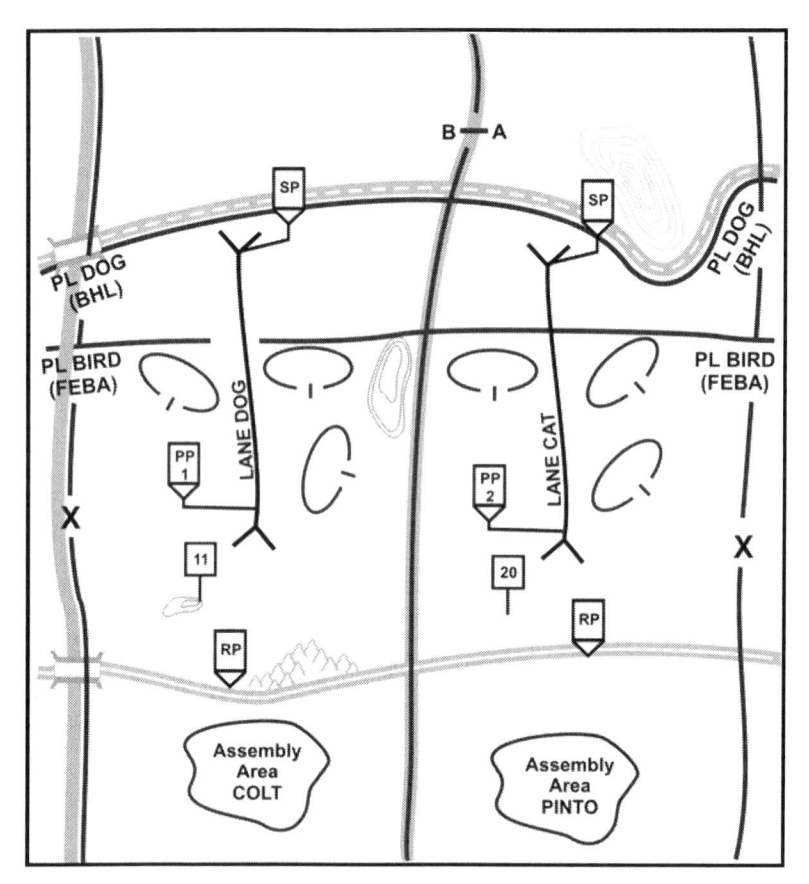

Figure 6-13. Forward passage line

Other Tactical Tasks

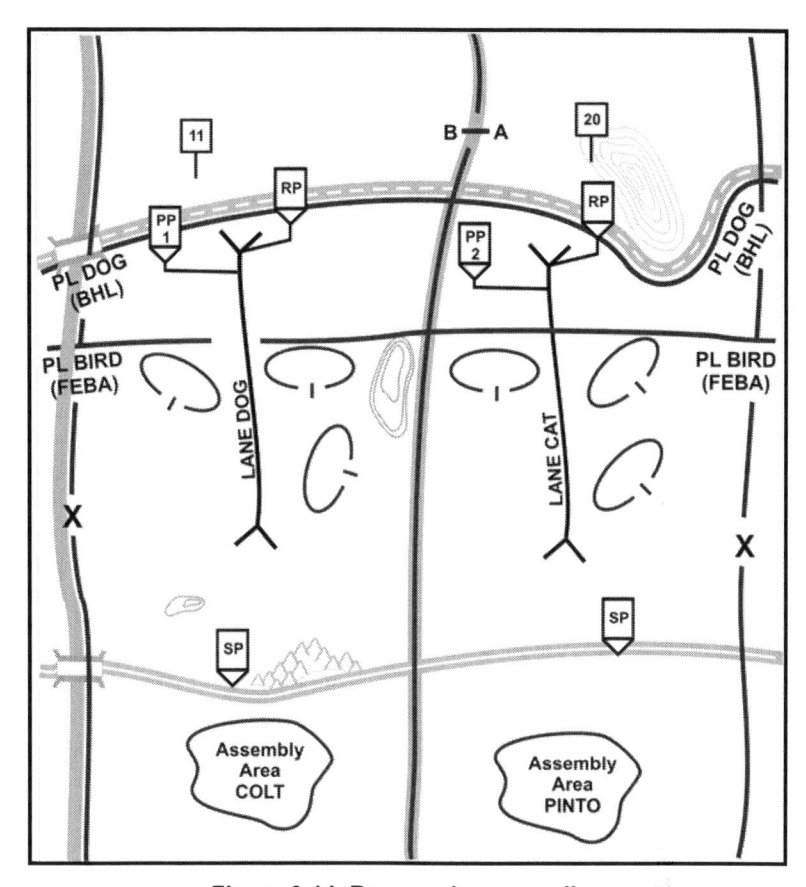

Figure 6-14. Rearward passage line

COORDINATION

6-159. Coordination for RHO/BHO occurs at a preplanned contact point where critical information is exchanged from the commander out of contact to the commander in contact. Coordination for the passage of lines and the handover should be conducted simultaneously.

6-160. The reconnaissance platoon leader plays a major role in coordination for passage of lines and handover, and is responsible for conducting reconnaissance to obtain information for use by the platoon and its parent unit. During reconnaissance, the platoon leader confirms the following factors and information related to the AO:
- The disposition of the stationary force through which the platoon and its parent unit passes.
- The location of contact points where both units are required to make physical contact at a predetermined time.

Chapter 6

- The location of passage lanes that provide a clear route through the stationary unit's position to facilitate a smooth and continuous passage. The areas selected for the passage should be unoccupied or on the flanks of units in position. If possible, the platoon leader should reconnoiter multiple routes that can reduce vulnerability during the mission.
- The rear boundary or assembly area (in a rearward passage) or the attack position (in a forward passage). This position should provide cover and concealment and be located where the passing unit does not interfere with the stationary unit.
- The initial locations for enablers and sustainment elements of the platoon's parent unit.

6-161. Based on this reconnaissance, the platoon leader coordinates the following information:
- Contact points (primary and alternate).
- Applicable passage points.
- Passage lanes, including the SP, RP, and critical points.
- The line of departure.
- Location and number of guides and guide vehicles.
- Routes through obstacles.
- Alternate routes.
- Sustainment plans, including resupply (Classes III and V), maintenance, MEDEVAC and CASEVAC, and disposition of EPWs.
- Traffic control factors, such as number of vehicles by type.
- Time of the passage.
- Rally points; the rear boundary or assembly area (rearward passage), or the attack position (forward passage).
- Actions on contact, if required during the passage.
- Times for transfer of responsibility for control of the sector, handover of the enemy, and RHL/BHL.
- Exchange of enemy and friendly information.
- Direct and indirect fire and obstacle plans.

ASSIST WITH A PASSAGE OF LINES

6-162. The platoon enhances the mission command function for the commander, who may require the platoon to assist other units in the passage of lines. The platoon may be required to conduct critical tasks of a stationary or passing unit, or assist its parent unit in the following ways:
- Elements of the platoon may help in securing contact and passage points where units meet and pass.
- The platoon may reconnoiter possible passage lanes (primary and alternate), clearing them of obstacles (within capability), and marking their locations.

Other Tactical Tasks

- The platoon may guide units from contact points to or through passage lanes. The platoon may also control traffic at the passage point and in the lane.
- The platoon may conduct area reconnaissance of attack positions (forward passage) and assembly area locations (rearward passage). This may include a requirement to check for CBRNE contamination.
- Platoon elements may be positioned in the passage area to act as a communications link in case units involved in the passage have trouble staying in contact with each other.
- The platoon may assist the commander by occupying OPs or conducting patrols to provide a continuous flow of information about the enemy situation.

EXECUTE A FORWARD PASSAGE OF LINES

6-163. A forward passage of lines is usually a column or staggered column formation along a covered and concealed route. The platoon ensures they maintain proper weapons orientation and follow weapons hold status at all times. The platoon makes sure that proper recognition signals, such as VS-17 and chem lights, are displayed properly. The platoon leader and PSG monitor the stationary unit's radio frequency throughout the passage of lines.

6-164. Upon reaching the contact point, the PSG positions himself with the stationary unit's representative. Together they count the vehicles and personnel to ensure all elements move into the passage lane.

6-165. Once the platoon enters the passage lane it does not stop or block it. All elements move through the passage lane until they reach the RP on the far side. If a vehicle becomes inoperable in the passage lane, the platoon attempts to self-recover. If recovery assets are required, the stationary unit dispatches a team to pull the inoperable vehicle back to the contact point and clear the passage.

6-166. If the platoon receives indirect fire during their passage, they continue movement to the RP as the stationary unit has responsibility for directing counterbattery fire. The platoon leader should give a spot report to the stationary unit CP to ensure they have SA.

6-167. If the platoon receives direct fire during the passage, they return fire as they maneuver to the RP. It is important that the platoon stay within the passage lane to avoid fratricide. The stationary unit returns fire on enemy positions, and has clear lanes of fire to effectively accomplish this.

6-168. Upon reaching the RP, the platoon deploys in sector. Elements cross the LD when adequate cover is available and permission is given prior to crossing. Once all elements reach the LD and assume covered positions to observe the assigned sectors, the platoon leader notifies the commander. The passing commander notifies

Chapter 6

the stationary commander and assumes responsibility of the battle. The platoon then starts their primary mission as outlined in the OPORD.

EXECUTE A REARWARD PASSAGE OF LINES

6-169. In a rearward passage of lines, the platoon is forward in defensive positions. The PSG or representative maneuvers to the contact point forward of the stationary unit's positions. It is very important that weapons orientation and recognition signals are displayed to avoid fratricide. Upon linkup at the contact point, the PSG verifies passage instructions with the stationary unit representative. Once all the information is collected, instructions are transmitted to the rest of the platoon. On the order of the higher commander, the platoon begins movement to the contact point.

6-170. As vehicles or personnel reach the contact point, they are counted and continue moving to the SP of the passage lane. Platoon elements may not all arrive at the contact point simultaneously but still continue movement to the rear. Once the passage lane is entered, elements do not stop until they reach the RP and the tactical assembly area located nearby. The PSG is the last element to enter the passage lane. After exiting the lane and passing the RP, the PSG notifies the commander that the platoon has cleared the passage lane.

6-171. The first platoon elements reaching the tactical assembly area take up the 12'oclock position and ensure the following elements take up positions on the perimeter. As elements set in the tactical assembly area, they report to the platoon leader. Once all elements have reached the tactical assembly area, the platoon leader notifies the commander and begins movement rearward.

SECTION VIII – RELIEF IN PLACE

6-172. Relief in place is a task where one unit replaces another unit in decisive action. Its primary purpose is to sustain the combat effectiveness of committed units. A relief is also conducted to allow a relieved unit to rest, reconstitute, decontaminate, or change missions. For the reconnaissance platoon, the relief may entail such tasks as serving as road guides for the supported unit, performing liaison with the relieved unit, or participating in the relief with its parent unit. (Refer to FM 3-20.96, FM 3-20.971, and ATTP 3-20.97 for more information.)

6-173. Relief in place is difficult to plan and conduct because of the nature of the task and the mission command, communications, and coordination required. It is important that the task not be disclosed to the enemy. Security, secrecy, and speed are critical. Though the platoon cannot always wait for optimum conditions, relief in place is best conducted during periods of limited visibility and lulls in the task. Limited visibility may be achieved by using obscurant munitions in key locations to block out the enemy's vision. Using obscuration over a large area can confuse the enemy as to the platoon's actual location.

Other Tactical Tasks

6-174. Relieving reconnaissance elements avoid sustaining casualties, hampering the operation of the elements being relieved, or allowing the enemy to detect the task. To reduce confusion and maintain security, the incoming platoon leader attempts to obtain the following information:
- Time that responsibility for the sector or zone is to pass.
- Operations security considerations.
- Deception plans.
- Time, method, and sequence of relief.
- Routes and critical control measures.
- Graphics for alternate and successive fighting positions.
- Contingency plans for changes of mission.
- Actions on enemy contact, if required before completion of the relief.
- Handover procedures for artillery, and air and missile defense.
- Obstacle locations and procedures covering the transfer of responsibility.
- Procedures for the transfer of ammunition, wire lines, and other items between outgoing and incoming units, if necessary. This also includes petroleum, oils, and lubricants (POL).

6-175. Radio traffic is kept to a minimum, and light and noise discipline is strictly enforced. If possible, the relieving platoon leader conducts a reconnaissance of the new positions. This is usually accomplished with the relieved platoon leader.

6-176. Once the reconnaissance is complete and orders are finalized, the platoon executes the relief using one of the following methods:
- **Sequential.** Vehicles move into position one at a time. This is the slowest but most secure method.
- **Simultaneously.** All of the relieved unit's vehicles pull out. Then the gaining unit's vehicles move at once. This is the quickest but least secure method, as it creates a large noise signature.
- **Staggered.** Platoons occupy adjacent or in-depth positions that cover the same area of responsibility. The relieving platoon is away from the relieved platoon and sections are replaced one at a time.
- **Exchange of vehicles and equipment.** This is typically used when secrecy is the overriding factor and the unit does not wish to be seen moving around. The relieving platoon moves to the relieved platoon's positions and assumes responsibility of the relieved platoon's vehicles and equipment, which remain in place. This is the most time-consuming method. The exchange method is also frequently used when units are in fixed surveillance sites or are taking part in peacekeeping missions where units rotate on a regular basis.

6-177. The actual relief in place can be conducted from a hide position with individual relieving vehicles moving forward to the relieved element's positions. The relieving platoon can also occupy alternate positions within the relieved element's sector or zone. The relieving element ensures that it covers the same sectors of fire as the relieved element. In some cases, the platoon may move into the primary positions as soon as the relieved vehicles back out. The relieved element may provide guides to ensure that relieving vehicles can locate those they are replacing.

6-178. Four important transmissions are made by the platoon leader, section leader, and squad leaders during the relief process to prevent fratricide:

- As the relieving platoon approaches from behind, it contacts the relieved platoon.
- When the relieving platoon's section sergeants are in their new positions, they contact the platoon leader or PSG with an established update. This is forwarded to the higher command and updated in FBCB2.
- When the relieving element's priorities of work and coordinating instructions are met, it reports again and announces that it is set (including the time).
- When the incoming platoon is in position and is prepared to conduct its next mission, the platoon leader or PSG contacts the commander.

Chapter 7

Augmenting Combat Power

Critical combat power augmentation provided by other units help support the maneuver of the reconnaissance platoon during reconnaissance missions. Combat power augmentation is employed by the commander to enhance the effectiveness of reconnaissance platoon missions. The unit commander and his subordinate leaders understand the capabilities and limitations of these elements to effectively incorporate them into unit missions.

The integration of enablers provides the platoon leader with the right assets to accomplish the mission while achieving the higher commander's intent. Enablers should complement the platoon mission, not detract from it. The platoon's integration of these assets begins during platoon planning and continues through rehearsals and execution.

SECTION I – FIRES

OVERVIEW

7-1 Reconnaissance platoons may receive indirect fire support from mortars, field artillery (FA), naval gunfire, aviation assets such as CAS, or rotary wing close combat attack. Most of these assets are not organic to the platoon, but are available through the platoon's parent unit. To make effective use of them, scouts understand the capabilities, limitations, and employment of fires assets. (Refer to FM 3-20.96, FM 3-20.971, FM 3-09.31, FM 3-22.90, and FM 6-20-40 for more information.)

7-2 Except as specifically directed, the reconnaissance platoon rarely engages the enemy with direct fire. When lethal fires are needed, the platoon usually employs indirect fire, CAS, or CCA assets, and may direct fires on specific targets to disengage from the enemy or to attack targets provided in the commander's high-payoff target list (HPTL).

7-4. Mortars and FA assets are the primary indirect fire support resources available to the reconnaissance platoon, although help can also come from aircraft and ships. In addition to understanding the capabilities and limitations of these assets, scouts know what fire request channels to use when calling for fires. The platoon leader is prepared to work with the troop and squadron/battalion FSOs to plan and coordinate fire support. (Refer to FM 3-09.32 for more information.)

Chapter 7

FIRE SUPPORT PERSONNEL

7-5. Fire support personnel may accompany or assist the reconnaissance platoon during the course of the platoon mission. These elements include the—
- Fire support team.
- Combat observation and lasing team.

7-6. Each troop has an organic FIST specifically designed to assist in the planning, coordination, and integration of fire support during missions. A FIST is capable of target acquisition under reduced visibility conditions, and has laser rangefinding and laser designating capabilities. Elements may assist the reconnaissance platoon in support of security tasks conducting calls for indirect fire support, and when target designation is required for laser-guided munitions engagements.

7-7. A COLT is controlled at the brigade level. It is capable of target acquisition under reduced visibility conditions, and has laser rangefinding and laser designating capabilities. The reconnaissance platoon may request indirect fire through the COLT, which has a secondary mission of processing these requests for the platoon.

7-8. The COLT may monitor the reconnaissance platoon net and handle the fire request and subsequent adjustments in the same manner as a normal FIST. It can enter the information gained through its primary mission, lasing targets for precision-guided munitions and CAS, directly into the Advanced Field Artillery Data System. When pushed forward with the reconnaissance platoon, the COLT may collocate with one of the platoon OPs for local security and protection. Leaders often link a COLTs observation of a TAI with a scout team's coverage of an NAI. This technique allows the scout team to act as a trigger, with the COLT executing and adjusting fires.

PLANNING CONSIDERATIONS

7-9. The reconnaissance platoon's main mission is reconnaissance rather than direct contact engagements with the enemy. Usually, indirect fires are used as a means of disengaging from the enemy. Depending on the commander's guidance, they may also employ indirect fires against HPTs that present themselves during platoon missions. One of the commander's greatest challenges is effectively synchronizing and concentrating all available assets at the critical time and place.

7-10. The planning process begins with receipt of the mission. The platoon leader and FSO interact throughout planning and execution to ensure that necessary support is continually provided. While developing plans for employment of forces, the commander and the FSO prepare for the best use of fires by determining:
- Fires and nonlethal assets that are tasked to support the platoon and subordinate elements.
- Targets to be attacked, including the HPTL.

- Indirect fires and nonlethal assets to be employed, along with ammunition and delivery provisions.
- Desired target effects.
- Engagement priorities.

7-11. The platoon leader clearly states the intent for fires, and ensures that the fires plan is developed to support each phase of the mission. The following list covers areas that the platoon leader coordinates with the FSO:
- **Scheme of maneuver.** This includes the AO, timing of advance, rate of movement, passage of lines, and Army aviation in the AO.
- **Priority of fires.** This identifies which section has priority of fires.
- **Priority targets.** These are identified, along with how long they are in effect.
- **High-payoff target list.** This is a list of targets whose loss to the enemy significantly contributes to the success of the friendly COA.
- **Close air support.** The platoon leader and FSO, in coordination with the squadron tactical air control party, determine what CAS assets are available, when they are available, and how they are used. This includes target selection and the desired effects.
- **Fire support coordination measures.** Existing or proposed, permissive or restrictive control measures are established, or recommended for establishment, by the appropriate commander.
- **Ammunition restrictions.** These place limitations on the use of obscurants, improved conventional munitions, or other ammunition including the established controlled supply rates.

7-12. The FS plan outlines how both lethal and nonlethal fires are used. The plan is developed by the platoon FSO and is constantly refined as the mission continues. It ranks targets in priority order, matches them with the available indirect fires systems, eliminates duplication with platoon targets, and allows fires to be executed quickly and without specific direction from the commander. An FS plan includes:
- The general concept of how indirect fires support the mission.
- A target list that includes planned locations of fires.
- Priority of fires.
- High-payoff target and priority targets.
- Allocation of priority targets and final protective fire, if available.
- Execution matrix.
- Required airspace coordination areas (ACAs).
- Fire support coordination measures.
- Rules of engagement.
- Clearance of fires.

7-13. The FSO disseminates the FS plan within the troop/company OPORD or by other means, such as a digital message. It contains all the elements listed above and is modified as platoon indirect fire plans are received. Updated fire plans are then returned to the platoon leaders.

FIRES IN CLOSE SUPPORT

7-14. Close supporting fires may be used in offensive or defensive situations depending on the nature of the mission, but are most commonly used to aid in disengaging from the enemy. The reconnaissance platoon mission does not usually engage in direct conflict with the enemy or require the use of indirect fires. Use of close supporting fires for disengagements is often to slow the enemy by degrading their effectiveness. Indirect fires may cause the enemy to seek cover or fight with their vehicles buttoned up. This gives the reconnaissance unit more freedom of maneuver to disengage. Suppression of the enemy and obscuration of friendly movements is usually the desired effect for the reconnaissance platoon.

Accuracy

7-15. Many variables affect the accuracy of the indirect fire weapon systems. The FSO has the technical knowledge to assist the platoon leader. Artillery and mortars are considered to be area weapon systems because they are high explosive rounds lacking an onboard guidance capability. Every round fired from the same tube at the same elevation and direction setting impacts an area around the target or aiming point in a standard dispersion pattern. This dispersion is greater in length than in width. Weather (wind, temperature, and humidity), proficiency of the crew, and trajectory of the round also affects accuracy.

Protection

7-16. If the unit is in well-prepared stationary positions with overhead cover, a final protective fire can be adjusted very close, just beyond bursting range. If required, the platoon leader can call for artillery fires right on his position using proximity or time fuses for airbursts. The platoon leader considers the terrain, breach site, and enemy positions to determine how close to adjust supporting indirect fires.

Integration of Suppresive Fires

7-17. When integrating indirect suppressive fires to support disengagements or other missions, the following points should be considered:
- Danger increases with the size of weapons. Mortars and artillery should be used on enemy positions further away from friendly units. Grenade launchers, 60-mm mortars, and direct fire weapons should be used for close suppression.
- If the rounds are coming over the head of friendly elements, the margin of safety is reduced.
- Unit mortars firing direct lay or direct alignment achieve quicker and greater success. They are able to observe the rounds' impact and adjust accordingly.

- Ideally, the firing units register prior to firing close support missions. If not, the first rounds fired might be off target by a considerable distance. Once the firing units are adjusted on a target, any shifts from that target are much more reliable.
- Risk estimate distances should always be considered when firing close to friendly units

MORTAR EMPLOYMENT

7-18. Mortars provide indirect fire support that is extremely responsive to the reconnaissance platoon needs. They provide a heavy volume of fires that are ideal for attacking targets on reverse slopes, in narrow ravines or trenches, and in forests, towns, and other areas that are difficult to strike with low-angle fires.

TYPES OF MORTAR SUPPORT

7-19. Suppression, obscuration, and illumination are the three types of mortar support available to the reconnaissance platoon. A discussion of these mortar supports follows.

Suppression

7-20. Without a direct hit, high explosive (HE) rounds generally do not completely destroy main battle tanks. Rounds hitting or detonating nearby can destroy or disable more lightly armored vehicles such as APCs and armored fighting vehicles, or incapacitate the crew. Suppressive fires can greatly disrupt enemy movement, and HE rounds can force mounted enemy units to button up or move to less advantageous positions. HE is very effective against dismounted threats and in urban environments.

Obscuration

7-21. Smoke rounds are used for obscuration and screening. Leaders use mortar-delivered obscurants to mark enemy positions, which can help enhance friendly maneuver and orient direct fires or CAS. They also employ obscurants to support infiltration and exfiltration. The platoon places a smokescreen on or just in front of enemy positions to obscure their vision and conceal movement. In urban environments, the platoon assesses wind conditions before using smoke. Calm conditions in urban environments may minimize the impact of winds that normally disperse the obscurant's effects. Care is taken that friendly smoke rounds do not cause unanticipated structure fires, or mark the platoon's position.

Illumination

7-22. Illumination rounds are used to light an area or enemy position during periods of limited visibility. This can increase the effectiveness of image intensification devices and sensors, and assist the reconnaissance platoon in gathering information, adjusting mortars or artillery, or engaging enemy targets with direct fire. Scouts use ground-burst illumination to mark enemy positions and provide a thermal TRP for control of direct and indirect fires. As with obscurants, leaders take care not to illuminate friendly positions. Because of the effectiveness of night observation devices (NODs), illumination can be unnecessary or even counterproductive. Whenever illumination is employed, scouts pay close attention to wind direction and speed to ensure proper deployment of the rounds.

MORTAR CAPABILITIES
7-23. Mortars are most effective—
- In urban areas or mountain terrain.
- When a fast response time is needed.
- Against low-density targets.

MORTAR LIMITATIONS
7-24. Drawbacks to using mortars are the—
- Short-range capability.
- Limited munitions selection.
- Vulnerability to enemy counterfire radars due to the high angle of fire.
- Limited basic loads of ammunition.

FIELD ARTILLERY SUPPORT

7-25. The brigade's organic fires battalion can potentially support the reconnaissance platoon. The fires battalion has several different munitions available such as HE dual-purpose improved conventional munitions (DPICMs), Copperhead, white phosphorus (WP), scatterable mines, HE rocket-assisted projectiles, Excalibur guided projectiles, obscuration, and illumination.

ARTILLERY CAPABILITIES
7-26. Artillery elements support the reconnaissance platoon by—
- Providing continuous all-weather and all-terrain fire support.
- Rapidly shifting and massing fires.
- Supporting in-depth with long-range fires.
- Employing a variety of conventional shell and fuze combinations.
- Accurately engaging stationary point targets with 155-mm Excalibur guided munitions or Guided Multiple Launch Rocket System munitions.
- Accurately engaging moving or stationary laser-designated targets with 155-mm Copperhead rounds.

ARTILLERY LIMITATIONS
7-27. Artillery elements supporting the platoon have—
- Limited effectiveness on moving targets.
- Limited ability to destroy point targets without considerable ammunition expenditure.
- Increased vulnerability to enemy counterfire due to firing signature.

Common Uses of Available Munitions

7-28. Field artillery employs a wide variety of munitions that can be tailored for the engagement of different types of targets. These ammunition types include—

- High explosives for use against personnel, field fortifications, and vehicles.
- Obscurants for obscuration and screening.
- Illumination.
- White phosphorus for obscuration, marking, screening, and incendiary effects against materiel targets. For example, a WP airburst over an easily recognizable feature assists disoriented personnel.
- Guided Multiple Launch Rocket System rockets and 155-mm Excalibur rounds for use against accurately located point targets.
- Copperhead 155-mm projectiles against stationary or moving point targets.
- Dual-purpose improved conventional munitions for use against personnel and light armored vehicles in the open.
- Scatterable mines.

7-29. Scatterable mines include area denial munitions for use against personnel, remote antiarmor mine systems, and armored vehicles. When firing a scatterable mines mission, the battery is not available for other fire missions because it requires slightly more lead time than other FA delivered munitions.

Elements and Sequence of Call for Fire

7-30. The format in Figure 7-1 is used to call for fire. (Refer to FM 6-30 for more information.)

Chapter 7

> **Initial transmission:** "*" indicates required elements. All other elements may be omitted, if desired.
>
> - * Observer's identification - call signs.
> - * Warning order:
>   - *Type of mission:
>   — Adjust fire.
>   — Fire for effect.
>   — Suppress.
>   - Size of element to fire for effect. (When the observer does not specify what size element to fire, the battalion fire direction center [FDC] decides.)
>   - * Method of target location:
>   — Polar plot.
>   — Shift from a known point (give TRP).
>   - * Location of target:
>   — 6-digit grid coordinate. Use eight digits if greater accuracy is required.
>   — Shift from a known point:
>   — Send observer to target (OT) direction:
>   — Mils (nearest 10).
>   — Degrees.
>   — Cardinal direction.
>   — Send lateral shift (right/left) (nearest 10 m).
>   — Send range shift (add/drop) (nearest 100 m).
>   — Send vertical shift (up/down). Use only if it exceeds 35 m (nearest 5 m).
>   — Polar plot:
>   — Send direction (nearest 10 mils).
>   — Send distance (nearest 100 m).
>   — Send vertical shift (nearest 5 m).
>   - * Description of target:
>   — Type.
>   — Activity.
>   — Number.
>   — Degree of protection.
>   — Size and shape (length/width or radius).

Figure 7-1. Example of a call for fire

- Method of engagement:
  - Type of adjustment. (When the observer does not request a specific type of fire control adjustment, area fire is issued.)
    - Area fire (moving target).
    - Precision fire (point target).
    - Danger close (when friendly troops are within 600 m for mortars and artillery).
- Mark (used to orient observer or to indicate targets).
- Trajectory:
  - Low angle (standard).
  - High angle (mortars, or if requested).
- Ammunition. (HE quick is used unless specified by the observer.)
  - Projectile (HE, ILLUM, ICM, SMOKE).
  - Fuze (quick, time, or other).
  - Volume of fire (observer may request the number of rounds to be fired).
- Distribution:
  - 100-m sheaf (standard).
  - Converged sheaf (used for small hard targets).
  - Special sheaf (any length, width, and attitude).
  - Open sheaf (separate bursts).
  - Parallel sheaf (linear target).
- Method of fire and control:
  - Specific guns and a specific interval between rounds. Normally adjust fire (one gun is used with a 5-second interval between rounds).
- Method of control:
  - AT MY COMMAND—FIRE. Remains in effect until observer announces, CANCEL AT MY COMMAND.
  - CANNOT OBSERVE. Observer can't see the target.
  - TIME ON TARGET. Observer tells the FDC when the rounds are to impact.
  - Continuous illumination. Calculated by the FDC, otherwise observer indicates interval.
  - Coordinated illumination. Observer may order the interval between ILLUM and HE shells.

Figure 7-1. Example of a call for fire (continued)

Chapter 7

> - CEASE LOADING to indicate the suspension of loading rounds.
> - CHECK FIRING. Immediate halt.
> - CONTINUOUS FIRE. Load and fire as fast as possible.
> - REPEAT. Fire another round with or without adjustments.
> - Authentication. Challenge and reply.
>
> • Message to observer:
>   - Battery(ies) to fire for effect.
>   - Adjusting battery.
>   - Changes to the initial call for fire.
>   - Number of rounds (per tube) to be fired for effect.
>   - Target numbers.
>   - Additional information:
>   - Time of flight. Moving target mission.
>   - Probable error in range (38 m or greater [normal mission]).
>   - Angle T (500 mils or greater).
>
> • Correction of errors. When the FDC has made an error when reading back the fire support data, the observer announces, CORRECTION and transmits the correct data in its entirety.

Figure 7-1. Example of a call for fire (continued)

Examples of Call for Fire Transmissions

7-31. Table 7-1 is an example of a GRID mission and Table 7-2 is an example of a shift from known point.

Table 7-1. Example of a GRID mission

Observer	Firing Unit
F24, this is J42, ADJUST FIRE, OVER.	J42, this is F24, ADJUST FIRE, OUT.
GRID WM 180513, DIRECTION 0530, OVER.	GRID WM 180513, DIRECTION 0530, OUT.
Infantry platoon dug in, OVER.	Infantry platoon dug in, OUT.

Table 7-1. Example of a GRID mission (continued)

Observer	Firing Unit
SHOT OUT.	SHOT OVER.
SLASH OUT.	SPLASH OVER.
End of mission, 15 casualties, platoon dispersed, OVER.	End of mission, 15 casualties, platoon dispersed, OUT.

Table 7-2. Example of a shift from known point

Observer	Firing Unit
J42, this is F24, ADJUST FIRE, SHIFT AB1001, OUT.	J42, this is F24, ADJUST FIRE, SHIFT AB1001, OUT.
DIRECTION 2420, RIGHT 400, ADD 400, OUT.	DIRECTION 2420, RIGHT 400, ADD 400, OUT.
5T72 Tanks at POL site, OVER.	5T72 Tanks at POL site, OUT.
I AUTHENTICATE Tango, OVER.	AUTHENTICATE Juliet, November, OVER.
SHOT OUT.	SHOT OVER.
SPLASH OUT.	SPLASH OVER.
End of mission, 2 tanks destroyed, 3 in wood line, OVER.	End of mission, 2 tanks destroyed, 3 in wood line, OUT.

7-32. In addition to the supporting cannon units, Multiple Launch Rocket System (MLRS)/High Mobility Artillery Rocket System elements may also provide fires. Unlike cannon artillery, MLRS units fire rocket and missile munitions delivering only HE, DPICM, or anti-personnel and anti-materiel warheads. They provide rocket or missile fires but do not offer special munitions such as obscuration, illumination, or WP. The maximum range of a MLRS rocket is 32,000 to 45,000 meters, depending upon the type of munitions. The planning range for MLRS missiles in the Army Tactical Missile System is 100,000 to 300,000 meters, depending upon the type of munitions.

CLOSE COMBAT ATTACK

7-33. Close combat attack is defined as a hasty or deliberate attack in support of units engaged in close combat. During CCA, attack reconnaissance helicopters engage enemy units with direct fire that impact near friendly forces. Targets may range from a few hundred to a few thousand meters. CCA is coordinated and directed by a team, platoon, or company-level ground-unit using standardized CCA procedures in unit SOPs. The reconnaissance platoon may require the use of Army aviation for CCA tasks.

Chapter 7

PLANNING CONSIDERATIONS

7-34. If available, digital transmission of information is faster and more accurate. Voice communications are necessary to verify information and clarify needs and intentions. The minimum information required by the Army aviation team to ensure accurate and timely support is listed below:

- Situation, including the location and composition of friendly forces; the enemy situation highlighting known air defense artillery threats in the mission request; and tentative EA coordinates.
- Brigade and battalion/squadron-level graphics update via FBCB2 or radio communications. Critical items such as LOA, fire-control measures, and maneuver graphics should be updated to better integrate into the friendly scheme of maneuver.
- Fighter squadron coordination information, location of direct support artillery and organic mortars, and call signs and frequencies.
- Ingress/egress routes in the AO. This includes passage points into a sector or zone, and the air route to the holding area or LZ.
- Call signs and frequencies of the battalion/squadron in contact, down to the platoon in contact. Air-ground coordination is done on command frequencies to provide SA for all elements involved.
- Global Positioning System (GPS) and Single-Channel Ground and Airborne Radio System time coordination. Ensure all units are operating on the same time.

MARKING

7-35. Ground units ensure aircraft positively identify and locate friendly units and targets. There are various ways to mark a location or target. The effectiveness of vision systems on helicopters compares to those found on ground vehicles. Simple, positive identification procedures are established and known to all so that aviation and ground forces do not become overloaded with tasks in the heat of battle.

Marking U.S. Troops

7-36. A method of target identification is direction and distance from friendly forces. Friendly forces can mark their own positions with infrared IR strobes, infrared tape, night vision goggles, lights, smoke, signal panels, body position, meals ready to eat heaters, chemical lights, and mirrors. Marking friendly positions is the least desirable method of target location and should be used with extreme caution as it can reveal friendly positions to the enemy.

Marking Enemy Positions

7-37. Target marking helps aircrews locate the target that the unit in contact desires them to attack. Ground commanders should provide the target mark whenever possible. To be effective, the mark is timely, accurate, and easily identifiable. It should not be confused with other fires on the battlefield, suppression rounds, detonations, and marks on other targets. Although a mark is not mandatory, it improves aircrew accuracy, enhances SA, and reduces the risk of fratricide.

Augmenting Combat Power

CLOSE COMBAT ATTACK REQUESTS

7-38. A request for CCA may be sent when targets of opportunity require engagement from Army aviation elements. Time is the primary constraining factor for coordinating aviation fires. Requests for CCA should follow the briefing format shown in Table 7-3. The CCA briefing is the joint standard five-line format with minor modifications for Army helicopters, and is also used for request for support from Specter gunships.

7-39. This briefing provides clear and concise information in a logical sequence, enabling aircrews to employ their weapons systems and provide appropriate control to reduce the risk of fratricide. Transmission of the brief constitutes clearance to fire except in a danger close situation. When applicable, danger close missions are declared in line 5.

Table 7-3. Close combat attack briefing

CLOSE COMBAT ATTACK BRIEFING (Ground to Air)
1. Observer-WARNORD: (Aircraft call sign) THIS IS (Observer call sign). FIRE MISSION. OVER.
2. Friendly Location/Mark: MY POSITION (TRP, GRID). MARKED BY (STROBE, BEACON, IR STROBE, or others).
3. Target Location: (Magnetic bearing and range (meters), TRP, Grid).
4. Target Description/Mark: (Target description) MARKED BY (IR, pointer, tracer, or others). OVER.
5. Remarks: "(Threats, danger close clearance,[1] restrictions, at my command,[2] or others.)"
As required: 1. Clearance: Transmission of the fire mission is clearance to fire, unless danger close. Danger close ranges are according to FM 3-09.32. For closer fire, the observer/commander accepts responsibility for increased risk. State, CLEARED DANGER CLOSE on line 5. This clearance may be preplanned.   2. At my command: For positive control of the gunship, state AT MY COMMAND on line 5. The gunship calls READY TO FIRE when ready.

AIR GROUND INTERGRATION

7-40. The platoon leader coordinates with the unit commander to employ attack reconnaissance assets as a maneuver force. The platoon leader considers basic fundamentals that are synchronized with unit operations and enhance overall effectiveness. These fundamentals include:

- Understanding the capabilities and limitations of attack reconnaissance assets.
- Adhering to established SOPs.
- Employing effective mission command.
- Synchronizing the efforts of air and ground forces.

CLOSE AIR SUPPORT

7-41. The reconnaissance platoon may employ CAS from fixed-wing aircraft to augment other supporting fires or to attack targets on the HPTL. The speed, range, and maneuverability of aircraft allow them to attack targets that other supporting arms may not be able to effectively engage due to limiting factors such as target type, range, terrain, or the ground scheme of maneuver.

7-42. Ground commanders are the ultimate authority for all supporting fires in their respective AOs. The ground commander at the lowest level is responsible for employment of CAS assets unless responsibility is specifically retained by a higher level commander in the ground force chain of command. (Refer to FM 3-09.32 for more information.)

Preplanned

7-43. Preplanned CAS missions are requested 72 hours in advance of the mission. They may or may not include detailed target information due to the lead time for the mission. These requests include potential targets, desired effects, proposed times, and a general priority.

7-44. Preplanned CAS is categorized as a scheduled mission or an alert mission. A scheduled mission entails CAS strikes on a planned target at a planned time or time on target (TOT). An alert (or on-call) CAS mission entails strikes on a planned target or target area executed upon request. Usually, this mission is launched (or scrambled) from a ground alert status, but may be flown from an airborne on-call alert status. Alert CAS allows the ground commander to designate a general target area and the specific targets to be attacked. The ground commander designates a conditional period within which to determine specific times for attacking targets.

Immediate

7-45. Requests for immediate CAS are used for requirements that are identified too late to meet the air tasking order cutoff time. If there are no immediate CAS sorties available and HPTs have been identified, then other aircraft may be diverted to engage these targets or provide CAS for reconnaissance platoon missions.

Close Air Support Planning Considerations

7-46. Close air support mission success is directly related to thorough planning based on these considerations:

- **Weather.** Weather is one of the most important considerations when visually employing weapons. It can hinder target identification and degrade weapon accuracy. Does the weather favor the use of aircraft? What is the cloud ceiling? What is the forecast for the immediate future?
- **Target acquisition.** Targets that are well camouflaged, small and stationary, or masked by natural and man-made terrain are difficult to identify from fast-moving aircraft. Marking rounds can enhance target identification and help ensure first-pass success.
- **Target identification.** This is critical if CAS aircraft are to avoid fratricide. It is accomplished by providing a precise description of the target in relation to terrain features easily visible from the air. Colored smoke and laser devices can also be used for marking purposes. The remotely operated video enhanced receiver by joint terminal attack controllers (JTACs) greatly enhances the ground commander's SA and simplifies the targeting process.
- **Identification of friendly forces.** This is a key consideration in using CAS or rotary-wing aircraft. The primary cause of fratricide is misidentification of friendly troops as threat forces. Safe means of friendly position identification include mirror flash, marker panels, and direction and distance from prominent land features or target marks.
- **General ordnance characteristics.** These identify types of targets to be engaged and the desired weapon effects.
- **Final attack heading.** The final attack heading depends on considerations of troop safety, aircraft survivability, and optimum weapon effects. Missiles or bombs are effective from any angle. Cannons are more effective against the flanks and rear of armored vehicles.
- **Suppression of enemy air defense (SEAD).** This is required based on the capabilities of the aircraft and presence of threat air defense systems in the target area.
- **CAS/artillery integration.** Army artillery and combat air power are complementary. Because artillery support is more continuous and is faster to respond than CAS, close air support missions are integrated with artillery so that limited firing restrictions are imposed. The airspace coordination area is the FSCM used to accomplish this integration.

Night Close Air Support Missions

7-47. As with weather considerations, the use of GPS and laser-guided munitions has enhanced the ability of CAS assets to provide support at night. The two most important requirements of a night CAS mission remain the same:

- Identification of the target.
- Positive marking/identification of friendly unit locations.

Chapter 7

7-48. Flares released from forward airborne air controllers, other CAS aircraft, or 'flare ships' can effectively illuminate target areas. Artillery and mortar-fired illumination is preferred because these assets provide a longer sustained rate of fire.

7-49. Tracers and infrared beacons can improve safety and provide target area references. Flares used during limited visibility conditions (such as fog or obscuration) can make it more difficult for aircraft to find targets. When used under a low cloud ceiling, flares can highlight the aircraft against the clouds. Strobe lights, used with blue or infrared filters, can be made directional by the use of any opaque tube. In overcast conditions they can be especially useful. Aside from obvious security considerations, almost any light that can be filtered, covered, and uncovered can be used for signaling aircraft.

Close Air Support Request

7-50. The CAS request provides SA and the information necessary for the crew of CAS aircraft to successfully engage their target(s). The terminal controller, normally a JTAC or joint operations center, transmits via radio to the attack aircraft, providing the aircrew with enough time to write down the information and set up their navigational equipment. The controller does not transmit the line numbers. Units of measurement are standard unless otherwise specified. Table 7-4 provides the CAS request format. (Lines 4 and 6 and any restrictions are mandatory read-back items [indicated by an '*'] in Table 7-4.) The controller may request read-back of additional items as required.

7-51. Leaders employ joint fires observers (JFOs) if no JTAC support is available. Reconnaissance platoons working forward and independent of the troop conduct emergency control of CAS missions in the absence of JTAC or JFO personnel. Referred to as, 'CAS by a nonqualified controller,' non-JTAC controllers clearly state to attacking aircraft that they are 'non-JTAC qualified' during aircraft check-in.

Table 7-4. Close air support nine-line request format

CAS Briefing (Nine-Line)
Do not transmit line numbers. Units of measure are standard unless briefed. Lines 4, 6, and restrictions are mandatory readback (*). JTAC may request additional readback. *"This is (aircraft call sign; JTAC)."*
"Type *(1, 2, or 3)* Control "   1. IP/BP: "___"

2. Heading: "___"
     (Degrees Magnetic; IP/BP to target)
     Offset: "___"
 (Left/right, when required)

3. Distance: "___"   *(IP to target in nautical miles, BP to target in meters).*
4.* Target Elevation: "___"   *(in feet/MSL)*
5. Target Description: "___"

Table 7-4. Close air support nine-line request format (continued)

CAS Briefing (Nine-Line)
6.* Target Location: "___" (Latitude and longitude, grid coordinates to include map datum such as WGS-84, offsets, or visual description)
7. Type Mark: "___" Code: "___" (WP, Laser, IR, Beacon) (Actual Code)
8. Location of friendlies: "___"   (From target, cardinal directions and distance in meters) Position marked by: "___"

9. Egress: "___"
    Remarks (as appropriate): "___"
    (Restrictions*, ordnance delivery, threats, FAH, hazards, ACAs, weather, target info, SEAD, LTL ,GTL {degrees magnetic north}, night vision, danger close [plus commander's initials]).
    Time on Target (TOT): "___" or
    Time to Target (TTT): "___"
    "_Standby plus, Hack._"
    (minutes) (seconds)
Note. When identifying position coordinates for joint operations, include map data. Grid coordinates include 100,000-meter grid identification.

Key ACA – airspace coordination area FAH – final attack heading GTL – gun-target line IP – initial position LTL – laser-to-target line MSP – mission support plan WGS – World Geodetic System

SNIPER EMPLOYMENT

7-52. Sniper teams play a critical role in tactical missions. Well-trained snipers provide commanders accurate and precisely targeted long-range small-arms fire. Unexpected sniper fires can affect enemy morale, their ability to move, and mission accomplishment.

7-53. Snipers are equipped to observe, collect, and provide critical, detailed information. It is in this role that they are often employed for reconnaissance units. The reconnaissance platoon leader or sniper squad leader controls the sniper teams from a central location. Once deployed, sniper teams may operate independently in support of the troop mission. They are effective only in areas with good fields of fire and observation, and should have the freedom of action to choose their own positions once on the ground. (Refer to FM 3-22.10 for more information.)

SECTION II – ENGINEERS

7-54. The reconnaissance platoon is likely to operate with a sapper squad from a combat engineer platoon. Sapper-qualified scouts enhance reconnaissance platoon capabilities and can provide support to attached engineer assets. (Refer to FM 3-34.170 for more information.)

SUPPORT IN RECONNAISSANCE TASKS

7-55. In reconnaissance tasks, an engineer team usually functions in direct support to a reconnaissance platoon and remain attached for the duration of the mission. The engineer team's primary objective is to collect obstacle intelligence (OBSTINTEL) and report the information back to the BCT engineer to facilitate breach planning and preparation. The engineer team may perform the following functions:

- Conduct limited reduction of obstacles, such as log cribs, abatis, and minefields. Reduction capabilities of the engineer reconnaissance team are limited to manual and explosive methods.
- Conduct tactical or technical reconnaissance.
- Conduct route and bridge classification.
- Assist in locating and marking bypasses around obstacles.
- Identify the exact composition and dimensions of an obstacle.
- Identify breach points and points of penetration.

7-56. Engineers conduct reconnaissance support in the offense as part of the combined arms team effort. Normally, they support reconnaissance elements to facilitate mission command and logistic support in an attached status.

7-57. Engineers conduct technical reconnaissance to collect specialized information about a designated target, area, or route. Engineers conduct this mission under low-level threat conditions in areas physically controlled by friendly forces. The technical reconnaissance mission is normally a specified task from higher HQ or derived from mission analysis.

7-58. Whenever possible, the attached engineer elements should have a habitual relationship with the reconnaissance platoon and be task organized with the platoon as early as possible in a mission. The platoon leader integrates them into troop-leading procedures, rehearsals, OPORD, and movement plans.

ENGINEER SUPPORT IN SECURITY TASKS

7-59. In security tasks, the reconnaissance platoon usually works under squadron/battalion or troop control and does not usually have any engineer assets operating under its control. However, the platoon leader has access to the squadron/battalion or troop obstacle plan, including the locations of lanes and gaps, to assist or facilitate the engineers as they emplace obstacles during a security mission.

7-60. The platoon may interact with the engineers in several roles during security tasks. The commander may direct the platoon to observe NAIs to trigger scatterable mine missions, overwatch obstacles, and call for indirect fires. The platoon may also guard, execute, and overwatch reserve demolition targets that engineers have prepared.

ENGINEER SUPPORT IN STABILITY TASKS
7-61. The reconnaissance platoon uses engineer support during stability and counterinsurgency tasks to:
- Construct fighting positions.
- Construct combat outposts.
- Provide barrier material for checkpoints, combat outposts, and other obstacles.

7-62. In stability tasks, the reconnaissance platoon does not usually have any engineer assets operating under its control, but provides security for them as they perform specific missions such as construction, utility restoration, or roadwork. The reconnaissance platoon leader has knowledge of the engineer mission to effectively plan for security.

SECTION III – INTELLIGENCE

SENSOR TEAMS
7-63. Sensor teams may augment reconnaissance platoons to enhance their surveillance capability. They detect targets and provide accurate range and azimuth readings to enemy locations during limited visibility conditions. Integration of tactical UASs by the reconnaissance platoon is critical for maximum effectiveness and survivability of dismounted scouts. (Refer to FM 3-20.971, FM 3-20.96, FM 2-22.3, and FM 3-04.155 for more information.)

7-64. Sensor teams employing ground surveillance systems may be attached or assigned OPCON for specific missions. The platoon leader plans the employment of this team and should work with the commander to position the sensor assets in conjunction with reconnaissance OPs in order to provide local security.

CAPABILITIES AND LIMITATIONS
7-65. Sensor teams provide mobile, all-weather surveillance. When employed, they can provide observation from a given vantage point twenty-four hours a day. Some systems can detect targets through light camouflage, obscuration, light snow and rain, haze, and darkness. However, foliage, and heavy rain and snow seriously reduce its capability.

7-66. Other systems do not require a background to detect moving targets and most are generally ineffective against an air target unless the aircraft is flying close to the ground. Sensor systems are vulnerable to enemy direction-finding and jamming

Chapter 7

equipment. The sensor team is sometimes equipped with a single radio. If employed forward with the reconnaissance platoon, the team usually sends all reports to the platoon leader for transmission to higher HQ.

EMPLOYMENT

7-67. The platoon leader assigns the sensor team a specific sector of surveillance and frequency of coverage. Surveillance tasks assigned to sensor teams include:

- Monitor avenues of approach or possible enemy positions on a scheduled or random basis to determine location, size, composition of enemy forces, and the nature of their activity.
- Monitor point targets such as bridges, defiles, or road junctions; and report quantity, type, and direction of enemy vehicles and personnel moving through the target area.
- Extend the observation capabilities of the scouts by enabling them to survey distant points and areas of special interest.
- Vector patrols to keep them oriented during limited visibility.

GROUND SURVEILLANCE SYSTEMS

7-68. Leaders emplace ground surveillance systems in an area that affords long-range observation, a wide field of view, and is generally free of clutter such as trees, thick vegetation, and buildings. Normally, the platoon leader assigns the team a general area and the surveillance team leader selects the specific position. To avoid enemy suppressive fires, the team should be prepared for rapid displacement and have several alternate positions selected and reconnoitered.

7-69. During reconnaissance tasks, leaders employ the surveillance equipment to the flanks of the reconnaissance platoon, or orient it on potential enemy locations. Since reconnaissance is a moving mission, the surveillance teams move as necessary to support the platoon.

7-70. In security tasks, the platoon leader uses surveillance teams to provide redundancy in surveillance of NAIs, and to add depth to the screen line by supplementing OPs.

HUMAN INTELLIGENCE COLLECTION

7-71. Human intelligence collection teams (HCTs) are the elements that collect information from human sources. HUMINT collectors deploy in groups of approximately four personnel.

7-72. The HUMINT collector's role is to gather foreign information from people and multiple media sources that identify adversary elements, intentions, composition, strength, dispositions, tactics, equipment, personnel, and capabilities. They use human sources and a variety of collection methods to gather information to satisfy the commander's information requirements and to cross-cue other intelligence disciplines.

7-73. Human intelligence collection teams conduct tasks throughout the platoon's AO. They have a crucial role supporting tactical forces by conducting debriefings, screenings, military source tasks, liaison, and interrogations, and supporting document and media exploitation. HUMINT activities focus on the threat and assist the platoon leader and unit commander in understanding the threat's decision-making process.

7-74. The HCT maintains constant contact with reconnaissance units and other assets (scouts, MISOs, CA teams, and MPs) to coordinate and deconflict operations, and to cross-check collected information.

UNMANNED AIRCRAFT SYSTEM TASKS

7-75. Unmanned aircraft system elements support reconnaissance missions by obtaining information about enemy or potential enemy activities and resources, or securing data concerning meteorological, hydrographic, or geographic characteristics of a particular area. A noncontiguous, expanded AO routinely creates gaps between friendly units. Reconnaissance of these gaps before, during, and after combat is an excellent mission for the UAS. These supported missions can provide information on the enemy or reconnaissance target using the SALUTE report categories:

- Size.
- Activity.
- Location.
- Unit.
- Time.
- Equipment.

7-76. Information derived from UAS assets helps the platoon leader determine which routes and cross-country terrain best accommodate reconnaissance tasks. In addition, the platoon takes information generated by UAS units and immediately sends SPOTREPs to organizations that need combat information. Information gathered by the UAS range from very near (over the next hill or around the next block) to hundreds of kilometers away. (Refer to FM 3-04.155 for more information.)

7-77. Platoons employ the man-portable RQ-11 Raven UAS, but also have direct access to real-time or near-real-time feeds from other UAS such as the BCT asset RQ-7 Shadow.

UAS SENSOR CHARACTERISTICS

7-78. Currently, two types of imagery sensors are available for use on man-portable and tactical UAS; electro-optical (EO) and IR. Each sensor has unique capabilities with distinct advantages and disadvantages. Table 7-5 is a matrix of characteristics for the EO and IR sensors currently available. Additional types of

Chapter 7

sensors and other tactical UAS payloads are currently under development and may be fielded as their respective technologies mature.

Table 7-5. UAS sensor characteristics

SENSOR TYPE	ADVANTAGES	DISADVANTAGES
Electro-optical (visible light)	Best tool for detailed analysis during daytime and clear weather. Affords a familiar view of a scene. Offers system resolution that cannot be achieved with other optical systems, thermal images, or radar. Preferred for detailed analysis and mensuration. Offers stereoscopic viewing.	Can be deceived by employment of camouflage and concealment techniques. Restricted by weather conditions; visible light cannot penetrate clouds or fog. Restricted by terrain and vegetation. Limited to daytime use only.
Infrared	Best tool for detailed analysis in darkness with clear weather. Passive sensor that is impossible to jam. Offers camouflage penetration. Provides good resolution. Offers nighttime imaging capability.	Not effective during thermal crossover (1 to 1.5 hours after sunrise or sunset). Tactical UASs can be threatened by enemy air defenses. Bad weather degrades quality of sensor images.

RELATIONSHIP OF THE UAS ELEMENT AND THE RECONNAISSANCE PLATOON

7-79. Unmanned aircraft systems are a significant asset in support of the ground commander's requirements. When operating with ground elements, the UAS element is normally under OPCON to the squadron or battalion. To be successful, the element communicates and coordinates directly with the most forward ground elements.

7-80. When working with the reconnaissance platoon, the UAS element normally operates the UAS forward of the ground elements. The exact distances are determined through a METT-TC analysis.

7-81. In a complementary relationship, the commander assigns the UAS and reconnaissance platoons different objectives or tasks. This allows more tasks or separate missions to be accomplished simultaneously. Often the UAS element performs missions to the flank or adjacent to the reconnaissance platoon, and may provide valuable information acquired during flights to and from its objective.

RECONNAISSANCE TASKS

7-82. The UAS normally operates 1 to 10 kilometers forward of the reconnaissance platoon (METT-TC dependent), conducting detailed reconnaissance of areas that are particularly dangerous to ground elements, such as open areas and defiles. Upon contact, the UAS provides early warning for the platoon and then maintains contact until they move up for handover.

Augmenting Combat Power

SECURITY TASKS

7-83. The UAS complements the reconnaissance platoon during security tasks by assisting in identifying enemy reconnaissance and main body elements, and providing early warning forward of the platoon. The UAS also has a critical role in providing security through the depth of the screen by observing dead space between OPs.

7-84. Because of the range of its sensors, the UAS does not require positions forward of the reconnaissance platoon to acquire enemy elements. The preferred practice is to position the aerial OPs forward of the ground OPs. This provides added depth to the screen, especially during operations in daylight. Ultimately, positioning of the UAS always depends on the specific METT-TC situation. (See Figure 7-2.)

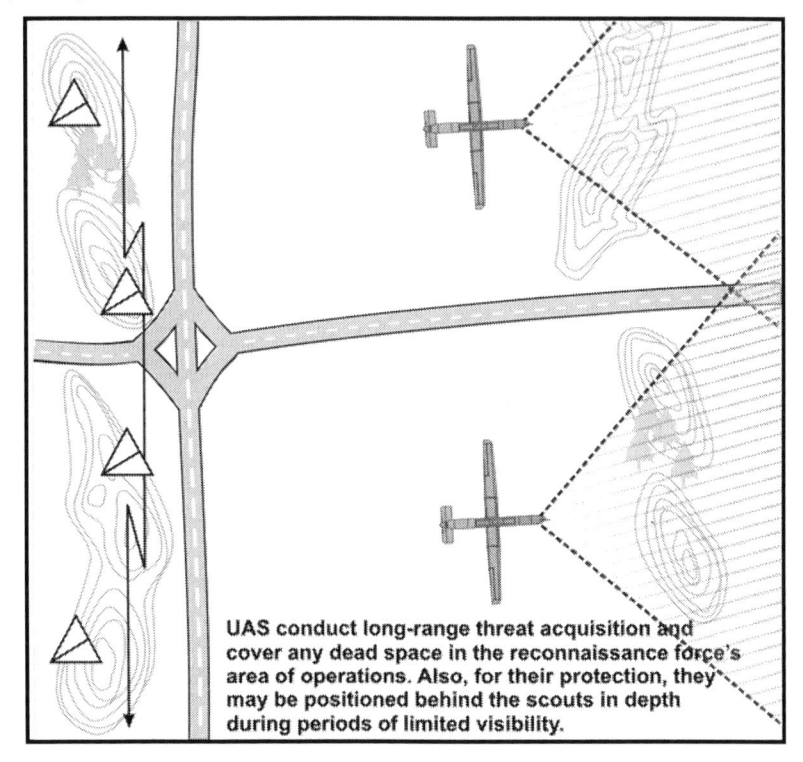

UAS conduct long-range threat acquisition and cover any dead space in the reconnaissance force's area of operations. Also, for their protection, they may be positioned behind the scouts in depth during periods of limited visibility.

Figure 7-2. UAS complementing a ground screen

Area Security

7-85. The UAS element can complement the reconnaissance platoon during area security missions by providing additional 360-degree security, or conducting reconnaissance for additional maneuver space. An air screen can provide early warning for a reconnaissance platoon executing a convoy escort mission or securing

Chapter 7

a critical point. (See Figure 7-3.) The UAS can identify enemy ambush positions forward of the convoy or find bypasses the convoy can use to move around an obstacle (as illustrated in Figure 7-4).

7-86. The UAS supporting the lead reconnaissance elements (section/squad and team) of the platoon can identify an enemy element before visual or physical contact with the Soldier. This prevents unwanted detection and direct fires. The lead vehicle and the overwatch element occupy positions allowing them to observe the enemy and, if necessary, destroy the enemy while the UAS provides the platoon with area security overhead. The UAS may also establish and maintain contact with a moving contact while units conduct a reconnaissance handover during a screen mission.

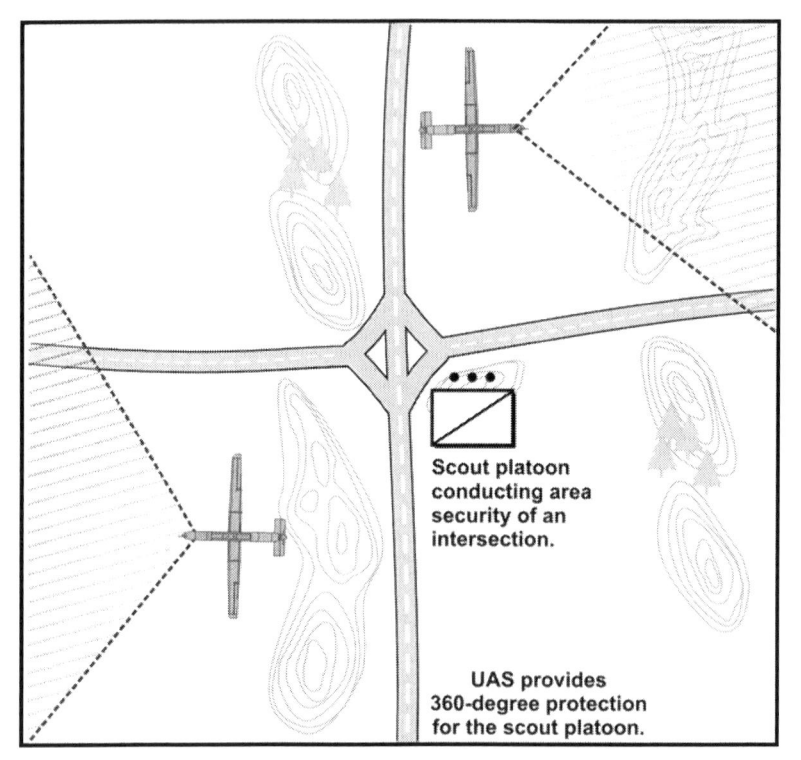

Figure 7-3. UAS providing additional security for a reconnaissance platoon

Augmenting Combat Power

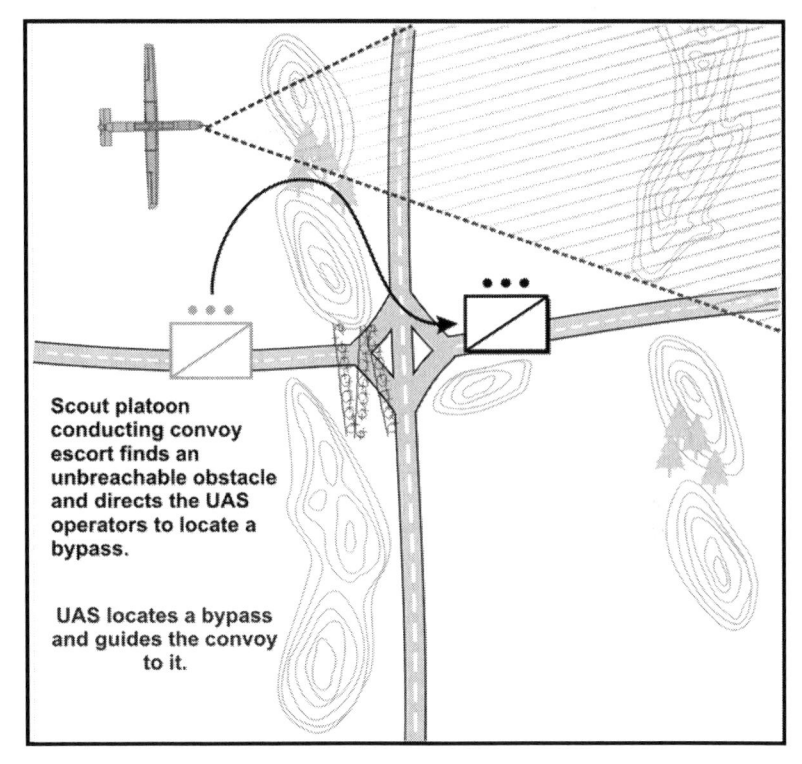

Figure 7-4. UAS reconnoitering for a bypass

MILITARY INTELLIGENCE COMPANY

7-87. The military intelligence company (MICO) mission is to conduct intelligence analysis, synchronization, and HUMINT collection supporting the unit and its subordinate commands across the range of military operations. It supports the unit S-2 by maintaining a timely and accurate picture of the enemy situation. This threat portion of the analysis aids in predicting future enemy COAs, and helps answer the unit commander's intelligence requirements. The MICO also assists the unit S-3 with intelligence, surveillance, reconnaissance synchronization, and integration tasks. It coordinates and executes tactical HUMINT tasks as directed by the unit S-3 and S-2.

SECTION IV – CHEMICAL, BIOLOGICAL, RADIOLOGICAL, NUCLEAR, AND HIGH-YIELD EXPLOSIVES

7-88. Chemical, biological, radiological, nuclear, and high yield explosives assets are limited within the reconnaissance platoon. External support is required for most circumstances involving CBRNE incidents.

7-89. Only the CBRNE officer and NCO are organic to the unit. The exception is the CBRNE reconnaissance platoon in the surveillance troop of the SBCT reconnaissance squadron. The unit CBRNE officer uses decision-support tools embedded in the joint Warning and Reporting System to plan defense, provide battle tracking during unit operations, and gain and maintain SA. The CBRNE battle staff assists the unit commander and the unit CBRNE NCO in defense through the integration of contamination avoidance, protection, and decontamination.

RECONNAISSANCE SUPPORT

7-90. CBRNE reconnaissance and surveillance elements locate, survey, detect, identify, quantify, sample collections, observe, monitor, mark, and report the presence or absence of CBRNE contamination. Information is obtained via observation, sensors, detectors, or other methods, and may include gathering information on enemy use of CBRNE weapons, associated hazards, or meteorological data for prediction purposes. (Refer to FM 3-11.19 for more information.)

7-91. When a CBRNE section or team is attached to a reconnaissance platoon during a zone, area, or route mission, the platoon leader ensures the CBRNE team leader understands the mission, their specific information requirements, the maneuver plan, and end state. They should deploy adjacent to forward elements of the reconnaissance platoon if CBRNE conditions are suspected. If these conditions are possible but not likely, the team is deployed in-depth for security purposes while continuing to monitor conditions and take samples.

SECTION V – OTHER COMBAT AUGMENTATION

7-92. The unit does not possess the organic assets to complete many of the detailed requirements of some complex tasks. Depending on METT-TC and the specific nature of the mission, unique enablers such as working dogs, interpreters, tactical military information support teams, EOD teams, or CA teams may be useful. If these assets are not immediately available, the unit commander and subordinate leaders clearly identify the request for additional support to or through the battalion/squadron.

MILITARY WORKING DOGS

7-93. Military police units can provide working dog support for mine and explosives detection, or to locate personnel, contraband, weapons, ammunition, and other items. These dogs are trained for a variety of purposes.

INTERPRETERS

7-94. Interpreters are valuable assets for reconnaissance tasks that require a close proximity to indigenous people. Early in the planning process, the commander should request an interpreter who is from or familiar with the AO. Using an interpreter improves communication between the local population and the reconnaissance platoon, helps improve intelligence gathering, and fosters acceptance of the unit within the particular AO. Interpreters often operate during searches, including tasks at roadblocks and checkpoints. It is very important to use only approved interpreters when collecting or verifying intelligence.

TACTICAL MILITARY INFORMATION SUPPORT TEAMS

7-95. Tactical MISO teams use various methods to influence the opinion of the population on or near the objective. They integrate with the inform and influence activities process at the battalion/squadron level to meet the commander's objectives. The commander should consider withdrawing reconnaissance elements from the area when employing MISO capabilities because the presence of each unit has the potential to compromise the mission of the other.

7-96. At the tactical level, MISO teams seek to influence targets directly through face-to-face encounters, dissemination of printed products, and use of loudspeakers. Tactical MISO teams can—

- Influence potential adversaries in the civil population to not interfere with friendly force efforts.
- Induce cooperation or reduce active opposition.
- Reduce collateral damage by giving instructions to noncombatants in the combat zone.

EXPLOSIVE ORDNANCE DISPOSAL

7-97. The reconnaissance platoon often requires EOD support to destroy threat ammunition and equipment, and ensure that IEDs and unexploded explosive ordnance (UXO) are rendered inoperable. Explosive ordnance disposal capabilities are not organic to the troop and augmentation of EOD personnel may be needed to clear an identified explosive hazard, or assist in the collection of explosive components. Requests for EOD support are processed through battalion/squadron operational channels to the unit's higher echelon, who forward the request to the supporting EOD headquarters. Once IEDs or UXOs are located and reported, the EOD headquarters determines which EOD assets can respond. If there is a constant presence of IED/UXO hazards, EOD teams can be attached to the reconnaissance platoon. This gives the security and mobility an EOD team needs to move to a location and execute their EOD mission.

CIVIL AFFAIRS TEAM

7-98. Civil affairs provide the commander with expertise on the civil component of the OE. They analyze and influence civil considerations through specific processes, dedicated resources, and personnel. Like other nonorganic assets, the CA team may have security provided by the reconnaissance platoon in order to conduct meetings with conventional forces, special operation forces, indigenous populations and institutions, intergovernmental organizations, NGOs, and interagency elements. (Refer to FM 3-57 for more information.)

Chapter 8

Sustainment

Sustainment for the reconnaissance platoon is a potentially challenging task due to the wide-ranging, low-profile, and sometimes decentralized nature of their mission. The platoon often operates well in front of maneuver forces while conducting reconnaissance and security missions. Sustainment or resupply for the platoon can be hindered by distance and the need to keep these tasks undetected by the threat. This chapter discusses planning and responsibilities, supply tasks, and functions of sustainment for the reconnaissance platoon.

SECTION I – PLANNING AND RESPONSIBILITIES

8-1. Planning for sustainment is primarily a troop- and squadron-level task. While the troop commander and executive officer plan the task(s), the platoon leader and PSG are responsible for the execution of the plan.

8-2. Effective sustainment tasks enable the platoon to accomplish the wide range of tasks it can be assigned without inhibiting operations. In conducting these tasks, leaders are guided by five imperatives:
- Anticipation.
- Integration.
- Continuity.
- Responsiveness.
- Improvisation

PLANNING CONSIDERATIONS

8-3. Sustainment elements arm, fuel, fix, feed, and provide transportation and personnel for the reconnaissance or scout platoon. This creates unique planning and operational challenges, with most of the responsibility falling to the PSG.

8-4. The PSG is the sustainment coordinator responsible for advising the platoon leader of the platoon's logistics requirements during preparation for combat. The PSG is also accountable for the current logistics status once sustainment and resupply tasks are under way. The platoon sergeant's NCOs assist in executing resupply tasks and determining the platoon's logistics needs. In combat, the PSG coordinates directly with the 1SG. With prior coordination, elements of one platoon can coordinate support with the 1SG of the troop that is nearest to them.

Chapter 8

8-5. Sustainment is planned in advance and aggressively pushed forward without the delay imposed by reacting to requests. FBCB2 provides sustainment functionality in the form of sustainment and personnel SITREPs, digital call for support and task order messaging, SA, and task management capabilities. These functions enhance the synchronization of all sustainment support in the AO.

8-6. The platoon's basic sustainment responsibilities are to report and request support requirements through the correct channels and ensure that sustainment tasks are properly executed. The PSG and section leaders submit accurate personnel and logistic reports, along with other necessary information and requests.

8-7. The platoon leader develops the sustainment plan by determining exactly what is on hand and accurately predicting the support requirements. This process validates the sustainment plan and ensures the platoon submits support requests as early as possible. The platoon leader formulates the plan and submits support requests to the company based on the maneuver plan. It is critical for the company to know what the platoon has on hand for designated critical supplies.

OPERATIONAL QUESTIONS

8-8. The sustainment plan should provide answers to the following types of operational questions:

- **Types of support:**
  - Based on the nature of the mission, what types of support does the platoon need?
  - How do specific tactical factors impact these types of support?
- **Quantities:**
  - What quantities are required by this support?
  - What is the estimated Class V requirement?
  - Are emergency resupplies required during the battle?
    — Potentially when and where?
  - Does this mission require prestocked supplies (cache points)?
- **Threat:**
  - What is the composition and disposition of the expected enemy threat?
    — What are its capabilities?
  - How does this affect sustainment tasks during the battle?
  - Contact is expected to occur where and when?
  - What are the platoon's expected casualties and equipment losses based on the nature and location of anticipated contact?
  - What impact do the enemy's special weapons capabilities (such as CBRNE) have on the battle and on expected sustainment requirements?
  - How many EPWs are expected, and where?

Sustainment

- **Terrain and weather:**
  - What ground provides the best security for CCPs?
  - What are the platoon's casualty evacuation routes?
  - What are the dirty routes for evacuating contaminated personnel and equipment?
- **Time and location:**
  - When and where does the platoon need sustainment?
  - Based on the nature and location of expected contact, what are the best sites for the CCP?
  - Where are the EPW collection points located?
    - Who secures them?
    - When does the platoon turn them over, and to whom?
- **Requirements:**
  - What are the support requirements by element and type of support?
  - Which section/team has priority for emergency Class V resupply?
- **Risk factor:**
  - Are support elements able to conduct resupply tasks in relative safety during lulls in the battle?
  - If no lulls are expected, how can the platoon best minimize the danger to the sustainment vehicles providing the required support?
- **Resupply technique:**
  - Based on operational factors, what technique is used to conduct sustainment for the platoon?
  - Can the sustainment be conducted during mission transition as opposed to during the reconnaissance mission?

INDIVIDUAL RESPONSIBILITIES

8-9. Sustainment is a requirement in all missions. Overall accountability for the platoon's sustainment belongs to the platoon leader, but every Soldier, leader, and unit has sustainment responsibilities. Duties include but are not limited to—

- Executing the platoon's sustainment plan.
- Coordinating with the higher command for the support required to conduct the mission.
- Ensuring, within the platoon's maintenance capabilities, that all vehicles, weapon systems, and equipment such as night-vision devices, mine detectors, and communications equipment are combat ready at all times.

Chapter 8

- Knowing the status of current platoon maintenance activities, including corrective actions for equipment faults, job orders to direct support (DS) maintenance elements, and requisition for repair parts. The platoon leader keeps the commander informed of the platoon's maintenance status.
- Planning and rehearsing a maintenance evacuation plan for every mission.

8-10. As the platoon's main sustainment operator, the platoon sergeant executes the logistics plan based on platoon and squadron SOP. The platoon sergeant's duties may include but are not limited to—

- Participating in sustainment rehearsals and integrating sustainment into the platoon's maneuver rehearsals.
- Receiving, consolidating, and forwarding all administrative, personnel, and casualty reports as directed or according to the unit SOP.
- Obtaining supplies, equipment (except Class VIII), and mail from the supply sergeant, and ensuring proper distribution.
- Supervising evacuation of casualties, KIAs, EPWs, and damaged equipment.
- Maintaining the platoon's manning roster.
- Cross-leveling supplies and equipment throughout the platoon.
- Coordinating logistics/personnel requirements with attached or OPCON units
- Using the FBCB2 System for recurring reports and coordination of sustainment assets moving forward.
- Directing and supervising unit maintenance of platoon equipment, vehicles, and weapon systems.
- Helping the platoon leader comply with responsibilities, and assuming these responsibilities in the platoon leader's absence.
- Coordinating with the 1SG to arrange organizational or DS maintenance.
- Collecting reports of the platoon's maintenance status in the field, and sending the appropriate consolidated reports to maintenance personnel.

8-11. Section/team leader's sustainment duties include—

- Ensuring Soldiers perform proper maintenance on assigned equipment.
- Ensuring Soldiers maintain personal hygiene.
- Compiling personnel and logistics reports for the platoon, and submitting them to the platoon sergeant as directed or according to the unit SOP.
- Obtaining supplies, equipment (except Class VIII), and mail from the platoon sergeant, and ensuring proper distribution.
- Cross-leveling supplies and equipment throughout the squad.

Sustainment

SECTION II – SUPPLY TASKS

CLASSES OF SUPPLY

8-12. There are ten categories, or classes, of supply. Each class has a major impact on any unit being able to accomplish the mission. (Refer to JP 1-02 for more information.) The classes of supply are—

- **Class I.** Rations and gratuitous issue of health, morale, and welfare items such as water and ice.
- **Class II.** Clothing, individual equipment, tentage, tool sets, and administrative and housekeeping supplies and equipment.
- **Class III.** Petroleum, oils, and lubricants.
- **Class IV.** Construction and engineering materials such as pickets, sandbags, and concertina wire.
- **Class V.** Ammunition, including mines and explosives.
- **Class VI.** Personal-demand items such as things normally sold through the exchange system, which can include candy, soaps, and cameras.
- **Class VII.** Major end items, including tanks, helicopters, and radios.
- **Class VIII.** Medical, including medical-peculiar repair parts supplied through the battalion medical platoon.
- **Class IX.** Repair parts and components for equipment maintenance, including the documents required for equipment maintenance tasks.
- **Class X.** Nonstandard items to support nonmilitary programs such as agriculture and economic development.
- **Miscellaneous.** Anything that does not fall into one of the existing classes of supply.

8-13. The platoon sergeant obtains supplies and delivers them to the platoon based upon the established priorities for delivery set by the platoon leader. Combat demands that Class I, III, V, and IX supplies and equipment take priority because they are the most critical to successful sustainment and resupply.

BASIC AND COMBAT LOADS
8-14. There are few, if any, contingencies where U.S. military forces have all the supplies needed for a mission. It is essential that every unit's daily logistics report accurately reflect its operational needs, and the supplies and equipment on hand.

Basic Load
8-15. The basic load includes supplies that the platoon keeps on its organic vehicles for use in combat. The amount of time the platoon sustains itself in combat without resupply determines the quantity of supply items. The higher command or the SOP specifies the Class V basic load.

Chapter 8

Combat Load

8-16. The platoon's combat load includes the supplies carried into the fight. The unit commander directs some minimum requirements, but the unit SOP or the platoon leader specifies most items for the combat load. Using organic transportation assets, the platoon's parent unit moves the combat load into battle in a single delivery.

METHODS OF RESUPPLY

8-17. A logistics package is the most common method of resupply, but tailgate resupply, service station resupply, a variation of one type, or a combination of both types, pre-positioning, and aerial resupply are also used. The tactical situation dictates which method of resupply the reconnaissance or scout platoon employs.

8-18. The situation also determines when resupply takes place. It's best to conduct resupply during mission transition, but this can be unavoidable during security missions of long duration

Routine Resupply

8-19. In the tailgate method, the PSG or another responsible individual brings fuel and ammunition forward to the reconnaissance sections or squads. The platoon uses this method when routes leading to vehicle positions are available (including successful infiltration routes) and the unit is not under direct enemy observation and fire. Tailgate resupply is time-consuming but stealthier in security missions when the scouts are not moving. The platoon further minimizes signatures by hand-carrying supplies to vehicle positions, if necessary. (See Figure 8-1.)

Sustainment

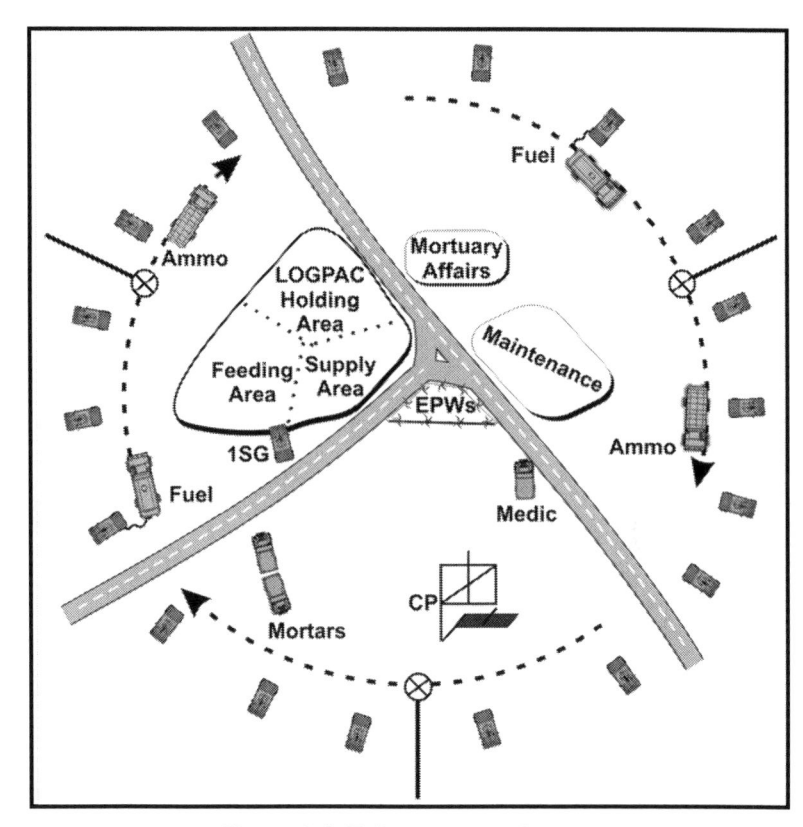

Figure 8-1. Tailgate resupply

8-20. Service station resupply is inherently faster than the tailgate method but can create security problems due to movement and concentration. During screening missions, the platoon is careful not to compromise the location of the OPs. Units commonly use this method during mission transition.

8-21. Depending upon the tactical situation, a vehicle, section or platoon moves out of its position, conducts resupply tasks, and moves back into position (refer to Figure 8-2). This process continues until the entire platoon receives its supplies. When using this method, vehicles enter the resupply point following a one-way traffic flow. Only vehicles that require immediate maintenance stop at the maintenance holding area. Vehicles move through each supply location.

Chapter 8

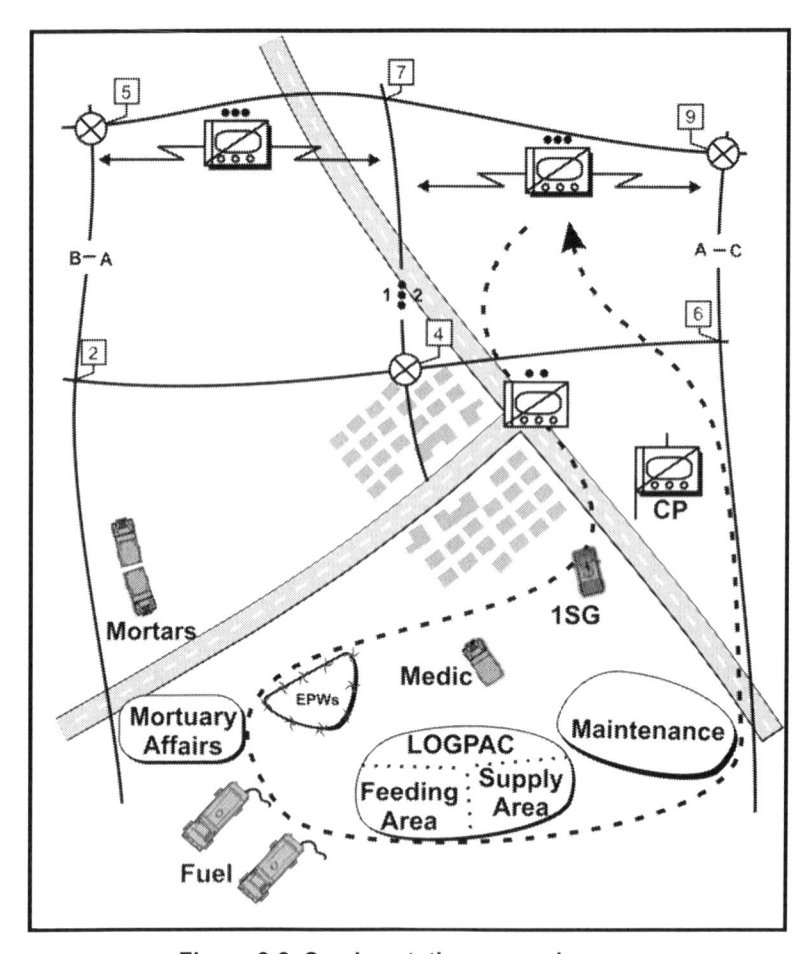

Figure 8-2. Service station resupply

8-22. The platoon leader can vary the specifics of the two basic methods or use them in combination. For example, during a screening mission the tailgate method can be used for the most forward OPs and the service station method for the OPs in-depth.

8-23. The crews rotate individually to eat, pick up mail and sundries, and refill or exchange water cans. When all platoon vehicles and crews have completed resupply, they move to a holding area. There, time permitting, the platoon leader and the PSG conduct a precombat inspection.

Prestock Resupply

8-24. At times the platoon usually needs prestocked supplies. These are also known as prepositioned or "cached" resupply. Normally, the platoon only pre-positions Classes IV and V items, but can also preposition Class III supplies. When the platoon conducts this type of resupply, the platoon leader directs the PSG to rotate vehicles or sections through prestock positions based on the enemy situation and shortages within the platoon. Security requires planning to prevent enemy dismounted/insurgent forces from destroying or sabotaging prestocked supplies.

8-25. All levels carefully plan and execute pre-stock requirements, and every leader knows the exact locations of pre-stock sites. During reconnaissance or rehearsals, these locations are verified, with the platoon taking steps to ensure the survivability of the pre-stocked supplies. These measures include selecting covered and concealed positions, and digging in the pre-stock positions. The plan should include a grid to the location of the sites, and have a removal and destruction plan to prevent the enemy from capturing pre-positioned supplies.

8-26. In addition to routine resupply systems, the reconnaissance or scout platoon uses several other methods to obtain needed materiels. These methods include:
- Aerial and airdrop resupply.
- Pre-positioning.
- Cache.

Aerial and Airdrop Resupply

8-27. Helicopters and fixed wing assets can be a vital lifeline when scouts are forced to operate forward of friendly lines for extended periods of time. Aerial assets are useful in resupplying dismounted scouts in restricted terrain OPs. This option is not always available due to lack of aircraft or degraded weather conditions. Careful choice of resupply routes, LZs, and DZs helps minimize the risk of signature resupply aircraft.

Prepositioning and Cache

8-28. The reconnaissance or scout platoon uses prepositioning and cache methods in a variety of missions. Also called prestock resupply, these two methods differ in the level of security allocated for the supplies. In prepositioning, units may leave supplies unattended or provide security as dictated by METT-TC. However, when it resupplies by cache, the platoon should take steps to prevent enemy detection.

8-29. During reconnaissance, the reconnaissance or scout platoon uses advance elements to establish prestock positions along the intended route of advance or near the objective. In security tasks, the platoon can set up prestock points throughout the AO. These points should be in alternate or supplementary OPs, and other locations throughout the depth of the sector. Scouts can also use prestock to provide resupply for patrols.

Chapter 8

8-30. The platoon carefully plans and executes cache tasks at every level. The platoon places cache points where someone who has never visited the site can find the point by following simple instructions. All leaders, down to squad leader and vehicle commander, know the exact locations of cache sites. The platoon leader takes steps to ensure the security and survivability of supplies by digging in cache positions, selecting covered and concealed positions, taking into account the effects of weather and terrain, and having a plan to remove or destroy cache supplies in order to prevent the enemy from capturing them.

SECTION III – FUNCTIONS OF SUSTAINMENT

MAINTENANCE

8-31. There are two levels of Army maintenance. Field maintenance primarily replaces parts on the user's system and sustainment maintenance repairs components off the user's platform.

FIELD MAINTENANCE

8-32. Field maintenance is on-system maintenance mainly involving preventive maintenance and replacement of defective parts. The goal of field maintenance is to repair and return equipment to the Soldier. It covers tasks previously assigned to operator/crew, organization/unit, and direct support maintenance levels; and includes some off-system maintenance critical to mission readiness.

8-33. The reconnaissance platoon leader and PSG ensure vehicle crews and equipment operators perform PMCS. Proper field maintenance keeps equipment and materiel in serviceable condition. This also includes inspecting, testing, servicing, repairing, requisitioning, recovering, and evacuating equipment and materiel whenever necessary.

SUSTAINMENT MAINTENANCE

8-34. Sustainment maintenance repairs components and returns them into the supply system. To maximize unit combat readiness, maintenance personnel repair and return the equipment to the user as quickly as possible. Repairs should be made as far forward as possible. Echelons above BCT perform this level of maintenance.

Vehicle Commander Responsibilities

8-35. Vehicle commanders are the platoon's first-line maintenance supervisors. The platoon's maintenance status and combat readiness depends on their commitment to proper maintenance procedures. The vehicle commander's duties in this area include—

- Ensuring operators fill out and update DA Forms 5988-E (Equipment Inspection Maintenance Worksheet (EGA)) and 2408-18 (Equipment Inspection List) in accordance with DA Pam 750-8.
- Training the crew in proper PMCS procedures.

Sustainment

- Ensuring the training and licensing for all crewmembers as drivers in preparing for continuous operations. At a minimum, ensuring the assigned vehicle driver or equipment operator is licensed.
- Ensuring that repair parts are installed upon receipt or are stored in authorized locations.
- Ensuring that all tools and basic issue items are properly marked, stored, maintained, and accounted for.
- Ensuring that the operator always tops off the vehicle in the garrison and that the vehicle receives as much fuel as possible at every opportunity in the field.
- Constantly updating the PSG on the maintenance and logistics status of the vehicle.

Operator Responsibilities

8-36. Operator maintenance includes the proper care, use, and maintenance of assigned vehicles and crew equipment such as weapons, CBRNE equipment, and NODs. The driver and other crewmembers perform daily services such as inspecting, servicing, tightening, lubricating, cleaning, preserving, and adjusting vehicles and equipment. The driver and gunner are required to use DA Form 5988-E to record these checks and services, and all equipment faults that cannot be immediately corrected. These reports are the primary means for reporting equipment faults through the vehicle commander to the PSG, platoon leader, and ultimately to organizational maintenance personnel.

8-37. Checks and services prescribed for the automotive system, weapon systems, and turret are divided into three groups:

- Before-mission.
- During-mission.
- After-mission.

8-38. The operator's manual explains these services. Although operators learn to operate equipment without referring to the manual, they always perform maintenance in accordance with the appropriate technical instructions.

FORCE HEALTH PROTECTION

8-39. Maintaining the health and fighting fitness of Soldiers is a vital responsibility of all leaders. The unit SOP should establish physical hygiene standards, sleep plans, safety procedures, and other measures to maintain the unit. Platoon and squad leaders ensure the health and fitness of their Soldiers by maintaining preventive medical measures, safety standards, and providing access to medical care. Small unit leaders are especially concerned about preventive health measures and stress control.

Chapter 8

PREVENTIVE MEDICINE

8-40. Leaders reduce health threats by monitoring and enforcing hygiene and sanitation practices, and emphasizing preventive measures. They are also actively involved in combat and operational stress reactions counseling.

8-41. Leaders emphasize high standards of health and hygiene. Soldiers shave daily so their protective masks seal correctly, and bathe and change clothes regularly to prevent disease. Each crewman carries shaving equipment, soap, a towel, and a change of clothing in a waterproof bag inside their pack.

8-42. Soldiers check their hands and feet regularly during cold weather to prevent frostbite, trench foot, and immersion foot. They are also aware of wind chill. A moving vehicle creates a wind chill effect even if the air is calm, causing exposed skin temperatures to be much lower than actual thermometer readings.

8-43. During hot weather, heat injuries can occur anywhere depending upon physical activity and the clothing worn. It is important for Soldiers to remain hydrated. Daily water requirements are increased due to the loss of body fluid through sweat. Dehydration leads to heat stress, reduces work performance, and degrades mission capabilities.

8-44. Field sanitation teams are trained in preventive medicine measures (PMM) and treatment of disease and nonbattle injuries (DNBI). They may advise the company/troop commander and platoon leader on the implementation of unit-level procedures for PMM and DNBI.

COMBAT AND OPERATIONAL STRESS CONTROL

8-45. Many factors cause operational stressors, including potential and actual enemy actions, the natural environment, and conducting missions in a combat environment. Sound leadership works to keep these operational stressors within tolerable limits. Some of the most potent stressors are interpersonal in nature and can be due to conflict in the unit or at home. For behavioral health, and combat and operational stress control support, Soldiers should contact the supporting medical company through the medical support section. (Refer to FM 4-02.51 and FM 6-22.5 for more information.)

CASUALTY EVACUATION PROCEDURES

8-46. It is the leader's responsibility to make sure that Soldiers wounded in action (WIA) receive immediate first aid, and the platoon leader or PSG is notified of all casualties. The use of combat lifesavers is absolutely critical. At a minimum, one member of each team is a trained combat lifesaver. Ideally, every member of the platoon should be a combat lifesaver. As per unit SOP, leaders need to mark their locations so that the unit medics can identify where casualties are located and who has priority.

Sustainment

8-47. If wounded crewmen require evacuation, the platoon leader or PSG takes one of the following steps:
- Coordinate with the supporting 1SG or troop medic for ground or aerial evacuation.
- Perform evacuation using organic platoon assets.

8-48. Regardless of the method of evacuation, all leaders have the necessary sustainment graphics available, including casualty collection points for the company/troop or combined arms battalion/squadron. Evacuation procedures are included in the platoon plan and should be rehearsed as part of mission preparation.

8-49. If available, aerial evacuation is preferred because of its speed. The platoon leader or PSG coordinate with higher HQ and then switch to the designated frequency to coordinate directly with aerial assets for MEDEVAC or CASEVAC services. The relatively flat, open, covered and concealed LZ location should be given to the aircraft by radio and marked with colored smoke as the aircraft approaches the area. The platoon provides local security until the evacuation is complete.

Note. Leaders should remove all key operational items and equipment from casualties before evacuation to the CCP or beyond. This includes signal operating instructions, maps, position-locating devices, and laser pointers. Every unit should establish their SOP for handling the weapons and ammunition of its wounded in action.

This page intentionally left blank.

Appendix A
Analog Reports

To facilitate common reporting formats, the following report arrangements can be used to ensure clear communications between units and echelons.

CONTACT AND BLUE REPORTS

A-1. A contact report is issued immediately upon contact with a threat or unknown force in the area of operations. This alert, which can be very brief, takes priority over all other communications traffic and is primarily sent by radio. If Soldiers are already in a hide position and have detected the enemy before being detected first (and time permits) this initial report may be sent digitally. State "CONTACT," followed by a description of the threat or unknown force and the cardinal direction from the sender.

BLUE 1 SPOT REPORT

A-2. A SPOTREP is used when scouts observe any known or suspected threat activity. It is also used when any characteristic of the AO likely to affect accomplishment of the mission is observed, or when required by the OPORD. Always send threat information in the clear. A SPOTREP takes priority over all other routine radio traffic. The initial SPOTREP should follow no more than one minute after the contact report. State "SPOTREP," or "UPDATED SPOTREP," followed by pertinent information on these lines:

- **Line ALPHA:** Observer or source (omit if it is the calling station, otherwise use call signs or description).
- **Line BRAVO:** Activity or characteristic being observed. Use the SALUTE format:
  - *Size:* The number of sighted personnel, vehicles, or other equipment.
  - *Activity:* What the threat is doing.
  - *Location:* Grid coordinates. (Report the center of mass for identical, closely grouped items.) Otherwise, report multiple grid coordinates of traces.
  - *Unit:* Patches, signs, or markings.
  - *Time:* Time the activity was observed.
  - *Equipment:* Description or identification of all equipment associated with the activity.

Appendix A

- **Line CHARLIE:** Actions the reporting Soldier has taken and personal recommendations. Actions usually involve conducting additional reconnaissance to determine the complete threat situation or recommending and executing a specific course of action.
- **Line DELTA:** Self-authentication (if required).

> **Example of a Blue 1 Spot Report**
>
> "YELLOW 4, THIS IS YELLOW 2. SPOTREP, OVER. ONE BRDM, STATIONARY, ORIENTED SOUTH AT GRID MS289546; 1725 HOURS. CONTINUING TO OBSERVE, OVER."

BLUE 2 SITUATION REPORT

A-3. The situation report (SITREP) is submitted by subordinate units to their higher HQ on the tactical situation and status. It is submitted daily, after significant events, or as otherwise requested by the platoon leader or commander. State "SITREP," followed by pertinent information on these lines:

- **Line 1:** The as-of DTG.
- **Line 2:** Brief summary of threat activity, casualties inflicted, and prisoners captured.
- **Line 3:** Friendly locations (encoded using control measures or TIRS points).
- **Line 4:** Combat vehicles, operational tanks.
- **Line 5:** Defensive obstacles (encoded using codes, control measures, or TIRS points). The type and location can be listed as:
  - *Obstacles.* Abbreviations can include MF (minefield), TD (tank ditch), AB (abatis), RC (road crater), and CW (concertina wire).
  - *Executed demolition targets.*
  - *Reserved demolition targets.*
- **Line 6:** Personnel strength, classified using the following status levels:
  - *GREEN:* Full strength; 90% or more fit for duty.
  - *AMBER:* Reduced strength; 80 to 89% fit for duty.
  - *RED:* Reduced strength; 60 to 79% fit for duty; the unit is mission-capable.
  - *BLACK:* Reduced strength; 59% or less fit for duty.
- **Line 7:** Classes III and V supplies available for combat vehicles. Status levels for ammunition and POL are the same ones used for personnel strength (GREEN, AMBER, RED, OR BLACK), with percentages referring to the amount of basic load level available. (Refer to Line 6 of this report.)
- **Line 8:** Summary of tactical intentions.

Analog Reports

Note. If an item is reported as status level BLACK on lines 6 or 7, the appropriate yellow (logistics) report follows this transmission.

Example of a Blue 2 Situation Report

"YANKEE 21, THIS IS YANKEE 02, SITREP, OVER. LINE 1: 062230. LINE 2: NEGATIVE CONTACT. LINE 3: VISIT 7. LINE 4B: 2. LINE 5: ABATIS, FROM X19 EAST ZERO POINT THREE NORTH ONE POINT SEVEN. LINE 6: GREEN. LINE 7A: GREEN. LINE 7B: AMBER. LINE 8: CONTINUING MISSION."

BLUE 4 – REPORT FOR BRIDGE, OVERPASS, CULVERT, UNDERPASS, OR TUNNEL

A-4. To send a bridge report (BRIDGEREP), state "BRIDGEREP," followed by pertinent information on these lines:

- **Line ALPHA:** Type and location (for a long tunnel, include the entrance and exit locations). Use either a TIRS point or grid coordinates.
- **Line BRAVO:** Overall length.
- **Line CHARLIE:** Width of roadway.
- **Line DELTA:** Height restrictions.
- **Line ECHO:** Length and number of spans.
- **Line FOXTROT:** Computed classification.
- **Line GOLF:** Bypass locations and conditions. Use a Blue 5 report if necessary.

BLUE 5 – REPORT FOR FORD, FERRY, OR OTHER CROSSING SITE

A-5. To send the crossing site report (CROSSREP), state "CROSSREP," followed by pertinent information on these lines:

- **Line ALPHA:** Type and location, using either a TIRS point or grid coordinates.
- **Line BRAVO:** Length of crossing in meters.
- **Line CHARLIE:** Usable width.
- **Line DELTA:** Current speed in meters per second.
- **Line ECHO:** Maximum depth in meters.
- **Line FOXTROT:** Bottom material and condition.
- **Line GOLF:** Capacity classification of any existing ferry equipment.
- **Line HOTEL:** Slope of entry bank.
- **Line INDIA:** Slope of exit bank.
- **Line KILO:** Other comments as necessary.

Appendix A

BLUE 7 – ROUTE RECONNAISSANCE REPORT

A-6. To report the results of a route reconnaissance, scouts should send an initial route reconnaissance report (ROUTEREP) at the SP. At a minimum, the initial report should be followed by updates at any obstructions, at each phase line, and whenever a route change becomes necessary. These update reports should include only the line(s) that have changed from the initial ROUTEREP. To send the report, state "ROUTEREP," followed by pertinent information on these lines:

- **Line ALPHA:** "From" location, reported using a control measure or TIRS point.
- **Line BRAVO:** "To" location, reported using a control measure or TIRS point.
- **Line CHARLIE:** Type of route, reported using the following designations:
  - *Highway:* Reported using the number "1."
  - *Road:* Number "2."
  - *Trail:* Number "3."
  - *Cross-country:* Number "4."
- **Line DELTA:** Classification of route. Check for height, width, and weight restrictions to determine the appropriate class, and report what vehicles the route is capable of handling using the following designations:
  - *All squadron/battalion vehicles* (70 class minimum), reported using the number "1."
  - *Tracked vehicles* only, number "2."
  - *CFVs* only (35 class restriction), number "3."
- **Line ECHO:** Seasonal limitations of route based on weather support capability, reported as follows:
  - *All-weather* (usable year-round), reported using the letter "X."
  - *Limited all-weather* (use limited during bad weather), letter "Y."
  - *Fair weather* (may be impassable during bad weather), letter "Z."
- **Line FOXTROT:** Rate of movement the route supports, reported as follows:
  - *Fast:* Reported using the number "1."
  - *Slow:* Reported using the number "2."
- **Line GOLF:** Location and type of any critical points (send the applicable report). Report the following obstructions in all cases:
  - *Curves* with a radius of 45 m or less.
  - *Uphill slopes* with grades of 5 percent or greater.
  - *Width restrictions* of 6 m or less for one-way traffic, 10 m or less for two-way traffic.
  - *Overhead clearance* of 4.3 m or less.

Analog Reports

BLUE 9 – OBSTACLE REPORT

A-7. Report all pertinent information using the following format:
- **Line ALPHA:** Type of obstacle or obstruction.
- **Line BRAVO:** Location, using grid coordinates. For large, complex obstacles, send the coordinates of the ends and of all turn points.
- **Line CHARLIE:** Dimensions and orientation.
- **Line DELTA:** Composition.
- **Line ECHO:** Threat weapons influencing obstacle.
- **Line FOXTROT:** Observer's actions.

BLUE 10 - BYPASS REPORT

A-8. Report all pertinent information using the following format:
- **Line ALPHA:** Observer or source.
- **Line BRAVO:** Length; width; surface type; grade.
- **Line CHARLIE:** Coordinates of "from" and "to" locations.
- **Line DELTA:** Seasonal/weather limitations. Use letter designation (X, Y, or Z) as described in the Blue 7 ROUTEREP (line Echo).
- **Line ECHO:** Bypass markings.
- **Line FOXTROT:** Observer's actions.

BLUE 11 - STAND-TO REPORT

A-9. The stand-to report (STANREP) is sent to the platoon leader or TOC, as applicable, when stand-to is completed. To send this report, state "STANREP," followed by pertinent information on these lines:
- **Line ALPHA:** Time stand-to was completed.
- **Line BRAVO:** Weapons on hand and functional. Use the term "UP" for functional weapons on hand. Use "EXCEPTION" for weapons that are not on hand or not functional.
- **Line CHARLIE:** Sensitive and accountable items on hand. Use "UP" or "EXCEPTION," as applicable.
- **Line DELTA:** Vehicles and radios on hand and functional. Use "UP" or "EXCEPTION," as applicable.
- **Line ECHO:** Report the on-hand/functional status of any other equipment using "UP" or "EXCEPTION."

Note. For lines B, C, D, and E, refer to the Yellow 1 ESTAT report for equipment line numbers.

Appendix A

> **Example of a Blue 11 Stand-To Report**
>
> "BLACK 3, THIS IS RED 1; BLUE 11. LINE ALPHA: COMPLETE TIME 0600. LINE BRAVO: UP. LINE CHARLIE: ITEM 38, MISSING 1 EACH. LINE DELTA: RED 3 WILL NOT START."

INTELLIGENCE REPORTS

A-10. Intelligence reports are routinely sent to account for friendly equipment, and captured enemy materiel and personnel. These reports are significant because they are used to relay information that has possible intelligence value in a concise format.

GREEN 2 – SENSITIVE ITEMS REPORT

A-11. The sensitive items report (SENSEREP) is sent daily at prescribed times (before and after significant movement, after significant events, and after any consolidation or reorganization). Items covered include machine guns, personal weapons, night vision devices, binoculars, nuclear, biological, and chemical (NBC) equipment, communications-electronics operating instructions (CEOI) materiels, maps/graphics, and special equipment assigned to platoons for particular missions. To send this report, state "SENSEREP," followed by pertinent information on these lines:

- **Line ALPHA:** Reporting unit (use call sign).
- **Line CHARLIE:** Results of sensitive items check. Use the term "UP" for on-hand/functional items. For missing items, report the line description and serial number, and provide an explanation. Use additional lines from the Yellow 1 report.
- **Line ECHO:** Initials of person sending report.

> **Example of a Green 2 Sensitive Items Report**
>
> "THIS IS RED 1. SENSEREP. LINE ALPHA: RED. LINE CHARLIE: ALL 'UP.' LINE ECHO: RWS."

GREEN 3 – SPLASH REPORT.

A-12. The splash report is used to report downed or missing aircraft. To send this report, provide all pertinent information on these lines:

- **Line 1:** Call sign.
- **Line 2:** Aircraft data (type and status).
- **Line 3:** Pilot status.

GREEN 4 – PATROL REPORT.

A-13. The patrol report may be submitted by radio or wire when required. The following debriefing format can be used to ensure all pertinent information is provided in the patrol report:

Analog Reports

- **Designation of patrol.** Include these elements:
  - *To:* _____
  - *From:* _____
  - *Maps:* _____
- **Size and composition of patrol.**
- **Task.**
- **Time of departure.**
- **Time of return.**
- **Routes (out and back).**
- **Terrain.** This includes a description of terrain by type (such as dry, swampy, and so forth), depth of ravines and draws, condition of bridges (type, size, and strength), and effect of terrain on tracked and wheeled vehicles.
- **Threat.** This includes details of threat strength, disposition, defenses, equipment, weapons, attitude, morale, exact location, and movements. The report should include the time threat activity was observed and coordinates for the location where the activity occurred.
- **Any map corrections.**
- **Miscellaneous information.** This includes pertinent details of NBC warfare, if applicable.
- **Results of encounters with the threat.** This includes threat prisoners and casualties, captured documents and equipment, identification of threat elements, and threat disposition after the contact.
- **Condition of the patrol.** This includes disposition arrangements for any dead or wounded.
- **Conclusions and recommendations.** This includes the extent to which the mission was accomplished and any recommendations as to patrol equipment and tactics.
- **Additional remarks by the debriefer.**

Note. The report should conclude with the name, rank/grade, and organization/unit of the patrol leader.

GREEN 6 – EPW/CAPTURED MATERIEL REPORT.

A-14. Use the EPW/captured materiel report only to inform the troop or battalion TOC of EPWs, or captured materiel of immediate tactical value. Usually, EPWs and captured materiel are tagged immediately to show the place, time, and circumstances of capture. This ensures information of intelligence value is not lost during evacuation of the EPW or materiel. Provide all pertinent information on the following lines (examples are in parentheses):

- **Line 1:** State "GREEN 6."
- **Line 2:** Item captured (state "EPW").
- **Line 3:** DTG of capture ("260845SEP83").

Appendix A

- **Line 4:** Place of capture, using grid coordinates ("NS 621434").
- **Line 5:** Capturing unit (appropriate call sign).
- **Line 6:** Circumstances of capture, described as briefly as possible.

Format for reporting captured materiel. Provide all pertinent information on the following lines (examples in parentheses):

- **Line 1:** State "GREEN 6."
- **Line 2:** Item captured (state "MATERIEL").
- **Line 3:** Type of document or equipment ("CEOI").
- **Line 4:** DTG of capture ("160900JUN83").
- **Line 5:** Place of capture, using grid coordinates ("NE824615").
- **Line 6:** Capturing unit (appropriate call sign).
- **Line 7:** Circumstances of capture, described as briefly as possible.

Note. After sending the report to the company team or troop commander, provide disposition instructions or recommendations, if necessary.

LOGISTICS REPORTS

A-15. Logistics reports are used to report the status of sustainment items and request resupply. Units should immediately follow a status report with a request report.

YELLOW 1 – EQUIPMENT STATUS REPORT

A-16. Each PSG sends the equipment status report (ESTAT) by courier or voice radio to the troop/task force TOC every day. The information is as of 1200 hours that same day. Equipment status is recorded using one of these terms: operational, inoperative, or combat loss. Provide all pertinent information using the following categories and lines:

- **Weapons.**
  - *Line 1:* Bayonet knife with scabbard, for M16 variants.
  - *Line 2:* Pistol, 9 mm, automatic, M9.
  - *Line 3:* Rifle, 5.56 mm, with equipment.
  - *Line 4:* Launcher, grenade, 40 mm, single shot, rifle-mounted, detachable, with equipment.
  - *Line 5:* Machine gun, M2, caliber .50, heavy barrel (HB).
  - *Line 6:* Machine gun, 7.62 mm.
  - *Line 7:* Squad automatic weapon, M249.
  - *Line 8:* Grenade launcher, 40 mm, MK19.
  - *Line 12:* Command launch unit, AAWS-M.

Note. Lines 13, 14, 15, and 16 are used as needed for additional weapons assigned to the platoon.

Analog Reports

- **Vehicles and vehicle equipment.**
  - *Line 17:* CFV, M3.
  - *Line 18:* Carrier, 107-mm mortar, self-propelled (less mortar), M106.
  - *Line 19:* Carrier, personnel, full-tracked, armored, M113.
  - *Line 20:* HMMWV, M1025/M1026.
  - *Line 21:* Tank, M1/M1A1/M1A2/M8-AGS.

Note. Lines 22, 23, and 24 are used as needed for additional vehicles and vehicle equipment assigned to the platoon.

- **NBC equipment.**
  - *Line 25:* Alarm, chemical agent, automatic, portable, for full-tracked APC and armored recovery vehicle (ARV).
  - *Line 26:* Alarm, chemical agent, automatic, portable, with power supply, for track, utility, ¼ ton.
  - *Line 27:* Charger, radiac detector, PP-1570/PD.
  - *Line 28:* Mask, chemical-biological, multipurpose.
  - *Line 30:* Alarm, chemical agent, automatic, portable, manpack.
  - *Line 33:* Radiacmeter, AN/VDR-1.

Note. Lines 34, 35, and 36 are used as needed for additional CBRNE equipment assigned to the platoon.

- **Radios.**

Note. Lines 46, 47, and 48 are used as needed for additional radios assigned to the platoon.

- **Miscellaneous equipment.**
  - *Line 49:* Demolition set, explosive, initiating, nonelectric.
  - *Line 51:* Detecting set, mine, portable, metallic, AN/PSS-11.
  - *Line 52:* Night vision goggles, AN/PVS-7B.
  - *Line 55:* Platoon early warning system (PEWS), AN/TRS-2(V).
  - *Line 56:* Binoculars, modular construction, military scale reticle, 7x50 mm, with equipment.
  - *Line 57:* Telescope, straight, military.
  - *Line 58:* Detector, radar signal, AN/PSS-1.

Note. Lines 61, 62, and 63 are used as needed for any other equipment assigned to the platoon.

Appendix A

> **Example of a Yellow 1 Equipment Status Report**
>
> "THIS IS RED 3. YELLOW 1. LINE 12: ALPHA. LINE 33: BRAVO. LINE 38: CHARLIE. LINE 55: CHARLIE. OVER."

YELLOW 1A – BATTLE LOSS SPOT REPORT.
A-17. The Yellow 1A report is transmitted by the platoon leader or PSG as soon as possible after items are lost or damaged in battle. Losses are reported using line numbers from the Yellow 1 report. Provide pertinent information on the following lines:

- **Line 1:** Time of loss.
- **Line 2:** Number of pieces of equipment to be evacuated to troop/battalion or higher for maintenance. Refer to the appropriate line numbers from the Yellow 1 report.
- **Line 3:** Number of pieces of equipment destroyed and abandoned in pieces. Refer to the appropriate line numbers from the Yellow 1 report.
- **Line 4:** Location (encoded) of abandoned equipment.

> **Example of a Yellow 1A Battle Loss Spot Report**
>
> "BLACK 3, THIS IS RED 4. YELLOW ONE ALPHA, BREAK. LINE 1: ONE FOUR THREE ZERO HOURS. LINE 2: REFERENCE SIX SLANT ONE; REFERENCE TWO-NINER SLANT THREE. LINE 3: REFERENCE TWO-NINER SLANT ONE. LINE 4: I SET VB, IDVRTG."

Note. Yellow 1A reports are not cumulative. A Yellow 1 report showing total unit status is sent daily not later than 1300 hours. It gives equipment status as of 1200 hours that day.

YELLOW 2 – AMMUNITION STATUS REPORT.
A-18. This report is transmitted once daily at 1300 hours or immediately upon completion of threat contact. The following status codes are used:

- **GREEN:** 90% or more on hand, all ammunition types.
- **AMBER:** 80% to 89% on hand, all ammunition types.
- **RED:** 60% to 79% on hand, all ammunition types.
- **BLACK:** 59% or less on hand, all ammunition types.

Note. BLACK status in a Yellow 2 report requires immediate follow-up with a Yellow 2A report. GREEN, AMBER, or RED status does not require submission of a Yellow 2A.

YELLOW 2A – AMMUNITION REQUEST.
A-19. The required quantity of each type of ammunition is requested using the following line numbers:
- **Line 1:** Report as-of DTG.
- **Line 2:** 105 mm/120 mm, HEAT.
- **Line 3:** 105 mm/120 mm, HEP.
- **Line 4:** 105 mm/120 mm, APERS.
- **Line 5:** 105 mm/120 mm, WP.
- **Line 6:** 105-mm/120 -mm, APDS.
- **Line 7:** 40 mm, HEDP.
- **Line 8:** Caliber .50 (M85).
- **Line 9:** Caliber .50 (M2).
- **Line 10:** 25 mm.
- **Line 11:** 7.62 mm (coax/M60).
- **Line 12:** 4.2 inch HE with fuze.
- **Line 13:** 4.2 inch WP with fuze.
- **Line 14:** 4.2 inch illumination with fuze.
- **Line 15:** 81 mm, HE with fuze.
- **Line 16:** 81 mm, WP with fuze.
- **Line 17:** 81 mm, illumination with fuze.
- **Line 18:** Fuze, prox (4.2 inch).
- **Line 19:** Fuze, PD (4.2 inch).
- **Line 20:** Fuze, prox (81 mm).
- **Line 21:** Fuze, PD (81 mm).
- **Line 22:** Fuze, blast, time.
- **Line 23:** Blasting cap, nonelectric.
- **Line 24:** Fuze, igniter.
- **Line 25:** 5.56 mm ball.
- **Line 26:** 5.56 mm tracer.
- **Line 28:** Grenade, fragmentation.
- **Line 29:** Grenade, smoke.
- **Line 30:** Grenade, thermite.
- **Line 31:** Grenade, 40 mm, HE.
- **Line 32:** Grenade, 40 mm, WP.
- **Line 33:** Grenade, 40 mm, AP.
- **Line 34:** Javelin.
- **Line 35:** AT4.
- **Line 37:** TOW.
- **Line 39:** Mine, AT.
- **Line 40:** Mine, AP.

Appendix A

- **Line 41:** Mine, Claymore.
- **Line 42:** 25 mm, HE.
- **Line 43:** 25 mm, AP.

Note. All Yellow 2A requests are for the quantity of ammunition required by the platoon, unless otherwise specified. When sending a Yellow 2A report, use only the lines required for specific requests. Additional lines (beginning with Line 45) are used to request any other types of ammunition required by the platoon. Attached units should coordinate with the S-4 for additional line numbers for their ammunition requirements.

Example of a Yellow 2A Ammunition Request

"BLACK 3, THIS IS RED 4. YELLOW TWO ALPHA, BREAK. LINE 1: 260941APR2011. LINE 37: 8. LINE 42: 1050."

YELLOW 3 – POL STATUS REPORT.
A-20. The POL report is sent twice daily or as required. The following status codes are used:
- **GREEN:** 90% or more of the required quantity on hand.
- **AMBER:** 80% to 89% on hand.
- **RED:** 60% to 79% on hand.
- **BLACK:** 59% or less on hand.

Example of a Yellow 3 POL Report

"BLACK 3, THIS IS RED 4. YELLOW THREE, AMBER, OVER."

YELLOW 3A – POL REQUEST.
A-21. The required quantity of each type of POL product is requested using the following line numbers:
- **Line 1:** Report as-of DTG.
- **Line 2:** MOGAS (gal).
- **Line 3:** Diesel (gal).
- **Line 4:** Oil, OE-10 (gal).
- **Line 5:** Oil, OE-30 (gal).
- **Line 6:** Oil, OE-50 (gal).
- **Line 7:** Oil, OE-90 (gal).
- **Line 8:** Antifreeze (gal).

- **Line 9:** Brake fluid (gal).
- **Line 10:** Hydraulic fluid, OHA (qt).
- **Line 11:** Hydraulic fluid, OHT (qt).
- **Line 12:** Hydraulic fluid, FRH (qt).
- **Line 13:** Oil, penetrating (qt).
- **Line 14:** Oil, PL-special (qt).
- **Line 15:** Oil, PL-medium (qt).
- **Line 16:** Bore cleaner (gal).
- **Line 17:** Oil, LSA (qt).
- **Line 18:** Grease, GAA (lb).
- **Line 19:** Grease, wheel bearing (lb).
- **Line 20:** Solvent (gal).

Note. Lines 61, 62, and 63 are used as needed for any other equipment assigned to the platoon. Additional lines (beginning with Line 21) are used to request any other POL products required by the platoon or attached elements.

> **Example of a Yellow 3A POL Request**
>
> "BLACK 3, THIS IS RED 1. YELLOW THREE ALPHA, BREAK. LINE 1: 251027APR2011 NOV. LINE 3: 900. LINE 8: 15."

PERSONNEL REPORTS

A-22. Personnel reports are used to notify the command group of casualties and request replacement personnel. Immediately follow a casualty report with a request for replacement.

RED 2 – PERSONNEL BATTLE LOSS REPORT.

A-23. A Red 2 report is transmitted to the troop/task force TOC as casualties occur. The unit also completes DA Form 1156 (Casualty Feeder Card), with witness statements, and submits them to the 1SG. Red 2 is an interim report to update information sent in the last Red 1 report. Provide all pertinent information using the following lines:

- **Line 1:** Battle roster number.
- **Line 2:** DTG of the incident.
- **Line 3:** Location of the incident (encoded).
- **Line 4:** Type of casualties, encoded by letter as follows:
  - *ALPHA:* KIA, hostile action.
  - *BRAVO:* KIA, nonhostile action.
  - *CHARLIE:* Body recovered.

Appendix A

- **DELTA:** Body not recovered.
- **ECHO:** Body identified.
- **FOXTROT:** Body not identified.
- **GOLF:** missing in action (MIA).
- **HOTEL:** Captured.
- **INDIA:** WIA, slight, hostile action.
- **JULIET:** WIA, serious, hostile action.
- **KILO:** WIA, slight, nonhostile action.
- **LIMA:** WIA, serious, nonhostile action.
- **MIKE:** Accident.
- **Line 5:** Location to which casualties are evacuated.

RED 3 – MEDICAL EVACUATION REQUEST.

A-24. A Red 3 report is sent to the medical team on the troop/company command net to request MEDEVAC support.

- **Ground evacuation format.** Provide pertinent information on the following lines:
    - **Line 1:** State "EVAC."
    - **Line 2:** Location for pickup (encoded).
    - **Line 3:** Number of casualties.
    - **Line 4:** Category of patient condition, encoded by letter designation as follows:
        — **ALPHA:** Urgent.
        — **BRAVO:** Priority.
        — **CHARLIE:** Routine.

Note. Use the letter designation with the number of patients in each category; for example, "TWO ALPHA" indicates that two patients require evacuation on an urgent basis.

- **Air evacuation format:**
    - **Line 1:** Location. Specify the grid coordinates for the six-digit grid location, preceded by the 100,000-meter grid identification.
    - **Line 2:** Radio frequency/call sign. The frequency and call sign should be that of the radio at the site of the unit requesting evacuation.
    - **Line 3:** Patient category of precedence. Classify the casualties' priority for evacuation using the following terms:
        — *Urgent.* Evacuation required within two hours to save life or limb.
        — *Priority.* Patient's medical condition will deteriorate, becoming urgent within four hours.

Analog Reports

— **Routine.** Evacuation required, but patient's condition is not expected to deteriorate for several hours.
— **Tactical immediate.** Evacuation required so casualties do not endanger the tactical mission.
- **Line 4:** Special equipment/emergency medical supplies.
- **Line 5:** Number and type of casualties.
- **Line 6:** Security of pickup site. Describe conditions for security at the LZ/pickup zone (PZ).
- **Line 7:** Signaling and site marking. Specify the signaling and marking methods to be used.
- **Line 8:** Patient nationality and status.
- **Line 9:** CBRN contamination area. Specify locations of any contaminated areas affecting the evacuation.

CHEMICAL, BIOLOGICAL, RADIOLOGICAL, NUCLEAR, AND HIGH YIELD EXPLOSIVES REPORTS

A-25. Chemical, biological, radiological, nuclear, and high yield explosives reports are used to describe contaminated areas, means of delivery, persistence, and initial agent identification. Units ensure that appropriate protective postures are assumed before gathering information for CBRNE reports.

CBRNE -1 – OBSERVER'S INITIAL REPORT

A-26. To send the CBRNE-1 report, state "CBRNE ONE" and give the type of CBRNE incident (nuclear, biological, or chemical). Other information that may be sent includes precedence of the report, date and time of the report (Universal Time [ZULU]), and security classification with "from" and "to" times the classification is applicable. Provide all pertinent information on the following lines:

- **Line ALPHA:** Strike serial number (if known).
- **Line BRAVO:** Position of observer (universal transverse Mercator [UTM] coordinates or name of place).
- **Line CHARLIE:** Grid or magnetic bearing (specify which is used) or azimuth of attack from observer (in degrees or mils; specify which is used).
- **Line DELTA:** DTG attack started, ZULU.
- **Line ECHO:** Illumination time in seconds (for nuclear burst); time the attack ended (toxic agent attack only).
- **Line FOXTROT:** Location of attack (UTM coordinates) and vicinity of attack (actual or estimated, specify which is given).
- **Line GOLF:** Means of delivery (if known).
- **Line HOTEL:** Type of burst (air, surface, unknown), type of toxic agent, or type of attack.
- **Line INDIA:** Number of shells, other data (for toxic attack only).
- **Line JULIET:** Flash-to-bang time (in seconds).

Appendix A

- **Line KILO:** Crater present or absent, diameter in meters (if known).
- **Line LIMA:** Cloud width (degrees or mils, specify which) five minutes after burst.
- **Line MIKE:** Cloud height (top or bottom, specify which) ten minutes after burst (degrees or mils, specify which).
- **Line SIERRA:** DTG of reading (local or ZULU time).

Note. DO NOT DELAY REPORTS in an attempt to provide complete format information. Omit information that is not applicable or available. Items that are always reported are the type of report; lines D and H; and one of the following lines: B, C, F, or G. Carefully specify the units of measure used (such as degrees, mils, or grid azimuth).

Example of a CBRNE-1 Observer's Initial Report

"THIS IS RED 1. CBRNE-1, CHEMICAL. LINE DELTA: 261003 ROMEO. LINE FOXTROT: NB783089. LINE GOLF: ARTILLERY. LINE HOTEL: VAPOR."

CBRNE -3 – IMMEDIATE WARNING OF EXPECTED CONTAMINATION

A-27. The CBRNE-3 report is sent by radio. State "NBC THREE," followed by pertinent information on these lines:

- **Line ALPHA:** Strike serial number (if known).
- **Line DELTA:** DTG when attack started.
- **Line FOXTROT:** Location of attack (specify actual or estimated).
- **Line PAPA:** Area of expected contamination.
- **Line YANKEE:** Bearing or azimuth of left, then right radial lines (specify degrees or mils, use four digits for each line).
- **Line ZULU:** Effective downwind speed (in km per mile, use three digits), downwind effective distance of zone (in km, use three digits), and cloud radius (in km, use two digits).

CBRNE -4 – REPORT OF RADIATION DOSE-RATE MEASUREMENT

A-28. The CBRNE-4 report, used for nuclear activity only, is submitted immediately after any radiation is detected and thereafter as required by the OPORD. To send this report, state "CBRNE FOUR," followed by pertinent information on these lines:

- **Line QUEBEC:** Location of reading, use friendly graphics or encryption. Omit this line when transmitting on a wire net.

- **Line ROMEO:** Dose rate in centigray per hour (cGy/hr) (average total dose rounded to the nearest 10 cGy). Specify whether the dose rate is "INITIAL," "INCREASING," "PEAK," or "DECREASING"; specify "SHIELDED" if the dose rate was measured inside a vehicle.
- **Line SIERRA:** DTG of reading. Specify the time zone.

Note. Repeat lines Q, R, and S as often as necessary. Radiation dose rates ideally are measured in the open, one meter above the ground. If the rate is measured in a shielded location, it is converted (as accurately as possible) to a rate in the open.

CBRNE -5 – REPORT OF AREAS OF CONTAMINATION

A-29. To send the CBRNE-5 report, state "CBRNE FIVE." Other information that may be sent includes precedence of the report, date and time of the report (ZULU), and security classification with "from" and "to" timeframe for the length of time the classification is applicable. Provide all pertinent information on the following lines:

- **Line ALPHA:** Strike serial number, if known.
- **Line OSCAR:** Reference DTG for estimated contours of contaminated areas.
- **Line SIERRA:** DTG when contamination was initially detected.
- **Line TANGO:** H+1 DTG or DTG of latest reconnaissance of contamination in the area.
- **Line UNIFORM:** Coordinates of contour lines marking dose rate of 1000 cGy/hr.
- **Line VICTOR:** Coordinates of contour lines marking dose rate of 300 cGy/hr.
- **Line WHISKEY:** Coordinates of contour lines marking dose rate of 100 cGy/hr.
- **Line X-RAY:** Coordinates of contour lines marking dose rate of 20 cGy/hr.

This page intentionally left blank.

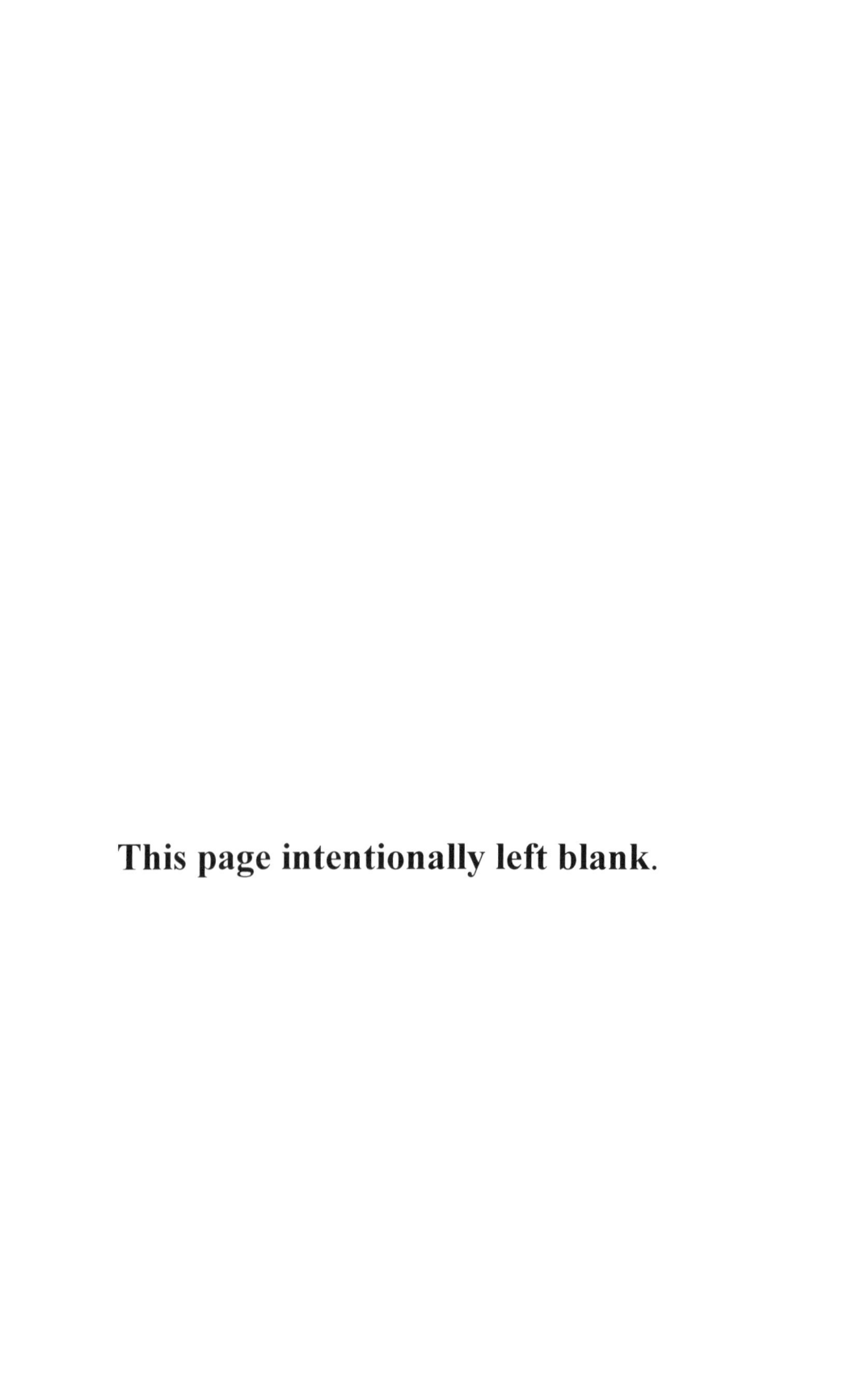

Glossary

Acronym/Term	Definition
1SG	first sergeant
A	
AA	*avenue of approach (graphic)*
AB	abatis
ACA	airspace coordination area
ABCT	Armored brigade combat team
AGL	*automatic grenade launcher (graphic)*
A/L	administrative/logistic
AO	area of operation
AOR	area of responsibility
APC	armored personnel carrier
ARNGUS	Army National Guard of the United States
ARV	armored recovery vehicle
ASCOPE	areas, structures, capabilities, organizations, and people
ASST	*assistant (graphic)*
ATGM	antitank guided missile
ATP	Army Techniques and Procedures
B	
BCT	brigade combat team
BFSB	battlefield surveillance brigade
BHL	battle handover line
BHO	battle handover
BP	battle position
BRIDGEREP	bridge, overpass, culvert, underpass, or tunnel report
C	
CA	civil affairs
CAB	combined arms battalion
CAS	close air support
CASEVAC	casualty evacuation
CBRNE	chemical, biological, radiological, nuclear, and high yield explosives
CCA	close combat attack
CCIR	commander's critical information requirement
CCN	combination class number

Glossary

Acronym/Term	Definition
CCP	casualty collection point
CEOI	communications-electronics operating instructions
CFV	cavalry fighting vehicle
cGy	centigray
cGy/hr	centigray per hour
CI	counter intelligence
CID	combat identification
Class I	rations and gratuitous issue of health, morale, and welfare items
Class III	petroleum, oils, and lubricants
Class IV	construction materials
Class V	ammunition
Class VIII	medical
Class IX	repair parts and components for equipment maintenance
COA	course of action
COLT	combat observation and lasing team
COMSEC	communications security
CO	*commanding officer (graphic)*
COP	common operational picture
CP	check point
CROSSREP	ford, ferry, or other crossing site report
CS	combat support
CSS	combat service support
CW	concertina wire
D	
DNBI	disease and nonbattle injuries
DOTD	Directorate of Training and Doctrine
DPICM	dual-purpose improved conventional munition
DRT	dismounted reconnaissance troop
DS	direct support
DSMTD	*dismounted (graphic)*
DTG	date-time, group
DZ	drop zone
E	
EA	engagement area
EO	electro-optical
EOD	explosive ordnance disposal

Glossary

Acronym/Term	Definition
EOF	escalation of force
EPLRS	Enhanced Position Location Reporting System
EPW	enemy prisoner of war
ESTAT	equipment status report
F	
FA	field artillery
FAH	final attack heading
FBCB2	Force XXI Battle Command Brigade and Below
FDC	fire direction center
FEBA	forward edge battle area
FIST	fire support team
five-S	secure, silence, separate, safeguard, and speed
FM	field manual
FOB	forward operating base
FPF	final protective fire
FRAGORD	fragmentary order
FS	fire support
FSCM	fire support coordination measure
FSO	fire support officer
G	
gal	gallon
GIRS	Grid Index Reference System
GTL	gun-target line
GPS	Global Positioning System
H	
H+1	time reference to the start of an operation
HB	heavy barrel
HCT	human intelligence collection team
HE	high explosive
HHC	headquarters and headquarters company
HMMWV	high-mobility multipurpose wheeled vehicle
HPT	high-payoff target
HPTL	high-payoff target list
HQ	headquarters
HQDA	Headquarters, Department of the Army
HUMINT	human intelligence

Glossary

Acronym/Term	Definition
I	
IAW	in accordance with
IBCT	Infantry brigade combat team
ID	identification
IE	information engagement
IED	improvised explosive device
IMINT	imagery intelligence
IP	initial position
IPB	intelligence preparation of the battlefield
IR	information requirement
IV	intervisibility
J	
JFO	joint fires observer
JTAC	joint terminal attack controller
K	
KIA	killed in action
km	kilometer
L	
lb	pound
LD	line of departure
LDR	*leader (graphic)*
LOA	limit of advance
LOC	line of communications
LRAS3	Long Range Advanced Scout Surveillance System
LRP	logistics release point
LT	*lieutenant (graphic)*
LTL	laser-to-target line
LZ	landing zone
M	
m	meter
MCoE	Maneuver Center of Excellence
MCS	Maneuver Control System
MEDEVAC	medical evacuation
MET	mission-essential task
METL	mission-essential task list

Glossary

Acronym/Term	Definition
METT-TC	mission, enemy, terrain and weather, troops and support available-time available and civil considerations
MF	minefield
MG	*machine gun (graphic)*
MGS	Mobile Ground System
MIA	missing in action
MICO	military intelligence company
MISO	military information support operation
MLC	military load classification
MLRS	Multiple Launch Rocket System
mm	millimeter
MOPP	mission-oriented protective posture
MOS	military occupational specialty
MP	military police
MSP	mission support plan
MSR	main supply route
N	
NAI	named area of interest
NBC	nuclear, biological, and chemical
NCO	noncommissioned officer
NFA	no fire area
NGO	nongovernmental organization
NOD	night observation device
O	
OA	operation area
OAKOC	observation, avenues of approach, key and decisive terrain, obstacles, and cover and concealment
OB	*obstruction (symbol)*
OBSTINTEL	obstacle intelligence
OE	operational environment
OP	observation post
ORP	objective rally point
OPCON	operational control
OPORD	operations order
OPSEC	operations security
OT	observer to target
P	

Glossary

Acronym/Term	Definition
P	*pedestrian ferry (symbol)*
PCI	precombat inspection
PEWS	platoon early warning system
PFC	*private first class (graphic)*
PIR	priority intelligence requirements
PL	*phase line (graphic)*
PMCS	preventive maintenance checks and services
PMESII-PT	political, military, economic, social, information, infrastructure, physical environment and time
PMM	preventive medicine measures
POL	petroleum, oils, and lubricants
PP	*passage point (graphic)*
PROPHET	a signals intelligence and electronic warfare system
PSG	platoon sergeant
psi	pounds per square inch
PZ	pickup zone

Q	
qt	quart

R	
RA	regular Army
R&S	reconnaissance and surveillance
RATELO	*radio telephone operator (graphic)*
RC	road crater
REDCON-1	readiness condition-1
RFL	restrictive fire line
RHL	reconnaissance handover line
RHO	reconnaissance handover
RHOCP	reconnaissance handover coordination point
RM	risk management
ROE	rules of engagement
POUTEREP	route reconnaissance report
RP	release point
RR	*railroad (symbol)*
RTO	radio telephone operator
RV	reconnaissance vehicle

S	
S	*screen (graphic)*

Glossary

Acronym/Term	Definition
S-1	adjutant (Army)
S-2	intelligence officer (Army)
S-3	operations staff officer
S-4	supply officer (Army)
SA	situational awareness
SALUTE	size, activity, location, unit, time, and equipment
SBCT	Stryker brigade combat team
SE	site exploitation
SEAD	suppression of enemy air defense
SENSEREP	sensitive items report
SGT	*sergeant (graphic)*
SIGINT	signals intelligence
SIR	specific information requirements
SITREP	situation report
SOI	signal operating instructions
SOP	standard operating procedure
SP	start point
SPC	*specialist (graphic)*
SPOTREP	spot report
SSG	*staff sergeant (graphic)*
STANAG	standardization agreement
STANREP	stand-to report
SU	situational understanding
SWEAT-MSO	sewage, water, electricity, academic, trash, medical, safety, and other considerations
T	
T	*snow blockage (symbol)*
TAC	tactical air coordinator
TACSAT	tactical satellite
TAI	target area of interest
T&EOS	training and evaluation outlines
TC	training circular
TD	tank ditch
TDA	table of distribution and allowance
TerraBase	terrain evaluation tool
TIRS	Terrain Index Reference System
TLP	troop-leading procedures
TM	*team (graphic)*
TOC	tactical operations center

Glossary

Acronym/Term	Definition
TOE	table of organization and equipment
TOT	time on target

Acronym/Term	Definition
TOW	tube-launched, optically tracked, wire-guided missile system
TRADOC	U.S. Army Training and Doctrine Command
TRP	target reference point
TTP	tactics, techniques, and procedures
U	
UAS	unmanned aircraft system
UTL	unit task list
UTM	universal transverse Mercator
UXO	unexploded explosive ordnance
V	
V	*vehicular ferry (symbol)*
VBS2	Virtual Battlespace 2
VC	vehicle commander
VEH	*vehicle (graphic)*
W	
W	*flooding (symbol)*
WARNORD	warning order
WFF	warfighting functions
WGS	World Geodetic System
WIA	wounded in action
WP	white phosphorus
X	
XO	executive officer
Z	
ZULU	Universal Time

References

SOURCES USED
These are the sources quoted or paraphrased in this publication.

ARMY PUBLICATIONS
ADP 3-0, *Unified Land Operations*, 10 October 2011.
ADP 5-0, *The Operations Process*, 17 May 2012.
ADRP 5-0, *The Operations Process*, 17 May 2012.
ATTP 3-06.11, *Combined Arms Operations in Urban Terrain*, 10 June 2011.
ATTP 3-20.97, *Dismounted Reconnaissance Troop*, 16 November 2010.
ATTP 3-90.4, *Combined Arms Mobility Operations*, 10 August 2011.
FM 1-02, *Operational Terms and Graphics*, 21 September 2004.
FM 2-22.3, *Human Intelligence Collector Operations*, 6 September 2006.
FM 3-04.155, *Army Unmanned Aircraft System Operations*, 29 July 2009.
FM 3-57, *Civil Affairs Operations*, 31 October 2011.
FM 3-06.20, *Cordon and Search Multi-Service Tactics, Techniques, and Procedures for Cordon and Search Operations*, 25 April 2006.
FM 3-07, *Stability Operations*, 6 October 2008.
FM 3-07.1, *Security Force Assistance*, 1 May 2009.
FM 3-09. 31, *Tactics, Techniques, and Procedures for Fire Support for the Combined Arms Commander*, 1 October 2002.
FM 3-09.32, *-FIRE Multi-Service Tactics, Techniques, and Procedures for the Joint Application of Firepower*, 20 December 2007.
FM 3-11.19, *Multiservice Tactics, Techniques, and Procedures for Nuclear, Biological, and Chemical Reconnaissance*, 30 July 2004.
FM 3-19.15, *Civil Disturbance Operations*. 18 April 2005.
FM 3-20.15, *Tank Platoon,* 22 February 2007.
FM 3-20.96, *Reconnaissance and Cavalry Squadron*, 12 March 2010.
FM 3-20.98, *Reconnaissance and Scout Platoon*, 3 August 2009.
FM 3-20.971, *Reconnaissance Calvary Troop*, 4 August 2009.
FM 3-21.8, *The Infantry Rifle Platoon and Squad*, 28 March 2007.

References

FM 3-21.94, *The Stryker Brigade Combat Team Infantry Battalion Reconnaissance Platoon*, 18 April 2003.

FM 3-22.10, *Sniper Training and Operations*, 19 October 2009.

FM 3-22.90, *Mortars*, 7 Dec 2007.

FM 3-25.26, *Map Reading and Land Navigation*, 18 January 2005.

FM 3-34, *Engineer Operations*, 4 August 2011.

FM 3-34.170, *Engineer Reconnaissance*, 25 March 2008.

FM 3-90-1, *Offense and Defense Volume 1*, 22 March 2013.

FM 4-02.51, *Combat and Operational Stress Control*, 6 July 2006.

FM 5-19, *Composite Risk Management*, 21 August 2006.

FM 6-02.53, *Tactical Radio Operations*, 5 August 2009.

FM 6-20-40, *Tactics, Techniques, and Procedures for Fire Support for Brigade Operations (Heavy)*, 5 January 1990.

FM 6-22, *Army Leadership: Competent, Confident, and Agile*, 12 October 2006.

FM 6-22.5, *Combat and Operational Stress Control Manual for Leaders and Soldiers*, 18 March 2009.

FM 6-30, *Tactics, Techniques, and Procedures for Observed Fire*, 16 July 1991.

TC 7-100, *Hybrid Threat*, 26 November 2010.

TC 31-34-4, *Special Forces Tracking and Countertracking*, 30 September 2009.

JOINT AND DEPARTMENT OF DEFENSE PUBLICATIONS

JP 1-02, *Department of Defense Dictionary of Military and Associated Terms*, 8 November 2010.

DODD 2310.01E, *Personnel Accounting – Losses Due to Hostile Acts*, 10 November 2003.

OTHER PUBLICATIONS

Geneva Convention, Article 3, Convention III relative to the Treatment of Prisoners of War, Geneva, 12 August 1949. http://www.icrc.org/ihl.nsf/WebART/375-590006

References

DOCUMENTS NEEDED
These documents must be available to the intended user of this publication.

STANAG 2010, *Military Load Classification Markings*, Ed: 6, 5 March 2004.

STANAG 2021, *Military Load Classification of Bridges, Ferries, Rafts, and Vehicles,* Ed: 6, 7 September 2006.

PAMPHLETS
DA PAM 750-8, *The Army Maintenance Management System (TAMMS) Users Manual,* 22 August 2005.

FORMS
DA forms are available on the Army Publishing Directorate Web site: www.apd.army.mil.

DD forms are available at http://www.dtic.mil/whs/directives/infomgt/forms/index.htm

DA Form 1156, *Casualty Feeder Card.*

DA Form 2028, *Recommended Changes to Publications and Blank Forms.*

DA Form 2408-18, *Equipment Inspection List.*

DA Form 5988-E, available in the PLL office at the unit motor pool.

DD Form 2745, *Enemy Prisoner of War (EPW) Capture Tag.*

READINGS RECOMMENDED
These sources contain relevant supplemental information.

FM 3-05.210, *Special Forces Air Operations,* 27 February 2009.

FM 3-06, *Urban Operations,* 26 October 2006.

FM 3-19.4, *Military Police Leaders' Handbook,* 4 March 2002.

FM 3-21.10, *The Infantry Rifle Company,* 27 July 2006.

FM 3-34.22, *Engineer Operations–Brigade Combat Team and Below,* 11 February 2009.

FM 3-50.1, *Army Personnel Recovery,* 21 November 2011.

FM 3-50.3, *Survival, Evasion, and Recovery Multi-Service Tactics, Techniques, and Procedures,* 20 March 2007.

FM 3-55.93, *Long-Range Surveillance Unit Operations,* 23 June 2009.

References

FM 3-97.6, *Mountain Operations*, 28 November 2000.

FM 4-02.17, *Preventive Medicine Services*, 28 August 2000.

WEBSITES

Most Army doctrinal publications and regulations are available online at:
  Army Publishing Directorate, http://www.apd.army.mil.
  Central Army Registry (CAR) on the Army Training Network (ATN), https://atiam.train.army.mil.
  Army Knowledge Online, https://akocomm.us.army.mil/usapa/doctrine/index.html.
  Standardization Agreements, https://nsa.nato.intl/protected/.
  StrykerNet, https://strykernet.army.mil

  Digital Training Management System, https://dtms.army.mil/DTMS

Most joint publications are available online at:
  http://www.dtic.mil/doctrine/doctrine/doctrine.htm.

Index

A

air defense artillery, 7-12
ambush, 4-34, 6-5
   reaction, 4-33
   techniques, 4-27
   urban area, 6-6
antitank guided missile (ATGM), 3-18, 4-3
area security, 4-1, 4-21, 4-23, 4-24, 5-11
   execution, 4-23
   planning, 4-22
   preparation, 4-22
artillery
   capability, 7-6
   common use, 7-7
   limitation, 7-6
ASCOPE, 1-11, 5-7
assembly area, 6-31
   characteristics, 6-31
   departure, 6-34
   occupation, 6-33
   reconnaissance, 6-32
   security, 6-34
   suitability, 6-32
   tasks, 6-33

B

BLUES, 4-14
brigade combat team (BCT), 3-6, 3-14, 3-34

C

cavalry fighting vehicle (CFV), 2-2, 2-4, 4-18, 4-35
CBRNE, 2-11, 4-12, 7-26, A-15
civil affairs (CA), 3-11, 4-24, 5-6, 5-17, 7-28
classes of supply, 8-5
close air support (CAS), 4-1, 4-27, 7-1, 7-14
   night operations, 7-15
   planning, 7-15
   preplanned, 7-14
   request, 7-16
close combat attack (CCA), 4-1, 7-11
   request, 7-13
combat observation and lasing team (COLT), 7-2
combat outpost, 4-27, 4-29, 6-26
engineer support, 7-19
command relationships, 1-9
commander's critical information requirement (CCIR), 2-1, 3-38
communication techniques, 1-8
   net control and discipline, 1-8
convoy escort, 4-30
counter-reconnaissance, 4-15, 4-17, 4-18, 6-23
cover mission, 4-1, 4-21, 6-37
curve radius formula, 3-30

D

decisive action, 1-3, 2-2
   inform and influence, 5-5
   operational considerations, 3-5
   relief in place, 6-46

Index

direct fire
 distributing, 6-27
 focusing, 6-27
 orienting, 6-28
 planning, 6-26
 SOP, 6-27
dismounted reconnaissance troop (DRT), 2-7, 2-8
disrupt and delay, 4-20, 4-21

E

enemy
 avenue of approach, 6-28
 engagement, 6-29
 scheme of maneuver, 6-29
engagement area, 6-28
engineer, 7-18
 security tasks, 7-18
 stability tasks, 7-19
executive officer (XO), 1-7, 5-16, 6-32
exfiltration, 6-20, 6-22
 execution, 6-22
 mounted, 6-22
 planning, 6-21
 urban areas, 6-21
explosive ordinance disposal (EOD), 1-10, 5-11, 7-27

F

fire support officer (FSO), 3-17, 3-19, 7-2, 7-3, 7-4
fire support team (FIST), 7-2
fires, 7-1, *See* mortars
 aviation, 7-13
 battalion, 7-6
 close support, 7-4
 indirect, 6-30, 7-2
 personnel, 7-2
 planning, 7-2
 sniper, 7-17
 suppressive, 7-4
first sergeant (1SG), 1-7, 5-16, 6-32, 6-36, 8-1
Force XXI Battle Command— Brigade and Below (FBCB2), 1-6, 2-2, 3-35, 4-40, 6-36, 7-12, 8-2
fratricide avoidance, 1-13

G

Global Positioning System (GPS), 7-12, 7-15
graphic control measures, 1-7, 3-11, 6-35, 6-38, 6-40

ground surveillance systems, 7-20
guard force, 4-21

H

health protection, 8-11
 CASEVAC, 8-12
 stressors, 8-12
high-payoff target list (HPTL), 7-1, 7-14
human intelligence (HUMINT), 1-10, 3-10, 4-30, 6-6, 7-20

I

improvised explosive device (IED), 5-10, 5-11, 6-7
infiltration, 6-17
 communications, 6-20
 execution, 6-18
 planning, 6-17
 purposes, 6-17
intelligence preparation of the battlefield (IPB), 1-7, 4-3
interpreter, 7-27

L

linkup, 6-34
 execution, 6-36
 planning, 6-35, 6-36

Index

preparation, 6-36

Long Range Advanced Scout Surveillance System (LRAS3), 2-2, 3-7, 6-4, 6-16

M

maintenance, 8-10
  field, 8-10
  responsibility, 8-10, 8-11
  sustainment, 8-10

marking
  enemy, 7-12
  friendly forces, 7-12
  target, 7-12

METT-TC, 1-11, 2-4, 3-12, 3-16, 3-19, 4-27, 5-9, 6-7, 6-16, 6-28, 7-22, 7-26

military load classification (MLC), 3-28
  temporary vehicle, 3-28
  tracked vehicle, 3-29
  wheeled vehicle, 3-29

MISO team, 7-27

mission command, 1-4

mission orders, 1-6

Mobile Ground System (MGS), 3-18, 4-3, 4-18, 4-24

mortars, 7-5, *See* fires
  illumination, 7-5
  obscuration, 7-5
  suppression, 7-5

mounted reconnaissance platoon, 2-4

movement techniques, 6-12
  bounding overwatch, 6-16
  traveling, 6-13
  traveling overwatch, 6-14

moving screen, 4-20

O

observation post (OP)
  communication, 4-13
  extended operations, 4-14
  improving position, 4-12
  manning, 4-11
  occupy, 4-10
  positioning, 4-8
  security, 4-13
  site selection, 4-10, 4-14

obstacles
  actions at, 4-40
  clearance, 6-32, 7-18
  critical task, 3-18, 4-12
  hasty, 4-12, 4-24
  planning, 6-30
  point-type, 4-40
  security, 4-40
  urban, 6-6

obstructions, 3-29

operational control (OPCON), 1-10, 4-19, 7-19

operational environment (OE), 1-2, 3-5

operations security (OPSEC), 5-4, 5-5, 5-8, 6-34

P

passage of lines, 6-37
  coordination, 6-43
  execute, 6-45, 6-46
  forward, 6-45
  graphic control measures, 6-40
  key elements, 6-37
  preparation, 6-40
  rearward, 6-46
  tasks, 6-39, 6-44

patrol base, 6-23

Index

activities, 6-25
clandestine, 6-26
occupation, 6-24
site selection, 6-23

patrol mission, 3-38
  execution, 3-47
  organization, 3-45
  preparation, 3-44
  rally points, 3-42
  routes, 3-41
  tasks, 3-38
  time schedule, 3-39

platoon formations, 6-8, 6-13
  coil, 6-10
  column, 6-9
  herringbone, 6-12
  line, 6-8
  staggered column, 6-10
  vee, 6-8
  wedge, 6-12

platoon leader, 1-4, 1-5, 1-7, 1-8, 1-11, 2-16, 3-3, 3-4, 3-6, 3-11, 3-12, 3-13, 3-17, 3-18, 3-33, 4-3, 4-18, 4-24, 4-31, 5-3, 5-8, 5-9, 5-14, 6-1, 6-3, 6-4, 6-9, 6-10, 6-13, 6-18, 6-20, 6-26, 6-28, 6-32, 6-33, 6-36, 6-38, 6-43, 6-44, 6-47, 7-3, 7-4, 7-14, 7-18, 7-20, 7-26, 8-2, 8-6, 8-9, 8-10
  sustainment, 8-3

platoon sergeant (PSG), 1-4, 1-8, 2-4, 3-17, 4-18, 5-15, 6-19, 6-45, 6-46, 8-1

R

reconnaissance
  area, 3-14, 3-15, 3-16, 3-17
  dismounted, 3-37
  handover (RHO), 3-33, 3-34, 3-35, 4-19, 6-37
  in force, 3-32
  obstacle, 3-13
  overlay symbols, 3-22
  passage of lines, 6-37
  route, 3-17, 3-18, 3-19
  zone, 3-9, 3-13

relief in place, 6-46, 6-48

reports
  Blue 1 SPOTREP, A-1
  Blue 10 bypass, A-5
  Blue 11 STANREP, A-5
  Blue 2 SITREP, A-2
  Blue 4 BRIDGEREP, A-3
  Blue 5 CROSSREP, A-3
  Blue 9 obstacle, A-5
  CBRNE-1 initial observer, A-15
  CBRNE-3 expected contamination warning, A-16
  CBRNE-4 radiation dose-rate, A-16
  CBRNE-5 areas of contamination, A-17
  contact, A-1
  Green 2 SENSEREP, A-6
  Green 3 splash, A-6
  Green 4 patrol, A-6
  Green 6 EPW, A-7
  Red 2 personnel battle loss, A-13
  Red 3 MEDEVAC, A-14

Index

Yellow 1 A battle loss, A-10
Yellow 1 ESTAT, A-8
Yellow 2 ammunition status, A-10
Yellow 2A ammunition request, A-11
Yellow 3 POL status, A-12
Yellow 3A POL request, A-12

resupply, 8-6
  aerial, 8-9
  prestock, 8-8, 8-9
  service station, 8-7
  tailgate, 8-6
risk management (RM), 1-12, 2-4
route classification formula, 3-26
route security, 4-25
  combat outpost, 4-29
  convoy, 4-28
  procedures, 4-27
  tasks, 4-26
  techniques, 4-26
routes
  Blue 7 ROUTEREP, A-4
  rules of engagement (ROE), 3-5, 5-3, 5-4, 5-7, 5-14, 6-5

S

S-2, 1-7, 3-13, 5-12, 7-25
S-3, 3-46, 7-25
SALUTE, 4-7, 7-21, A-1
scatterable mines, 7-7, 7-19
scouts, 3-4, 3-13, 4-3, 4-5, 4-7, 4-8, 4-11, 4-13, 4-18, 4-19, 4-28, 4-42, 6-2, 6-4, 6-5, 6-7, 6-12, 6-16, 7-1
quartering party, 6-31
security tasks
  execution, 4-6
  local, 4-41
  organization, 4-4
  planning, 4-3
  reconnaissance, 4-2
  screen, 4-3
sensor team, 7-19
  tasks, 7-20
signal intelligence (SIGINT), 3-11, 4-3
situation template, 1-7
slope percentage formula, 3-30
sniper, 7-17
stability tasks, 5-1, 5-2, 5-3, 5-5, 5-8
  civil disturbance, 5-13
  civil services, 5-3
  civilian security, 5-14
  engagement, 5-6
  environment, 5-3
  force protection, 5-4

T

tactical air coordinator (TAC), 6-39
tactical movement, 6-1
  covered and concealed, 6-2
  danger areas, 6-4
  dismounted, 6-3, 6-7
  fundamentals, 6-2
  lateral mobility, 6-7
  open areas, 6-4
  terrain, 6-2
  urban areas, 6-6
  wooded areas, 6-5
tactical satellite (TACSAT), 1-8
tracking, 3-48

Index

box method, 3-50
concepts, 3-48
footprints, 3-50
indicators, 3-48, 3-51
organization, 3-48

traffic flow capability, 3-27
troop-leading procedure (TLP), 1-12

U

unmanned aircraft system (UAS), 1-7, 2-11, 3-6, 3-10, 3-12, 3-14, 4-26, 6-7, 6-17, 6-32, 7-21, 7-22, 7-23

W

working dog, 7-27

ATP 3-20.98
(FM 7-92 and FM 3-21.94)
5 April 2013

By Order of the Secretary of the Army:

RAYMOND T. ODIERNO
*General, United States Army
Chief of Staff*

Official:

JOYCE E. MORROW
*Administrative Assistant to the
Secretary of the Army*
1309504

DISTRIBUTION:

Active Army, Army National Guard, and United States Army Reserve: To be distributed in accordance with initial distribution number (IDN) 111029, requirements for ATP 3-20.98.

Made in the USA
Middletown, DE
04 October 2016